Thirteenth Edition

The State
of
Church Giving
through 2001

John L. Ronsvalle

Sylvia Ronsvalle

empty tomb,®*inc.*
Champaign, Illinois

The State of Church Giving through 2001
by John and Sylvia Ronsvalle
published by empty tomb, inc.
First printing, October 2003

empty tomb, inc.
301 N. Fourth Street
P.O. Box 2404
Champaign, IL 61825-2404
Phone: (217) 356-9519
Fax: (217) 356-2344
www.emptytomb.org

ISBN 0-9679633-3-8
ISSN 1097-3192

The Library of Congress has catalogued this publication
as follows:
The state of church giving through …—19uu- Champaign, Ill. :
Empty Tomb, Inc.,
v. : ill. ; 28 cm. Annual.
1. Christian giving Periodicals.
2. Christian giving Statistics Periodicals.
3. Church finance—United States Periodicals.
4. Church finance—United States Statistics Periodicals.
  BV772 .S32 98-640917

CONTENTS_____

TABLES AND FIGURES

PREFACE

Are we all actually busier than we ever were before, or does it only seem like it? Conveniences like e-mail, faxing, and computers were supposed to simplify our lives. Instead, we live in a tyranny of the immediate. People expect responses and results in a matter of minutes rather than days.

The preservation of history can lose as a priority under these pressures. That is why the faithful work of denominational officials is of such great value. In addition to all the other demands on their time, these administrators collect, aggregate, and make available their denominational numbers in a published tradition that began in 1916 and has continued through the present in the *Yearbook of American and Canadian Churches* (*YACC*) and its predecessors. The work of these officials makes an important contribution to the knowledge bank about the church in the United States, and their efforts are gratefully acknowledged.

The National Council of the Churches of Christ in the U.S.A. (NCC) has carried on the publication that began with the *Federal Council Year Book* in 1916. By continuing this rich tradition, Robert W. Edgar, NCC General Secretary, has displayed true church statesmanship.

Eileen Lindner, *YACC* editor, and her assistants, Marcel Welty and Elizabeth During, continue to survey the denominations and publish the data. It is a privilege to work with them. Their preservation of this information base benefits not only current but also future researchers and others who will want to know about the church in the U.S.

Once again this year, we joyfully acknowledge the staff members of empty tomb who remain courageous in their pursuit of faithful servant leadership, and supportive of the vision of a more faithful church. In particular, Peter Helfrich, Administrative Assistant, has played a key role in the production of this volume and we thank him. Financial supporters and volunteers are another key component of the works through empty tomb. We want to express appreciation to volunteer John K. Jones for his assistance.

Again this year, we offer the analyses on the following pages with the hope that they will be one means to "spur one another on toward love and good deeds (Hebrews 10:24, NIV)."

John L. Ronsvalle, Ph.D.
Sylvia Ronsvalle

Champaign, Illinois
September 2003

SUMMARY_____

The State of Church Giving through 2001 is the most recent report in an annual series that began with *The State of Church Giving through 1989*. These analyses consider denominational giving data for a set of denominations first analyzed in a study published in 1988. The present report reviews data for a composite set of denominations from 1968 to 2001 that includes 28.7 million full or confirmed members, and just over 100,000 of the estimated 350,000 religious congregations in the U.S.

The findings of the present church member giving analysis include the following.

- Per member giving to Total Contributions and Congregational Finances increased as a portion of income between 1968 and 2001, with giving to Congregational Finances recovering to the level of the early 1970s. In 2001, per member giving as a portion of income to Benevolences improved slightly from that in the year 2000, when it reached its lowest point in the 1968-2001 period.

- Data for an additional 15 denominations was available for 2000-2001, allowing an analysis that included 41 Protestant communions for those two years. As a percentage of income, giving to Total Contributions and Congregational Finances increased at a higher rate in the original composite set, while the increase to Benevolences was at a higher rate when the set was expanded to 41 denominations.

- An analysis of data for a subset of mainline Protestant denominations and a subset of evangelical Protestant denominations found giving higher in the evangelical Protestant denominations, but a steeper decline in giving patterns among the evangelicals over the 1968-2001 period. Evangelical denominations were increasing in membership during these years, but their members were giving a smaller contribution as a portion of income. In the mainline denominations, giving as a portion of income to Congregational Finances was higher in 2001 than in 1968; however, Benevolences continued to decline, along with these denominations' membership.

- A review of giving and membership patterns in 11 Protestant denominations from 1921 to 2001 found that per member giving as a portion of income began to decline in 1961, and membership began to decline as a percent of U.S. population in 1962. Giving as a percentage of income was lower in 2001 than in either 1921 or 1933.

- Data was analyzed using both linear and exponential regression. The increase in giving as a portion of income to Congregational Finances apparent in recent years produced levels that were higher than either the linear or exponential regression series for 1968-2001 suggested. Both the linear and the exponential regressions for Benevolences suggested that giving to that category will be much reduced by the year 2050.

- Membership analyses of various groupings of communions suggested that there was a decline in church membership as a portion of U.S. population in the 1968-2001 period.

- If church members were to reach a congregation-wide average of 10% giving, an additional $143 billion dollars would be available to assist both local and global neighbors in need.

- The third annual Report Card on Philanthropy Measurement evaluated the contributions of twelve entities to public knowledge about charitable giving in the United States. The overall quality of philanthropy measurement merited a C-.

- The last chapter builds on the recommendations in *The State of Church Giving through 2001*. In this edition of the series, it is proposed that developing a country-by-country analysis of needs will assist in reversing the decline in giving to Benevolences as a portion of income.

INTRODUCTION

An historical series of financial and membership data in the United States extends back to 1916. Church statesmen took a broad overview of organized religion as a major social institution. They collected and preserved the data through publications and archives.

This information tradition continues through the present. Individual congregations initially provide the data to the regional or national denominational office with which the congregation is affiliated. The denominational offices then compile the data. The *Yearbook of American and Canadian Churches* (*YACC*), of the National Council of the Churches of Christ in the U.S.A., requests the data from the national denominational offices, publishing it in annual *YACC* editions.

The data published by the *YACC*, in some cases combined with data obtained directly from a denominational source (as noted in the series of tables in Appendix B), serves as the basis for the present report. The numbers on the following pages are not survey reports. Rather, they represent the actual dollar records included in reports submitted by pastors and lay congregational leaders to their own denominational offices.

By following the same data set of denominations over a period of years, trends can be seen among a broad group of church members. In addition, since the data set includes communions from across the theological spectrum, subsets of denominations within the larger grouping provide a basis for comparing patterns between communions with different perspectives.

In an ongoing fashion, efforts are made to use the latest information available. As a result, *The State of Church Giving through 2001* provides information available to date.

Definition of Terms. The analyses in this report use certain terms that are defined as follows.

Full or Confirmed Members are used in the present analysis because it is a relatively consistent category among the reporting denominations. Certain denominations also report a larger figure for Inclusive Membership, which may include, for example, children who have been baptized but are not yet eligible for confirmation in that denomination. In this report, when the term "per member" is used, it refers to Full or Confirmed Members, unless otherwise noted.

The terms "denomination" and "communion" are used interchangeably. Both refer to a group of church people who share a common identity defined by traditions and stated beliefs.

The phrase "historically Christian church" refers to that combination of believers with a historically acknowledged confession of the faith. The broad spectrum of communions represented in the National Church Leaders Response Form list indicates the breadth of this definition.[1]

---

[1] John Ronsvalle and Sylvia Ronsvalle; "National Church Leaders Response Form"; *The State of Church Giving through 1998* (2000 edition); <http://www.emptytomb.org/survey1.html>.

Total Contributions Per Member refers to the average contribution in either dollars or as a percentage of income which is donated to the denominations' affiliated congregations by Full or Confirmed Members in a given year.

Total Contributions combines the two subcategories of Congregational Finances and Benevolences. The definitions used in this report for these two subcategories are consistent with the standardized *YACC* data request questionnaire.

The first subcategory of Congregational Finances includes contributions directed to the internal operations of the individual congregation, including such items as the utility bills and salaries for the pastor and office staff, as well as Sunday school materials and capital programs.

The second subcategory is Benevolences. This category includes contributions for the congregation's external expenditures, beyond its own operations, for what might be termed the larger mission of the church. Benevolences includes international missions as well as national and local charities, through denominational channels as well as programs of nondenominational organizations to which the congregation contributes directly. Benevolences also includes support of denominational administration at all levels, as well as donations to denominational seminaries and schools.

As those familiar with congregational dynamics know, an individual generally donates an amount to the congregation which underwrites both Congregational Finances and Benevolences. During the budget preparation process, congregational leadership considers allocations to these categories. The budget may or may not be reviewed by all the congregation's members, depending on the communion's polity. However, the sum of the congregation's activities serves as a basis for members' decisions about whether to increase or decrease giving from one year to the next. Also, many congregations provide opportunities to designate directly to either Congregational Finances or Benevolences, through fundraising drives, capital campaigns, and special offerings. Therefore, the allocations between Congregational Finances and Benevolences can be seen to fairly represent the priorities of church members.

When the terms "income," "per capita income," and "giving as a percentage of income" are used, they refer to the U.S. Per Capita Disposable (after-tax) Personal Income series from the U.S. Department of Commerce Bureau of Economic Analysis (BEA), unless otherwise noted.

The Implicit Price Deflator for Gross National Product was used to convert current dollars to 1996 dollars, thus factoring out inflation, unless otherwise specified.

Appendix C includes both U.S. Per Capita Disposable Personal Income figures and the Implicit Price Deflator for Gross National Product figures used in this study.

Analysis Factors. *Chained Dollars.* The analyses in *The State of Church Giving through 2001* are keyed to the U.S. BEA series of "chained (1996) dollars."

Income Series. The U.S. Department of Commerce Bureau of Economic Analysis has published the 11th comprehensive revision of the national income and product accounts, with the benchmark year being 1996. The U.S. Per Capita Disposable Personal Income series used in the present *The State of Church Giving through 2001* is drawn from this national accounts data.

Rate of Change Calculations, 1985-2001. The following methodology is used to calculate the rate of change between 1985 and the most recent calendar year for which data is available, in the present case, 2001.

The rate of change between 1968 and 1985 was calculated by subtracting the 1968 giving as a percentage of income figure from the 1985 figure and then dividing the result by the 1968 figure.

The rate of change between 1985 and 2001 was calculated as follows. The 1968 giving as a percentage of income figure was subtracted from the 2001 figure and divided by the 1968 figure, producing a 1968-2001 rate of change. Then, the 1968-1985 rate of change was subtracted from the 1968-2001 figure. The result is the 1985-2001 rate of change, which may then be compared to the 1968-1985 figure.

Rounding Calculations. In most cases, Total Contributions, Total Congregational Finances, and Total Benevolences for the denominations being considered were divided by Full or Confirmed Membership in order to obtain per capita, or per member, data for that set of denominations. This procedure occasionally led to a small rounding discrepancy in one of the three related figures. That is, by a small margin, rounded per capita Total Contributions did not equal per capita Congregational Finances plus per capita Benevolences. Similarly, rounding data to the nearest dollar for use in tables and graphics led on occasion to a small rounding error in the data presented in tabular or graphic form.

Giving in Dollars. Per member giving to churches can be measured in dollars. The dollar measure indicates, among other information, how much money religious institutions have to spend.

Current dollars indicate the value of the dollar in the year it was donated. However, since inflation changes the amount of goods or services that can be purchased with that dollar, data provided in current dollars has limited information value over a time span. If someone donated $5 in 1968 and $5 in 2001, on one level that person is donating the same amount of money. On another level, however, the buying power of that $5 has changed a great deal. Since less can be bought with the $5 donated in 2001 because of inflation in the economy, on a practical level the value of the donation has shrunk.

To account for the changes caused by inflation in the value of the dollar, a deflator can be applied. The result is inflation-adjusted 1996 dollars. Dollars adjusted to their chain-type, annual-weighted measure through the use of a deflator can be compared in terms of real growth over a time span since inflation has been factored out.

The deflator most commonly applied in this analysis designated the base period as 1996, with levels in 1996 set equal to 100. Thus, when adjusted by the deflator, the 1968 gift of $5 was worth $19.02 in inflation-adjusted 1996 dollars, and the 2001 gift of $5 was worth $4.57 in inflation-adjusted 1996 dollars.

Giving as a Percentage of Income. There is another way to look at church member giving. This category is giving as a percentage of income. Considering what percentage or portion of income is donated to the religious congregation provides a different perspective.

Rather than indicating how much money the congregation has to spend, as when one considers dollars donated, giving as a percentage of income indicates how the congregation rates in light of church members' total available incomes. Has the church sustained the same level of support from its members in comparison to previous years, as measured by what portion of income is being donated by members from the total resources available to them?

Percentage of income is a valuable measure because incomes change. Just as inflation changes the value of the dollar so $5 in 1968 is not the same as $5 in 2001, incomes, influenced by inflation and real growth, also change. For example, per capita income in 1968 was $3,119 in current dollars; if a church member gave $312 that year, that member would have been tithing, or giving the standard of ten percent. In contrast, 2001 per capita income had increased to $25,957 in current dollars; and if that church member still gave $312, the member would have been giving only a little more than 1% of income. The church would have commanded a smaller portion of the member's overall resources.

Thus, while dollars donated provide a limited picture of how much the church has to spend, giving as a percentage of income provides some measure of the church member's level of commitment to the church in comparison to other spending priorities. One might say that giving as a percentage of income is an indication of the church's "market share" of church members' lives.

In most cases, to obtain giving as a percentage of income, total income to a set of denominations was divided by the number of Full or Confirmed Members in the set. This yielded the per member giving amount in dollars. This per member giving amount was divided by per capita disposable personal income.

Data Appendix and Revisions. Appendix B includes the aggregate denominational data used in the analyses in this study. In general, the data for the denominations included in these analyses appears as it was reported in editions of the *YACC*. In some cases, data for one or more years for a specific denomination was obtained directly from the denominational office or another denominational source. Also, the denominational giving data set has been refined and revised as additional information has become available. Where relevant, this information is noted in the appendix.

chapter 1

Church Member Giving, 1968-2001

HIGHLIGHTS

- Per member giving to churches increased in both current and inflation-adjusted 1996 dollars between 1968 and 2001. Because dollars did not keep pace with increases in income, giving as a percentage of income declined between 1968 and 2001.
  - Per Member Giving to Total Contributions increased from $368.16 to $631.48 in inflation-adjusted dollars, an increase of 72%, from 1968 to 2001.
  - U.S. per capita Disposable (after-tax) income increased 100% in inflation-adjusted dollars, from $11,864 in 1968 to $23,731 in 2001.
  - Per Member Giving as a Percentage of Income declined from 3.10% in 1968 to 2.66% in 2001, a decline of 14% in the portion of income donated to the church from the 1968 base.
- Congregational Finances, funding local operations, increased in inflation-adjusted dollars from $290.42 in 1968, to $536.16 in 2001. Giving as a portion of income to this category declined from 2.45% in 1968 to 2.26% in 2001, a decline of 8%. A general increase in giving to Congregational Finances began in 1993. By 2001, giving as a portion of income to this category had recovered to the level of the early 1970s.
- Benevolences, funding the larger mission of the church, increased in inflation-adjusted dollars from $77.73 in 1968 to $95.31 in 2001. As a portion of income, Benevolences declined 39% from 0.66% in 1968 to 0.40% in 2001.
- In 1968, 21¢ of every dollar donated funded Benevolences. By 2001, 15¢ of every dollar went to Benevolences. Of each additional inflation-adjusted dollar donated to the church between 1968 and 2001, 93¢ went to Congregational Finances.
- If the portion of income donated to the church had not declined between 1968 and 2001, congregations and denominations would have had, in aggregate dollars, 8% more for Congregational Finances and 61% more for Benevolences in 2001.

NARRATIVE

The Composite Denominations The first study that provided a basis for the present series was published in 1988. The *Yearbook of American and Canadian Churches* (*YACC*) series publishes church member giving data. Data for the years 1968 and 1985 could be confirmed for 31 denominations.[1] The data year 1968 was selected because, beginning that year, a consistent distinction was made between Full or Confirmed Membership and Inclusive Membership in the *YACC* series. The denominations that published data for both 1968 and 1985 included 29,477,705 Full or Confirmed Members in 1985. They comprise approximately 100,000 of the estimated 350,000 religious congregations in the U.S.

The present church member giving report series extended the analysis for the original set of denominations beyond 1985. The current report analyzes the data set through 2001, the most recent year for which data was available at the time the report was written.[2] Also, data for the intervening years of 1969 through 1984, and 1986 through 1998, was included in the composite data set, as available.[3]

Giving Categories. When a dollar is given to the church, it is allocated into one of two major subcategories, as defined by the annual reporting form of the *YACC*. Congregational Finances refers to those expenditures that support the operations of the local congregation, such as utilities, pastor and staff salaries, insurance and Sunday school materials. Benevolences refers to expenditures for what might be termed the broader mission of the church, beyond the local membership. Benevolences includes everything from regional

---

[1]John Ronsvalle and Sylvia Ronsvalle, *A Comparison of the Growth in Church Contributions with United States Per Capita Income* (Champaign, IL: empty tomb, inc., 1988).

[2]Two of the original 31 denominations merged in 1987, bringing the total number of denominations in the original data set to 30. As of 1991, one denomination reported that it no longer had the staff to collect national financial data, resulting in a maximum of 29 denominations from the original set which could provide data for 1991 through 2001. Of these 29 denominations, one reported data for 1968 through 1997, but did not have financial data for 1998 through 2001 available in time for this report; this communion indicated its intention to supply the missing years' data in late 2002 or 2003. A second denomination merged with another communion not included in the original composite set but since added; having merged, this new denomination did not plan to collect financial data for 2001-2002 from its congregations, although conversations continue about the preservation of the historical data stream that extends back to at least 1968. A third denomination did not report financial data although it had previously done so since 1921. Therefore, the composite data for 2001 includes information from 26 communions in the data set. Throughout this report, what was an original set of 31 denominations in 1985 will be referred to as the composite denominations. Data for 31 denominations will be included for 1968 and 1985, as well as for intervening years, as available.

[3]For 1986 through 2001, annual denominational data has been obtained which represented for any given year at least 98.84% (the 2001 percentage) of the 1985 Full or Confirmed Membership of the denominations included in the 1968-1985 study. For 1986 through 2001, the number of denominations for which data was available varied from a low of 26 denominations of a possible 30 in 2001 to a high of 29 in 1987 through 1997. For the years 1969 through 1984, the number of denominations varied from a low of 28 denominations of a possible 31 in 1971-1972 and 1974-1975 to 31 in 1983, representing at least 99.74% of the membership in the data set. The denominational giving data considered in this analysis was obtained either from the *Yearbook of American and Canadian Churches* series, or directly in correspondence with a denominational office. For a full listing of the data used in this analysis, including the sources, see Appendix B-1.

and national denominational offices to the local soup kitchen, from seminaries to international ministries. Total Contributions is the sum of Congregational Finances and Benevolences.

Financial Categories. Calculating contributions on a per member basis accounts for any changes in membership, either through growth or decline, that might have taken place during the period under review. The dollars given can be considered from two points of view. The *number of dollars given* by members indicates how much money the church has to spend. On the other hand, *giving as a percentage of income* places donations in the larger context of income available to church members.

Within the category of dollars given, there are two approaches as well: (1) current dollars; and (2) inflation-adjusted dollars.

Current dollars refers to the value that the dollar had in the year it was donated. However, inflation affects the value of dollars. A dollar in 2001 bought fewer goods or services than it did in 1968, an issue that members understand at the grocery store but seem to have greater difficulty understanding at church. In order to account for this factor, giving in inflation-adjusted dollars factors out the economic impact of inflation.

The second general category is giving as a percentage of income. This category considers not only the dollars given, but what portion those dollars represent of the resources available to the donor. One might say that looking at the amount of dollars donated indicates how much churches had to spend, while considering giving as a percentage of income reflects how the donation rated in the donor's overall lifestyle choices.

Giving in Dollars. Table 1 presents per member contributions in both current and inflation-adjusted dollars for the composite denominations data set.

Each data series is considered in the three categories of Total Contributions Per Member and the two subcategories of Congregational Finances and Benevolences.

Current Dollars, 1968-2001. As can be seen in Table 1, the per member amount given to Total Contributions, Congregational Finances, and Benevolences increased in current dollars each year during the 1968-2001 period.

Overall, from 1968 to 2001, Total Contributions to the church in current dollars increased $593.92 on a per member basis. Of this amount, $510.10 was directed to increase the per member Congregational Finances expenditures, for the benefit of members within the congregation. Benevolences, or outreach activities of the congregation, increased by $83.82.

One effect of this allocation distribution was that Benevolences shrank as a portion of Total Contributions. In 1968, 21¢ of each dollar went to Benevolences. By 2001, the amount had decreased to 15¢.

Inflation-adjusted Dollars, 1968-2001: The U.S. Bureau of Economic Analysis (U.S. BEA) publishes the deflator series that are used to factor out inflation. These deflators allow dollar figures to be compared more precisely across years. The current year of base comparison in the U.S. BEA series is 1996. By applying the

Implicit Price Deflator for Gross National Product to the current-dollar church member giving data, the data can be reviewed across years with inflation factored out. The result of this process is also listed in Table 1. The arrows next to the three inflation-adjusted columns are included to provide a quick reference as to whether giving increased or decreased from one year to the next.

When the effects of inflation were removed, one may note that per member giving decreased in more years than in the current dollar columns. For example, although per

Table 1: Per Member Giving to Total Contributions, Congregational Finances and Benevolences, Current and Inflation-Adjusted 1996 Dollars, 1968-2001

| | Per Full or Confirmed Member Giving to Congregations, in Dollars | | | | | | | | |
| | *Current Dollars* | | | Inflation-Adjusted 1996 Dollars | | | | | |
Year	*Total*	*Cong. Finances*	*Benevol.*	Total	↑↓	Cong. Finances	↑↓	Benevol.	↑↓
1968	*$96.79*	*$76.35*	*$20.44*	$368.16		$290.42		$77.73	
1969	*$100.82*	*$79.34*	*$21.47*	$365.41	↓	$287.58	↓	$77.83	↑
1970	*$104.36*	*$82.87*	*$21.49*	$359.25	↓	$285.27	↓	$73.98	↓
1971	*$109.55*	*$87.07*	*$22.48*	$358.95	↓	$285.30	↑	$73.65	↓
1972	*$116.97*	*$93.16*	*$23.81*	$367.61	↑	$292.78	↑	$74.83	↑
1973	*$127.37*	*$102.01*	*$25.36*	$379.06	↑	$303.59	↑	$75.47	↑
1974	*$138.87*	*$110.79*	*$28.08*	$379.21	↑	$302.54	↓	$76.68	↑
1975	*$150.19*	*$118.45*	*$31.73*	$375.18	↓	$295.91	↓	$79.28	↑
1976	*$162.87*	*$129.15*	*$33.72*	$384.95	↑	$305.24	↑	$79.71	↑
1977	*$175.82*	*$140.23*	*$35.60*	$390.46	↑	$311.40	↑	$79.05	↓
1978	*$193.05*	*$154.74*	*$38.31*	$400.19	↑	$320.78	↑	$79.41	↑
1979	*$212.42*	*$170.17*	*$42.25*	$406.47	↑	$325.62	↑	$80.85	↑
1980	*$233.57*	*$186.90*	*$46.67*	$409.41	↑	$327.61	↑	$81.80	↑
1981	*$256.60*	*$205.15*	*$51.44*	$411.34	↑	$328.88	↑	$82.46	↑
1982	*$276.72*	*$223.93*	*$52.79*	$417.63	↑	$337.96	↑	$79.66	↓
1983	*$293.52*	*$237.69*	*$55.83*	$426.07	↑	$345.02	↑	$81.05	↑
1984	*$316.25*	*$257.63*	*$58.62*	$442.62	↑	$360.57	↑	$82.05	↑
1985	*$335.44*	*$272.95*	*$62.48*	$455.14	↑	$370.35	↑	$84.78	↑
1986	*$354.20*	*$288.74*	*$65.47*	$470.26	↑	$383.34	↑	$86.92	↑
1987	*$367.87*	*$301.73*	*$66.14*	$474.19	↑	$388.93	↑	$85.25	↓
1988	*$382.55*	*$313.15*	*$69.40*	$476.87	↑	$390.36	↑	$86.51	↑
1989	*$403.23*	*$331.07*	*$72.16*	$484.19	↑	$397.54	↑	$86.65	↑
1990	*$419.65*	*$346.48*	*$73.17*	$484.98	↑	$400.42	↑	$84.56	↓
1991	*$433.58*	*$358.68*	*$74.90*	$483.53	↓	$400.00	↓	$83.53	↓
1992	*$445.01*	*$368.29*	*$76.73*	$484.55	↑	$401.01	↑	$83.54	↑
1993	*$457.49*	*$380.55*	*$76.94*	$486.38	↑	$404.58	↑	$81.80	↓
1994	*$488.84*	*$409.36*	*$79.48*	$509.10	↑	$426.32	↑	$82.78	↑
1995	*$497.71*	*$416.01*	*$81.71*	$507.30	↓	$424.02	↓	$83.28	↑
1996	*$538.39*	*$453.34*	*$85.05*	$538.39	↑	$453.34	↑	$85.05	↑
1997	*$554.60*	*$466.07*	*$88.52*	$544.09	↑	$457.25	↑	$86.84	↑
1998	*$587.91*	*$495.57*	*$92.34*	$569.84	↑	$480.34	↑	$89.50	↑
1999	*$624.80*	*$527.98*	*$96.82*	$597.04	↑	$504.52	↑	$92.52	↑
2000	*$664.27*	*$563.55*	*$100.72*	$621.63	↑	$527.38	↑	$94.25	↑
2001	*$690.71*	*$586.46*	*$104.25*	$631.48	↑	$536.16	↑	$95.31	↑

Details in the above table may not compute to the numbers shown due to rounding

member contributions to Total Contributions increased in the majority of years, the six years of 1969, 1970, 1971, 1975, 1991 and 1995 posted declines.

Congregational Finances also generally increased in inflation-adjusted 1996 dollars. Declines appear in six years: 1969, 1970, 1974, 1975, 1991 and 1995.

Benevolences also increased in the majority of years. Decreases occurred in eight years in the 1968-2001 period, in the years 1970, 1971, 1977, 1982, 1987, 1990, 1991 and 1993.

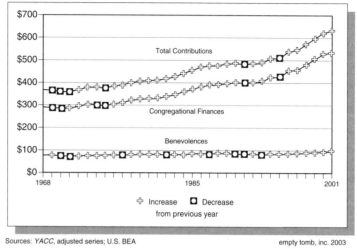

Figure 1: Changes in Per Member Giving in Inflation-Adjusted 1996 Dollars, Total Contributions, Congregational Finances, and Benevolences, 1968-2001

Sources: *YACC*, adjusted series; U.S. BEA   empty tomb, inc. 2003

Figure 1 presents the changes in inflation-adjusted dollar contributions to the three categories of Total Contributions, Congregational Finances and Benevolences.

Over the 1968-2001 period, per member donations to Total Contributions in inflation-adjusted dollars increased from $368.16 to $631.48, an increase of $263.32, or 72%.

Of the total increase, $245.74 was directed to Congregational Finances. This subcategory increased 85% between 1968 and 2001, from $290.42 to $536.16.

In contrast, Benevolences increased 23%, from $77.73 in 1968 to $95.31 in 2001, a difference of $17.58.

Of the total inflation-adjusted dollar increase between 1968 and 2001, 93% was directed to Congregational Finances. Stated another way, of each additional inflation-adjusted dollar donated in 2001 compared to 1968, 93¢ was directed to Congregational Finances. This emphasis on the internal operations of the congregation helps explain the finding that Benevolences represented 21% of all church activity in 1968, and 15% in 2001.

Figure 2 provides a comparison of per member giving to the categories of Congregational Finances and Benevolences with changes in U.S. per capita disposable personal income in inflation-adjusted 1996 dollars.

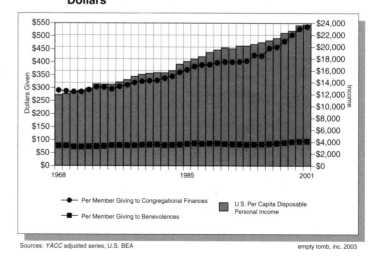

Figure 2: Per Member Giving to Congregational Finances and Benevolences, and U.S. Per Capita Disposable Personal Income, 1968-2001, Inflation-Adjusted 1996 Dollars

Sources: *YACC* adjusted series; U.S. BEA   empty tomb, inc. 2003

Giving as a Percentage of Income, 1968-2001. The second approach to considering giving is as a portion of income. Unlike dollars, there is no distinction between current or inflation-adjusted dollars when one is considering giving as a percentage of income. So long as one compares current dollar giving to current dollar income when calculating the percentage of income—or inflation-adjusted giving with inflation-adjusted income—the percentage will be the same.

Table 2: Per Member Giving as a Percentage of U.S. Per Capita Disposable Personal Income, 1968-2001

Per Full or Confirmed Member Giving to Congregations as a Percentage of Income						
Year	Total Contributions Per Member	↑↓	Congregational Finances	↑↓	Benevolences	↑↓
1968	3.10%		2.45%		0.66%	
1969	3.03%	↓	2.38%	↓	0.65%	↓
1970	2.91%	↓	2.31%	↓	0.60%	↓
1971	2.84%	↓	2.26%	↓	0.58%	↓
1972	2.83%	↓	2.25%	↓	0.58%	↓
1973	2.76%	↓	2.21%	↓	0.55%	↓
1974	2.77%	↑	2.21%	↑	0.56%	↑
1975	2.75%	↓	2.17%	↓	0.58%	↑
1976	2.73%	↓	2.17%	↑	0.57%	↓
1977	2.70%	↓	2.15%	↓	0.55%	↓
1978	2.66%	↓	2.13%	↓	0.53%	↓
1979	2.64%	↓	2.12%	↓	0.53%	↓
1980	2.63%	↓	2.11%	↓	0.53%	↑
1981	2.63%	↓	2.10%	↓	0.53%	↑
1982	2.67%	↑	2.16%	↑	0.51%	↓
1983	2.66%	↓	2.15%	↓	0.51%	↓
1984	2.59%	↓	2.11%	↓	0.48%	↓
1985	2.59%	↑	2.11%	↑	0.48%	↑
1986	2.61%	↑	2.13%	↑	0.48%	↑
1987	2.58%	↓	2.12%	↓	0.46%	↓
1988	2.50%	↓	2.05%	↓	0.45%	↓
1989	2.48%	↓	2.04%	↓	0.44%	↓
1990	2.44%	↓	2.02%	↓	0.43%	↓
1991	2.45%	↑	2.03%	↑	0.42%	↓
1992	2.40%	↓	1.99%	↓	0.41%	↓
1993	2.41%	↑	2.00%	↑	0.41%	↓
1994	2.49%	↑	2.09%	↑	0.40%	↓
1995	2.44%	↓	2.04%	↓	0.40%	↓
1996	2.56%	↑	2.15%	↑	0.40%	↑
1997	2.53%	↓	2.13%	↓	0.40%	↑
1998	2.55%	↑	2.15%	↑	0.40%	↓
1999	2.63%	↑	2.22%	↑	0.41%	↑
2000	2.63%	↑	2.23%	↑	0.40%	↓
2001	2.66%	↑	2.26%	↑	0.40%	↑

Details in the above table may not compute to the numbers shown due to rounding

In Table 2, giving as a percentage of income is presented for per member Total Contributions, and the related subcategories of Congregational Finances and Benevolences. As in Table 1 the arrows indicate whether the percentage of income in that category increased or decreased from the previous year. Inasmuch as the percent figures are rounded to the second decimal place, the arrows indicate the direction of a slight increase or decrease for those situations in which the percentage provided appears to be the same numerical figure as the previous year.

Figure 3 presents per member giving as a percentage of income to Total Contributions, Congregational Finances and Benevolences

A review of Table 2 yields the following information.

Overall, per member giving as a percentage of income to Total Contributions decreased from 3.10% to 2.66%, a decline of 14% in the portion of income donated to the church. Giving as a percentage of income to Total Contributions decreased 21 times out of a possible 33 times, or 64% of the time.

The decline in giving as a percentage of income to Total

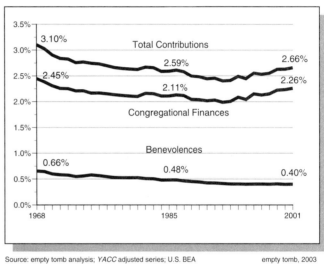

Figure 3: Per Member Giving as a Percentage of Income to Total Contributions, Congregational Finances and Benevolences, 1968-2001

Source: empty tomb analysis; *YACC* adjusted series; U.S. BEA   empty tomb, 2003

Contributions is in contrast to the increase to Total Contributions in both current and inflation-adjusted dollars. Giving as a percentage of income takes into account changes in the resources available to the donor. U.S. per capita disposable (after-tax) personal income serves as an average income figure for the broad spectrum of church members included in the composite denominations data set.

U.S. per capita disposable personal income was $3,119 in current dollars in 1968. When that figure is calculated in inflation-adjusted 1996 dollars, U.S. per capita disposable personal income in 1968 was $11,864.

The current-dollar income figure for 2001 was $25,957. When inflation was factored out, 2001 U.S. per capita disposable personal income was $23,731.

Thus, after-tax per capita income in inflation-adjusted dollars increased by $11,867, an increase of 100% from 1968 to 2001. Even though per member Total Contributions increased 72% in inflation-adjusted dollars from 1968 to 2001, the income increase of 100% during the same period explains how church member contributions could be increasing in inflation-adjusted dollars in most of the years from 1968 to 2001, and yet decreasing as a percentage of income in most of the years from 1968 to 2001.

Congregational Finances decreased 20 times during the 33 two-year sets in the 1968-2001 period, or 61% of the time. Congregational Finances declined from 2.45% in 1968 to 2.26% in 2001, a percent change of 8% from the 1968 base in giving as a percentage of income.

Benevolences declined from 0.66% of income in 1968 to 0.40% in 2001, a decline of 39% as a portion of income. In unrounded figures, the 0.40% level of per member giving as a portion of income in the year 2001 increased slightly over the year 2000 figure, which was the lowest level in the 1968-2001 period. Out of the 33 two-year sets in the 1968-2001 interval, the portion of income that went to Benevolences declined 23 times, or 70% of the time.

Giving in Inflation-adjusted Dollars, 1968, 1985 and 2001. The first report, that served as the basis for the present series on church member giving, considered data for the denominations in the composite for the years 1968 and 1985. With the data now available through 2001, a broader trend can be reviewed for the period under discussion, the 34-year range from 1968 to 2001.

Table 3 presents per member gifts to Total Contributions, Congregational Finances and Benevolences in inflation-adjusted 1996 dollars for the years 1968, 1985 and 2001.

The per member amount donated to Total Contributions in inflation-adjusted 1996 dollars was $86.98 greater in 1985 than it was in 1968 for the denominations in the composite data set. This amount represented an average increase of $5.12 a year in per member contributions. There was an overall increase during the 1985-2001 sixteen-year period as well. In 2001, the per member contribution to the composite denominations, which represented 98.8% of the total 1985 membership of the denominations originally studied, was $176.34 more per member in inflation-adjusted dollars than in 1985. The average annual increase was $11.02 between 1985 and 2001.

Gifts to Congregational Finances also increased between 1968 and 1985, as well as from 1985 to 2001. As in the case of Total Contributions, the annual rate of increase accelerated. Per member contributions to Congregational Finances were $290.42 in 1968, in inflation-adjusted 1996 dollars, and increased to $370.35 in 1985, a total increase of $79.93, with an average annual rate of change of $4.70. From 1985 to 2001, the average

Table 3: Total Contributions, Congregational Finances and Benevolences, Per Member Giving in Inflation-Adjusted 1996 Dollars, 1968, 1985 and 2001

Year	Giving Per Member in Inflation-Adjusted 1996 Dollars								
	Total Contributions			Congregational Finances			Benevolences		
	Per Member Giving	Diff. from Previous $ Base	Average Annual Diff. in $s Given	Per Member Giving	Diff. from Previous $ Base	Average Annual Diff. in $s Given	Per Member Giving	Diff. from Previous $ Base	Average Annual Diff. in $s Given
1968	$368.16			$290.42			$77.73		
1985	$455.14	$86.98	$5.12	$370.35	$79.93	$4.70	$84.78	$7.05	$0.41
2001	$631.48	$176.34	$11.02	$536.16	$165.81	$10.36	$95.31	$10.53	$0.66

Details in the above table may not compute to the numbers shown due to rounding

annual rate of change more than doubled to $10.36, with per member gifts growing from $370.35 in 1985 to $536.16 in 2001, an increase of $165.81.

In inflation-adjusted 1996 dollars, gifts to Benevolences were $77.73 in 1968 and grew to $84.78 in 1985, an increase of $7.05, with an annual average rate of change of $0.41. Between 1985 and 2001, per member gifts to Benevolences increased to $95.31, an increase of $10.53, with an annual average rate of change of $0.66 for the 1985-2001 period. The rate of change increased from 1985 to 2001, compared to the 1968 to 1985 period.

Giving as a Percentage of Income, 1968, 1985 and 2001. Between 1968 and 1985, Total Contributions declined from 3.10% to 2.59% as a portion of income. The percentage change in giving as a percentage of income from the 1968 base was -16% in the 17 years from 1968 to 1985.

From 1985 to 2001, giving as a percentage of income to Total Contributions changed from 2.59% in 1985 to 2.66% in 2001. The percentage change in giving as a percentage of income was 2.2% in this sixteen-year interval of 1985-2001. Therefore, the annual percent change in the portion of per capita income donated to Total Contributions measured 0.14% in the 1985-2001 period, compared to the rate of -0.97% in the 1968-1985 period. This data suggests that the rate of annual change in giving as a percentage of income reversed from a decline in the first seventeen years to a slow increase during the last sixteen years of the 1968 to 2001 period.

Table 4 presents data for Total Contributions per member as a percentage of income in summary fashion for the years 1968, 1985 and 2001.

Per member gifts to Congregational Finances measured 2.45% of income in 1968, 2.11% in 1985 and 2.26% in 2001. The annual average percent change in giving as a percentage of income changed direction from -0.81% a year between 1968 and 1985, from the 1968

Table 4: Per Member Giving as a Percentage of Income to Total Contributions, 1968, 1985 and 2001[4]

Year	Total Contributions Per Member as a Percentage of Income			
	Total Contributions Per Member as a Percentage of Income	Difference in Total Contributions Per Member as a Percent of Income from Previous Base	Percent Change in Total Contributions Per Member as a Percent of Income Calculated from Previous Base	Annual Average Percent Change in Total Contributions Per Member as a Percent of Income
1968	3.10%			
1985	2.59%	-0.51%	-16.47% from 1968	-0.97%
2001	2.66%	0.07%	2.22% from 1985	0.14%

Details in the above table may not compute to the numbers shown due to rounding

[4]An explanation as to how the 1968-1985 and 1985-2001 rates of change were calculated may be found in the Introduction.

Table 5: **Per Member Giving as a Percentage of Income to Congregational Finances, 1968, 1985 and 2001**

Year	Congregational Finances Per Member as a Percentage of Income			
	Congregational Finances Per Member as a Percentage of Income	Difference in Congregational Finances Per Member as a Percent of Income from Previous Base	Percent Change in Congregational Finances Per Member as a Percent of Income Calculated from Previous Base	Annual Average Percent Change in Congregational Finances Per Member as a Percent of Income
1968	2.45%			
1985	2.11%	-0.34%	-13.84% from 1968	-0.81%
2001	2.26%	0.15%	6.13% from 1985	0.38%

Details in the above table may not compute to the numbers shown due to rounding

base, to an increase of 0.38% a year between 1985 and 2001, from the 1985 base. Table 5 presents these numbers. A sporadic trend of increased giving to Congregational Finances began in 1993, and by 2001, the level of giving as a percentage of income had recovered to the level of the early 1970s.

Table 6 presents Benevolences as a percentage of income in 1968, 1985 and 2001. Between 1985 and 2001, the annual average percent decline in giving as a percentage of income to Benevolences was smaller than that during the 1968-1985 period. From 1968 to 1985, the portion of member income directed to Benevolences decreased from 0.66% to 0.48%. This figure translated to a percent change in giving as a percentage of income of 26% from the 1968 base, with an annual average percent change of -1.55%. In the sixteen-year period from 1985 to 2001, giving as a percentage of income directed to Benevolences

Table 6: **Per Member Giving as a Percentage of Income to Benevolences, 1968, 1985 and 2001**

Year	Benevolences Per Member as a Percentage of Income			
	Benevolences Per Member as a Percentage of Income	Difference in Benevolences Per Member as a Percent of Income from Previous Base	Percent Change in Benevolences Per Member as a Percent of Income Calculated from Previous Base	Annual Average Percent Change in Benevolences Per Member as a Percent of Income
1968	0.66%			
1985	0.48%	-0.17%	-26.31% from 1968	-1.55%
2001	0.40%	-0.08%	-12.39% from 1985	-0.77%

Details in the above table may not compute to the numbers shown due to rounding

declined from 0.48% to 0.40%. The 1985-2001 percent change in giving as a percentage of income of –12.39% produced an annual average percent change of –0.77%, a slowing in the rate of decline compared to the 1968-1985 rate.

Giving in 2000 Compared to 2001. Per member giving as a percentage of income to Total Contributions in 2000 measured 2.63%. In 2001, the figure increased to 2.66%.

Congregational Finances increased from 2.23% in 2000 to 2.26% in 2001, continuing a recent trend of increase in this category that varies from an earlier overall pattern of decline.

In 2000, per member giving to Benevolences as a portion of income rounded to 0.40%, but was, as noted earlier, at the lowest in the 1968-2001 period. In the year 2001, giving to Benevolences increased slightly, but also rounded to 0.40%.

The implications of these changes, slight though they seem, can be understood when translated to dollars. The unrounded difference between 2000 and 2001 Benevolences as a portion of income was 0.0023873% of per capita income. When multiplied by the current dollar U.S. per capita income figure of $25,957 in 2001, that figure translated into an increase of only $0.62 more donated per member. However, this group of denominations had 28,728,958 members in 2001. As a result of this slight increase in per member giving as a portion of income to Benevolences, the composite communions had $17,802,262 more to spend in 2001 on the larger mission of the church compared to the 2000 level.

Potential Giving. What would have been the situation in 2001 if giving had at least maintained the 1968 percentages of income donated?[5]

The implications of the difference become clearer when the aggregate totals are calculated by multiplying the theoretical per member giving at 1968 levels by the number of members reported by these denominations in 2001. Aggregate Total Contributions would then have been $23.0 billion rather than $19.8 billion, a difference of $3.1 billion (unrounded), or an increase of 16%.

Aggregate Congregational Finances would have been $18.1 billion rather than $16.8 billion, a difference of $1.3 billion, or an increase of 8%.

There would have been a 61% increase in the total amount received for Benevolences. Instead of receiving $3.0 billion in 2001, as these church structures did, they would have received $4.8 billion, a difference of $1.8 billion for the larger mission of the church.

---

[5]For this comparison, only 26 denominations that provided data for both 1968 and 2001 were included.

chapter 2

Church Member Giving
for 41 Denominations,
2000 to 2001

HIGHLIGHTS

- The composite denominations data set was expanded to include fifteen additional denominations that reported 2000 and 2001 data to the *YACC*.

- In both the composite set and the expanded set, from 2000 to 2001 per member contributions in current and inflation-adjusted dollars increased to Total Contributions and the two subcategories of Congregational Finances and Benevolences.

- In both the composite set and the expanded set, from 2000 to 2001 per member giving as a percentage of income increased to Total Contributions, Congregational Finances, and Benevolences.

- The rate of increase in giving as a percentage of income to Total Contributions from 2000 to 2001 was higher in the composite set of communions than in the expanded set.

- The rate of increase in giving as a percentage of income to Benevolences from 2000 to 2001 was higher in the expanded set of communions than in the composite set.

NARRATIVE

The 1968-2001 analysis in chapter one considers data for a group of denominations that published their membership and financial information for 1968 and 1985 in the *Yearbook of American and Canadian Churches* (*YACC*) series. That initial set of communions, considered in the first report on which the present series on church giving is based, has served as a denominational composite set analyzed for subsequent data years. Twenty-six of the communions in the 1968-2001 data set provided information for both 2000 and 2001.

Data for both 2000 and 2001 for an additional fifteen denominations was either published in the relevant editions of the *YACC* series, or obtained directly from denominational offices.

By adding the data for these 15 denominations to that of the composite group for these two years, giving patterns in an expanded set of communions can be considered.

In this enlarged comparison, the 2001 member sample increased from 28.7 million to 39,622,918 Full or Confirmed Members, and the number of denominations increased from 26 to 41. The larger group of denominations included both The United Methodist Church and The Episcopal Church, which were not included in the original 1968-1985 analysis because of the unavailability of confirmed 1968 data at the time of that study. A list of the denominations included in the present analysis is contained in Appendix A.

Per Member Giving in Inflation-Adjusted 1996 Dollars. As noted in the first chapter of this report, per member giving to Total Contributions increased from 2000 to 2001 for the composite denominations data set in inflation-adjusted 1996 dollars. Specifically, Total Contributions Per Member increased by $9.85 in inflation-adjusted 1996 dollars, from $621.63 in 2000 to $631.48 in 2001. When the group was expanded to 41 denominations, Total Per Member giving increased by $8.81, from $641.54 in 2000 to $650.35 in 2001. The rate of change in giving in inflation-adjusted dollars was higher in the composite group

The composite denominations increased per member giving in inflation-adjusted dollars to Congregational Finances by $8.79, from $527.38 in 2000 to $536.16 in 2001. The expanded group increased the lower amount of $6.42, from $541.35 in 2000 to $547.77 in 2001.

In the composite communions, per member contributions to Benevolences increased from $94.25 to $95.31, an increase of $1.06. The expanded group of 41 denominations increased by $2.39, from $100.19 to $102.58.

Table 7 presents per member giving data for 2000 and 2001 for the expanded group of 41 denominations, both in inflation-adjusted 1996 dollars, and also as a percentage of income. In addition, the change from 2000 to 2001 in per member contributions in inflation-adjusted

Table 7: Per Member Giving in 41 Denominations, 2000 and 2001, in Inflation-Adjusted 1996 Dollars and as a Percentage of Income

Year	Total Contributions Per Member		Congregational Finances		Benevolences	
	$s Given in Inflation Adj. '96 $	Giving as % of Income	$s Given in Inflation Adj. '96 $	Giving as % of Income	$s Given in Inflation Adj. '96 $	Giving as % of Income
2000	$641.54	2.72%	$541.35	2.29%	$100.19	0.42%
2001	$650.35	2.74%	$547.77	2.31%	$102.58	0.43%
Difference from the 2000 Base	$8.81	0.02%	$6.42	0.02%	$2.39	0.01%
% Change in Giving as % of Income from the 2000 Base		0.89%		0.70%		1.90%

Details in the above table may not compute to the numbers shown due to rounding.

1996 dollars, in giving as a percentage of income, and in the percent change in giving as a percentage of income from the 2000 base are also included.

Per Member Giving as a Percentage of Income. In the composite denominations set, from 2000 to 2001, giving as a percentage of income increased to Total Contributions, Congregational Finances, and Benevolences. The percent given to Total Contributions increased from 2.63% in 2000 to 2.66% in 2001. Congregational Finances increased from 2.23% in 2000 to 2.26% in 2001. Benevolences measured 0.40% in 2000, and increased in 2001, although the rounded level still measured 0.40%.

In the expanded group of 41 denominations, giving as a percentage of income also increased to Total Contributions, Congregational Finances, and Benevolences. In this expanded set, the percent of income given on a per member basis to Total Contributions measured 2.72% in 2000 and 2.74% in 2001. Congregational Finances was 2.29% in 2000 and increased to 2.31% in 2001. Benevolences measured 0.42% in 2000 and 0.43% in 2001, posting a stronger increase than that evident in the composite denominations.

A comparison of the rate of percent change in giving as a percentage of income from the 2000 base resulted in the following. For Total Contributions, the composite denominations posted a 1.10% change from the 2000 base, compared to 0.89% for the expanded group of 41 denominations. For Congregational Finances, the composite denominations had a rate of 1.18% percent increase, compared to 0.70% for the expanded group of 41 denominations. Benevolences for the composite denominations posted a 0.64% percent increase, compared to a rate of 1.90% when the group was expanded to include 41 denominations.

Thus, the composite set of denominations had a larger rate of increase to both Total Contributions and Congregational Finances, while the expanded set had a larger rate of increase to Benevolences.

chapter 3

Church Member Giving in Denominations Defined by Organizational Affiliation, 1968, 1985, and 2001

HIGHLIGHTS

- During the 1968-2001 period, members of evangelical Protestant denominations gave larger dollar amounts and larger portions of income to their churches than did members of mainline Protestant denominations.

- In 2001, mainline Protestant church members were giving a higher portion of income to the category of Congregational Finances than they did in 1968. All other categories for both groups declined as a portion of income from 1968 to 2001.

- The 1968-2001 rate of decline in giving as a portion of income to Total Contributions was greater among the members of the evangelical denominations than it was among the members of the mainline denominations. While giving as a portion of income to Congregational Finances declined among the National Association of Evangelicals (NAE)-affiliated denominations, it reversed in the National Council of Churches (NCC)-affiliated denominations. Per member giving as a portion of income to Benevolences declined to both the evangelical and the mainline communions between 1968 and 2001.

- Membership in the evangelical denominations grew between 1968 and 2001, in contrast to the mainline denominations, which decreased in membership. Therefore, although evangelicals were receiving a smaller portion of income per member in 2001 than in 1968, aggregate donations were higher in 2001 than in 1968 for this group.

- Among the mainline denominations, the increase in giving was directed to Congregational Finances. This fact, combined with the loss in membership, may account for the finding that aggregate Benevolences donations in inflation-adjusted dollars were 13 percent smaller in 2001 than in 1968 for these communions.

NARRATIVE_____

The communions included in the composite denominations data set considered in chapter 1 of this volume span the theological spectrum. Reviewing data for defined subsets within the composite group allows for additional analysis.

For example, the theory that evangelical Protestants donate more money to their churches than do members of mainline Protestant denominations can be tested by comparing giving patterns in two subgroups of communions within the composite denominations data set.

In the composite group, membership and financial data is available for 1968, 1985 and 2001 for eight communions affiliated with the National Association of Evangelicals (NAE).

Seven communions affiliated with the National Council of the Churches of Christ in the U.S.A. (NCC) also had membership and financial data available for 1968, 1985 and 2001.

Of course, there is diversity of opinion within any denomination, as well as in multi-communion groupings such as the NAE or the NCC. For purposes of the present analysis, however, these two groups may serve as general standards for comparison, since they have been characterized as representing certain types of denominations. For example, the National Association of Evangelicals has, by choice of its title, defined its denominational constituency. And traditionally, the National Council of the Churches of Christ in the U.S.A. has counted mainline denominations among its members.

Recognizing that there are limitations in defining a denomination's theological perspectives merely by membership in one of these two organizations, a review of giving patterns of the two subsets of denominations may nevertheless provide some insight into how widely spread current giving patterns may be. Therefore, an analysis of 1968-2001 giving patterns was completed for the two subsets of those denominations which were affiliated with one of these two interdenominational organizations.

Using 1985 data, the eight denominations affiliated with the NAE as of 2001 represented 18% of the total number of NAE-member denominations as listed in the *Yearbook of American and Canadian Churches* (*YACC*) series; 21% of the total number of NAE-member denominations with membership data listed in the *YACC*; and approximately 21% of the total membership of the NAE-member denominations with membership data listed in the *YACC*.[1]

Data for 2001 was also available for seven NCC-member denominations. In 1985, these seven denominations represented 21% of the total number of NCC constituent bodies as listed in the *YACC*; 23% of the NCC constituent bodies with membership data

_____

[1]The 1985 total church membership estimate of 3,388,414 represented by NAE denominations includes *YACC* 1985 membership data for each denomination where available or, if 1985 membership data was not available, membership data for the most recent year prior to 1985. Full or Confirmed membership data was used except in those instances where this figure was not available, in which case Inclusive Membership was used.

listed in the *YACC*; and approximately 28% of the total membership of the NCC constituent bodies with membership data listed in the *YACC*.[2]

Per Member Giving to Total Contributions, 1968, 1985 and 2001. As noted in Table 8, per member giving as a percentage of income to Total Contributions for a composite of those eight NAE-member denominations was 6.15% in 1968. That year, per member giving as a percentage of income to Total Contributions was 3.30% for a composite of these seven NCC denominations.

Table 8: Per Member Giving as a Percentage of Income to Total Contributions, Eight NAE and Seven NCC Denominations, 1968, 1985 and 2001

	Total Contributions									
	NAE Denominations					NCC Denominations				
Year	Number of Denom. Analyzed	Total Contrib. Per Member as % of Income	Diff. in Total Contrib. as % of Income from Previous Base	Percent Change in Total Contrib. as % of Income Figured from Previous Base	Avg. Annual Percent Change in Total Contrib. as % of Income	Number of Denom. Analyzed	Total Contrib. Per Member as % of Income	Diff. in Total Contrib. as % of Income from Previous Base	Percent Change in Total Contrib. as % of Income Figured from Previous Base	Avg. Annual Percent Change in Total Contrib. as % of Income
1968	8	6.15%				7	3.30%			
1985	8	4.74%	-1.41%	-22.94% from '68	-1.35%	7	2.85%	-0.45%	-13.74% from '68	-0.81%
2001	8	4.27%	-0.47%	-7.65% from '85	-0.48%	7	3.17%	0.32%	9.79% from '85	0.61%

Details in the above table may not compute to the numbers shown due to rounding.

In 1985, the NAE denominations' per member giving as a percentage of income level was 4.74%, while the NCC level was 2.85%.

The data shows the NAE-member denominations received a larger portion of their members' incomes than did NCC-affiliated denominations in both 1968 and 1985. This information supports the assumption that denominations identifying with an evangelical perspective received a higher level of support than denominations that may be termed mainline.

The analysis also indicates that the decline in levels of giving observed in the larger composite of 29 denominations was evident among both the NAE-member denominations and the NCC-member denominations as well. While giving levels decreased for both sets of denominations between 1968 and 1985, the decrease in Total Contributions was more pronounced in the NAE-affiliated communions. The percent change in the percentage of income donated in the NAE-member denominations, in comparison to the 1968 base, was

---

[2]The 1985 total church membership estimate of 39,621,950 represented by NCC denominations includes *YACC* 1985 membership data for each denomination where available or, if 1985 membership data was not available, membership data for the most recent year prior to 1985. Full or Confirmed membership data was used except in those instances where this figure was not available, in which case Inclusive Membership was used.

-23% between 1968 and 1985, while the percent change in percentage of income given to the NCC-member denominations was -14%.

A decline in giving as a percentage of income continued among the eight NAE-member denominations during the 1985-2001 period. By 2001, per member giving as a percentage of income to Total Contributions had declined from the 1985 level of 4.74% to 4.27%, a percentage change of -8% in the portion of members' incomes donated over that sixteen-year period.

In contrast, the seven NCC-affiliated denominations increased in giving as a percentage of income to Total Contributions during 1985-2001, from the 1985 level of 2.85% to 3.17% in 2001, a percentage increase of 10% in the portion of income given to these churches.

Because of the decline in the portion of income given in the NAE-affiliated denominations and increase among the NCC-affiliated denominations, in 2001 the difference in per member giving as a percentage of income between the NAE-affiliated denominations and the NCC-affiliated denominations was not as large as it had been in 1968. Comparing the two rates in giving as a percentage of income to Total Contributions between the NAE-member denominations and the NCC-member denominations in this analysis, the NCC-affiliated denominations received 54% as much of per member income as the NAE-member denominations did in 1968, 60% as much in 1985, and 74% in 2001.

For the NAE-affiliated denominations, during the 1985 to 2001 period, the rate of decrease in the average annual percent change in per member giving as a percentage of income to Total Contributions slowed in comparison to the 1968-1985 annual percent change from the 1968 base. The 1968-1985 average annual percent change was -1.35%. The figure for 1985-2001 was -0.48%.

In the NCC-member denominations, the trend reversed. While the average annual percent change from the 1968 base in giving as a percentage of income was -0.81% between 1968 and 1985, the average annual change from 1985 was an increase of 0.61% between 1985 and 2001.

Per Member Giving to Congregational Finances and Benevolences, 1968, 1985 and 2001. Were there any markedly different patterns between the two subsets of denominations defined by affiliation with the NAE and the NCC in regards to the distribution of Total Contributions between the subcategories of Congregational Finances and Benevolences?

In the subcategory of Congregational Finances, a difference was observable. The NCC-related denominations posted an increase from 1968 levels in the portion of income directed to this category. In the NAE-related denominations, the portion of income declined. Table 9 presents the Congregational Finances giving data for the NAE and NCC denominations in 1968, 1985 and 2001.

In the subcategory of Benevolences, both groups posted declines in the portion of income directed to that category. Table 10 presents the Benevolences giving data for the NAE and NCC denominations in 1968, 1985 and 2001.

In 1968, the NAE-affiliated members were giving 6.15% of their incomes to their churches. Of that, 5.01% went to Congregational Finances, while 1.14% went to Benevolences. In 1985, of the 4.74% of income donated to Total Contributions, 3.82% was

Table 9: Per Member Giving as a Percentage of Income to Congregational Finances, Eight NAE and Seven NCC Denominations, 1968, 1985 and 2001

| | Congregational Finances | | | | | | | | | |
| | NAE Denominations | | | | | NCC Denominations | | | | |
Year	Number of Denom. Analyzed	Cong. Finances Per Member as % of Income	Diff. in Cong. Finances as % of Income from Previous Base	Percent Change in Cong. Finances as % of Income Figured from Previous Base	Avg. Annual Percent Change in Cong. Finances as % of Income	Number of Denom. Analyzed	Cong. Finances Per Member as % of Income	Diff. in Cong. Finances as % of Income from Previous Base	Percent Change in Cong. Finances as % of Income Figured from Previous Base	Avg. Annual Percent Change in Cong. Finances as % of Income
1968	8	5.01%				7	2.67%			
1985	8	3.82%	-1.19%	-23.71% from '68	-1.39%	7	2.40%	-0.27%	-10.07% from '68	-0.59%
2001	8	3.56%	-0.26%	-5.15% from '85	-0.32%	7	2.78%	0.38%	14.21% from '85	0.89%

Details in the above table may not compute to the numbers shown due to rounding.

Table 10: Per Member Giving as a Percentage of Income to Benevolences, Eight NAE and Seven NCC Denominations, 1968, 1985 and 2001

| | Benevolences | | | | | | | | | |
| | NAE Denominations | | | | | NCC Denominations | | | | |
Year	Number of Denom. Analyzed	Benevol. Per Member as % of Income	Diff. in Benevol. as % of Income from Previous Base	Percent Change in Benevol. as % of Income Figured from Previous Base	Avg. Annual Percent Change in Benevol. as % of Income	Number of Denom. Analyzed	Benevol. Per Member as % of Income	Diff. in Benevol. as % of Income from Previous Base	Percent Change in Benevol. as % of Income Figured from Previous Base	Avg. Annual Percent Change in Benevol. as % of Income
1968	8	1.14%				7	0.63%			
1985	8	0.92%	-0.22%	-19.51% from '68	-1.15%	7	0.44%	-0.18%	-29.36% from '68	-1.73%
2001	8	0.71%	-0.21%	-18.60% from '85	-1.16%	7	0.39%	-0.06%	-9.05% from '85	-0.57%

Details in the above table may not compute to the numbers shown due to rounding.

directed to Congregational Finances. This represented a percent change in the portion of income going to Congregational Finances of -24% from the 1968 base. Per member contributions to Benevolences among these NAE-member denominations declined from 1.14% in 1968 to 0.92% in 1985, representing a percent change of -20% from the 1968 base in the portion of income donated to Benevolences.

In 2001, the 4.27% of income donated by the NAE-member denominations to their churches was divided between Congregational Finances and Benevolences at the 3.56% and 0.71% levels, respectively. The percent change between 1985 and 2001 in contributions to Congregational Finances as a percent of income was a decline of -5%. In contrast, the percent change in contributions to Benevolences as a percent of income was a decline of

19% in the same sixteen-year period. The annual rate in the percent change in giving as a percentage of income to Benevolences remained relatively constant at -1.15%. from 1968 to 1985 and -1.16% from 1985 to 2001.

In 1968, the NCC-member denominations were giving 3.30% of their incomes to their churches. Of that, 2.67% went to Congregational Finances. In 1985, of the 2.85% of income donated to these communions, 2.40% went to Congregational Finances. This represented a percent change from the 1968 base in the portion of income going to Congregational Finances of -10%. In contrast, per member contributions as a percent of income to Benevolences among these same NCC-affiliated denominations had declined from 0.63% in 1968 to 0.44% in 1985, representing a percent change of -29% from the 1968 base in the portion of income donated to Benevolences.

In 2001, the 3.17% of income donated by the NCC-affiliated members to their churches was divided between Congregational Finances and Benevolences at the 2.78% and 0.39% levels, respectively. The increase in per member Total Contributions as a percent of income was directed to Congregational Finances, which increased from 2.40% in 1985 to 2.78% in 2001. The 2001 percent change in contributions to Congregational Finances as a percent of income from 1985 was an increase of 14%. The 2001 level of giving to this category was higher than that posted by these communions in 1968.

The portion of income directed to Benevolences by these NCC-member denominations declined from 1968 to 1985, and continued to decline from 1985 to 2001. The percent change in contributions to Benevolences as a percent of income declined from 0.44% in 1985 to the 2001 level of 0.39%, a decline of 9% in this sixteen-year period. The annual percent change from 1985 in giving as a percentage of income to Benevolences indicated a lower rate of decline at –0.57% between 1985 and 2001, compared to the 1968-1985 annual rate of –1.73%.

Figure 4: Per Member Giving as a Percent of Income to Total Contributions, Congregational Finances and Benevolences, Eight NAE and Seven NCC Denominations, 1968, 1985 and 2001

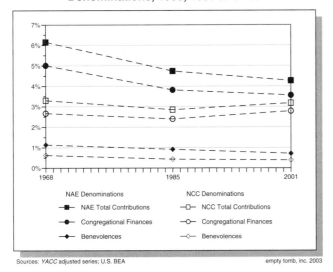

Sources: *YACC* adjusted series; U.S. BEA   empty tomb, inc. 2003

Figure 4 presents data for giving as a percentage of income to Total Contributions, Congregational Finances and Benevolences for both the NAE and NCC denominations in graphic form for the years 1968, 1985 and 2001.

Changes in Per Member Giving, 1968 to 2001. For the NAE-affiliated denominations, per member giving as a percentage of income to Congregational Finances declined from 5.01% in 1968 to 3.56% in 2001, a change of -29% from the 1968 base. In Benevolences, the -38% change reflected a decline from 1.14% in 1968 to 0.71% in 2001.

For the NCC-affiliated denominations, between 1968 and 2001 in the subcategory of Congregational Finances, per member giving as a percentage of income increased from 2.67% to 2.78%, a change of 4% from the 1968 base. That compared to the 38% decline in the subcategory of Benevolences that changed from 0.63% in 1968 to 0.39% in 2001.

Table 11 presents the 1968-2001 percent change in per member giving as a percentage of income to Total Contributions, Congregational Finances and Benevolences in both the NAE- and NCC-affiliated communions.

Table 11: Percent Change in Per Member Giving as a Percentage of Income, Eight NAE and Seven NCC Denominations, 1968 to 2001

Year	NAE Denominations				NCC Denominations			
	Number of Denom. Analyzed	Total Contrib.	Cong. Finances	Benevol.	Number of Denom. Analyzed	Total Contrib.	Cong. Finances	Benevol.
1968	8	6.15%	5.01%	1.14%	7	3.30%	2.67%	0.63%
2001	8	4.27%	3.56%	0.71%	7	3.17%	2.78%	0.39%
% Chg. 1968-01	8	-31%	-29%	-38%	7	-4%	4%	-38%

Details in the above table may not compute to the numbers shown due to rounding.

Per Member Giving in Inflation-Adjusted 1996 Dollars. The NAE-affiliated group's level of per member support to Total Contributions in inflation-adjusted 1996 dollars was $730.03 in 1968. This increased to $832.67 in 1985, and by 2001 increased to $1,013.65.

For the NAE-affiliated denominations, per member contributions in inflation-adjusted 1996 dollars to the subcategory of Congregational Finances increased from 1968 to 1985, and again from 1985 to 2001. Per member contributions in inflation-adjusted 1996 dollars to Benevolences increased between 1968 and 1985, and, at a slower rate, between 1985 and 2001. Of the increased per member giving in inflation-adjusted dollars between 1968 and 2001, 89% went to Congregational Finances.

The NCC-affiliated group also experienced an increase in inflation-adjusted per member Total Contributions between 1968 and 2001. The 1968 NCC level of per member support in inflation-adjusted 1996 dollars was $391.66. In 1985, this had increased to $500.01, and in 2001 the figure was $752.44.

The NCC-member denominations experienced an increase in inflation-adjusted per member donations to Congregational Finances in both 1985 and 2001 as well. Although 95% of the increase between 1968 and 2001 was directed to Congregational Finances, gifts to Benevolences increased in inflation-adjusted 1996 dollars between 1968 and 1985, and again between 1985 and 2001.

As a portion of Total Contributions, the NAE-member denominations directed 19% of their per member gifts to Benevolences in 1968, 19% in 1985, and 17% in 2001. The NCC-member denominations directed 19% of their per member gifts to Benevolences in 1968, 16% in 1985, and 12% in 2001.

Table 12: Per Member Giving, Eight NAE and Seven NCC Denominations, 1968, 1985 and 2001, Inflation-Adjusted 1996 Dollars

Year	NAE Denominations					NCC Denominations				
	Number of Denom. Analyzed	Total Contrib.	Cong. Finances	Benevol.	Benevol. as % of Total Contrib.	Number of Denom. Analyzed	Total Contrib.	Cong. Finances	Benevol.	Benevol. as % of Total Contrib.
1968	8	$730.03	$594.59	$135.44	19%	7	$391.66	$317.11	$74.54	19%
1985	8	$832.67	$671.33	$161.34	19%	7	$500.01	$422.09	$77.93	16%
2001	8	$1,013.65	$846.00	$167.65	17%	7	$752.44	$660.60	$91.83	12%
$ Diff. '68-'01		$283.62	$251.41	$32.21			$360.78	$343.49	$17.29	
% Chg. '68-'01		39%	42%	24%			92%	108%	23%	

Details in the above table may not compute to the numbers shown due to rounding.

Figure 5: Per Member Giving to Total Contributions, Congregational Finances and Benevolences, Eight NAE and Seven NCC Denominations, 1968, 1985 and 2001, Inflation-Adjusted 1996 $

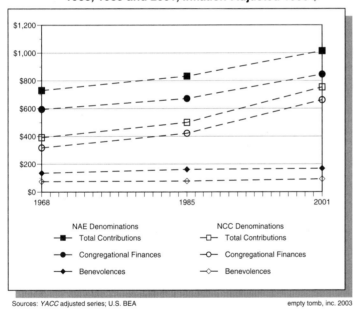

NAE Denominations
- ■ Total Contributions
- ● Congregational Finances
- ◆ Benevolences

NCC Denominations
- □ Total Contributions
- ○ Congregational Finances
- ◇ Benevolences

Sources: *YACC* adjusted series; U.S. BEA   empty tomb, inc. 2003

Table 12 presents the levels of per member giving to Total Contributions, Congregational Finances and Benevolences, in inflation-adjusted 1996 dollars, and the percentage of Total Contributions which went to Benevolences in 1968, 1985 and 2001, for both sets of denominations. In addition, the percent change from 1968 to 2001, from the 1968 base, in per member inflation-adjusted 1996 dollar contributions is noted.

Figure 5 presents the data for per member contributions in inflation-adjusted 1996 dollars in graphic form for the years 1968, 1985 and 2001.

Aggregate Dollar Donations, 1968 and 2001. The NCC-member denominations and the NAE-member denominations differed in terms of changes of membership. The impact of this difference was evident at the aggregate dollar level.

Table 13 considers aggregate giving data for the eight NAE-member denominations included in this analysis. Membership in these eight NAE-member denominations increased 60% from 1968-2001.

As measured in current aggregate dollars, giving in each of the three categories of Total Contributions, Congregational Finances and Benevolences was greater in 2001 than in 1968

Table 13: Aggregate Giving, Eight NAE Denominations, 1968 and 2001,
Current and Inflation-Adjusted 1996 Dollars

Year	Number of Den. Analyzed	Member-ship	Current Dollars			Inflation-Adjusted 1996 Dollars		
			Total Contributions	Cong. Finances	Benevol.	Total Contributions	Cong. Finances	Benevol.
1968	8	535,865	$102,845,802	$83,765,677	$19,080,125	$391,197,421	$318,621,822	$72,575,599
2001	8	856,742	$949,893,096	$792,790,452	$157,102,644	$868,433,988	$724,803,851	$143,630,137
% Chg.		60%	824%	846%	723%	122%	127%	98%

Details in the above table may not compute to the numbers shown due to rounding.

for the NAE-member denominations. This was true even though per member giving as a portion of income declined to all three categories during this period.

The same can be said for the three aggregate categories when inflation was factored out by converting the current dollars to inflation-adjusted 1996 dollars. These denominations have been compensated for a decline in giving as a percentage of income to all three categories by the increase in total membership. As long as these denominations continue to grow in membership, their national and regional programs may not be affected in the immediate future by the decline in the portion of income donated.

Table 14 below considers aggregate data for the seven NCC-member denominations. The NCC-related denominations experienced a membership decline of 29% between 1968 and 2001. The increase in current dollar donations was sufficient to result in an increase in aggregate current dollars in each of the three categories of Total Contributions, Congregational Finances and Benevolences.

However, the inflation-adjusted 1996 dollar figures account for the acknowledged financial difficulties in many of these communions, particularly in the category of Benevolences. The impact of the decline in membership was evident at the aggregate dollar level. The increase in giving to Congregational Finances as a portion of income noted above was tempered by a loss of members. Between 1968 and 2001, while the NCC-related communions experienced an increase of 92% in per member giving to Total Contributions in inflation-adjusted 1996 dollars—from $391.66 in 1968 to $752.44 in 2001—

Table 14: Aggregate Giving, Seven NCC Denominations, 1968 and 2001,
Current and Inflation-Adjusted 1996 Dollars

Year	Number of Den. Analyzed	Member-ship	Current Dollars			Inflation-Adjusted 1996 Dollars		
			Total Contributions	Cong. Finances	Benevol.	Total Contributions	Cong. Finances	Benevol.
1968	7	12,688,864	$1,323,017,450	$1,071,215,356	$251,802,094	$5,032,398,060	$4,074,611,472	$957,786,588
2001	7	9,106,351	$7,494,676,664	$6,579,961,822	$914,714,842	$6,851,962,575	$6,015,690,091	$836,272,483
% Chg.		-29%	466%	514%	263%	36%	48%	-13%

Details in the above table may not compute to the numbers shown due to rounding.

aggregate Total Contributions in 2001 to these seven denominations measured only 36% larger in inflation-adjusted 1996 dollars in 2001 than in 1968.

Further, Congregational Finances absorbed all of the increased giving at the aggregate level. The 13% decline in aggregated Benevolences receipts in inflation-adjusted 1996 dollars between 1968 and 2001 provides insight into the basis for any cutbacks at the denominational level.

chapter 4

Church Member Giving in Eleven Denominations, 1921-2001

HIGHLIGHTS

Eleven denominations reported data on a fairly consistent basis from 1921 through 2001.

- Per member giving as a portion of income was above three percent from 1922-1933 and again from 1958-1962. However, unlike after 1933, when the country was experiencing the Great Depression followed by World War II, no major national catastrophes explain the drop below 3% after 1962, and the following decline.

- Per member giving as a percent of income began to decline in 1961, and membership as a percent of U.S. population began to decline in 1962. While giving as a portion of income showed a slight upward trend beginning in 1993, the decline in membership as a percent of U.S. population continued uninterrupted through the year 2001.

- Considered in five-year segments as inflation-adjusted dollars between 1950 and 2001, the highest average annual rate of growth in per member giving in inflation-adjusted dollars was from 1995-2000. However, when the increase in dollars given was considered as a portion of average annual income increase, the highest rate was in the 1950-1955 segment, followed by 1955-1960.

- Considered in five-year segments as a percentage of income between 1950 and 2001, the highest annual average in giving as a percent of Disposable Personal Income was in 1950-1955, followed by 1955-1960. The period 1960-1980 posted declines.

- Giving as a percentage of income was lower in 2001 than in 1921 or in 1933, the depth of the Great Depression.

NARRATIVE

A continuing feature in this ongoing series reviewing church member giving is an analysis of available giving data throughout this century. Because of the fixed nature of the data source, the analysis remains fairly static. However, the data can now be updated to include information through 2001. This data makes use of the U.S. BEA income series, with the benchmark year being 1996.

For the period 1921 through 2001, the preferable approach would be to analyze the entire composite denominations data set considered in chapter one of this volume. Unfortunately, comparable data since 1921 is not readily available for these communions. However, data over an extended period of time is available in the *Yearbook of American and Canadian Churches* series for a group of 11 Protestant communions, or their historical antecedents. This set includes ten mainline Protestant communions and the Southern Baptist Convention.

The available data has been reported fairly consistently over the time span of 1921 to 2001.[1] The value of the multiyear comparison is that it provides a historical time line over which to observe giving patterns.

Giving as a Percentage of Income. The period under consideration in this section of the report began in 1921. At that point, per member giving as a percentage of income was 2.9%. In current dollars, U.S. per capita disposable (after-tax) personal income was $555, and per member giving was $16.10. When inflation was factored out by converting both income and giving to 1996 dollars, per capita income in 1921 measured $4,705 and per member giving was $136.58.

From 1922 through 1933, giving as a percent of income stayed above the 3% level. The high was 3.7% in 1924, followed closely by the amount in 1932, when per member giving measured 3.6% of per capita income. This trend is of particular interest inasmuch as per capita income was increasing steadily between 1921 and 1927, with the exception of a decline in 1925. Even as people were increasing in personal affluence, they also continued to maintain a giving level of more than 3% to their churches. Even after income began to decline because of the economic reverses in the Great Depression, giving measured above 3% from 1929 through 1933.

The year 1933 was the depth of the Great Depression. Per capita income was at the lowest point it would reach between 1921 and 2001, whether measured in current or inflation-adjusted dollars. Yet per member giving as a percentage of income was 3.3%. Income had decreased by 17% between 1921 and 1933 in inflation-adjusted 1996 dollars, from $4,705 to $3,904. Meanwhile, per member giving had decreased 6%, from $136.58 in 1921 to $127.81 in 1933, in inflation-adjusted dollars. Therefore, giving as a percentage of income actually increased from 2.9% in 1921 to 3.3% in 1933, an increase of 13% in the portion of income contributed to the church.

Giving in inflation-adjusted 1996 dollars declined from 1933 to 1934, although income began to recover in 1934. Giving then began to increase again in 1935. In inflation-adjusted dollars, giving did not surpass the 1927 level of $209.62 until 1953, when giving grew from $201.58 in 1952 to $221.68 in 1953.

---

[1]Data for the period 1965-1967 was not available in a form that could be readily analyzed for the present purposes, and therefore data for these three years was estimated by dividing the change in per member current dollar contributions from 1964 to 1968 by four, the number of years in this interval, and cumulatively adding the result to the base year of 1964 data and subsequently to the calculated data for the succeeding years of 1965 and 1966 in order to obtain estimates for the years 1965-1967.

During World War II, incomes improved rapidly. Meanwhile, church member giving increased only modestly in current dollars. When inflation was factored out, per member giving was at $132.12 in 1941, the year the United States entered the war. It declined to $128.01 in 1942, increased in 1943 to $129.71 and then to $142.86 in 1944. However, income in inflation-adjusted dollars grew from $6,379 in 1941 to $7,401 in 1942, $7,907 in 1943, and reached a high for this period of $8,368 in 1944, a level that would not be surpassed again until 1953. Thus, giving as a percentage of income reached a low point during the three full calendar years of formal U.S. involvement in World War II, at levels of 1.73% in 1942, 1.64% in 1943, and 1.71% in 1944.

In 1945, the last year of the war, U.S. per capita income was $8,260 in inflation-adjusted dollars. Giving in inflation-adjusted dollars increased from 1944 to 1945, to $161.78, the highest amount it had been since 1930. Although per member giving increased 27% between 1933 and 1945, per capita income had increased 112%. Giving as a percentage of income therefore declined from the 3.3% level in 1933, to 2.0% in 1945.

The unusually high level of per capita income slumped after the war but had recovered to war levels by the early 1950s. By 1960, U.S. per capita income was 11% higher in inflation-adjusted 1996 dollars than it had been in 1945, increasing from $8,260 in 1945 to $9,134 in 1960. Meanwhile, per member giving in inflation-adjusted dollars had increased 77%, from $161.78 in 1945 to $285.64 in 1960. Giving recovered the level it had been from 1922 through 1933, and stayed above 3% from 1958 through 1962. Giving as a percentage of income reached a postwar high of 3.13% in 1960, and then began to decline.

For the second time in the century, giving levels were growing to, or maintaining a level above, three percent of income even while incomes were also expanding. From 1921-1928, incomes expanded 24%. During this time giving grew to above 3% and stayed there. From 1950-1962, incomes grew 20%. Again, giving grew to above 3% in 1958 and stayed there through 1962. In both cases, church members increased or maintained their giving levels even as their incomes increased.

In the 1920s, the economic expansion was interrupted by the Great Depression, followed by World War II. In contrast to the economic upheaval earlier in the century, however, the economy continued to expand through the 1960s. Yet the portion of income given was not sustained above 3%. By 1968, giving as a percentage of income had declined to 2.6% for this group of 11 communions. U.S. per capita income increased 30% in inflation-adjusted 1996 dollars between 1960 and 1968, from $9,134 in 1960 to $11,864 in 1968. In comparison, per member giving increased 10% in inflation-adjusted dollars, from the 1960 level of $285.64 to the 1968 level of $314.08.

By 1985, per member giving had increased 33% in inflation-adjusted 1996 dollars, from $314.08 in 1968 to $419.30 in 1985. U.S. per capita income measured $17,559, an increase of 48% over the 1968 level of $11,864. Giving as a percentage of income, therefore, measured 2.4% in 1985, representing a 10% decline from the 1968 level of 2.6%.

The year 2001 was the latest year for which membership data was available for the eleven denominations considered in this section, and financial data for ten. In that year, per member giving as a percentage of income was 2.6%, a 7% increase from the 1985 level. Per member giving increased 44% in inflation-adjusted 1996 dollars, from $419.30 in 1985 to $605.14 in 2001. U.S. per capita income increased 35% during this period, from the 1985 level of $17,559 to the 2001 level of $23,731. Thus, the percentage of income given increased.

Figure 6: **Per Member Giving as a Percent of Income in 11 Denominations, and U.S. Per Capita Income, 1921-2001**

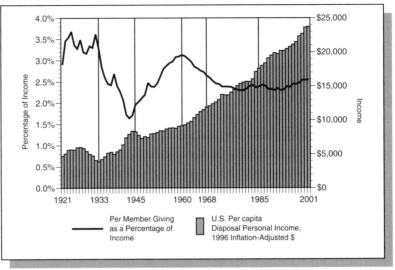

Source: empty tomb analysis; *YACC* adjusted series; U.S. BEA   empty tomb, inc. 2003

Figure 6 contrasts per member giving as a percent of income for a composite of eleven Protestant denominations, with U.S. disposable personal income in inflation-adjusted 1996 dollars, for the period 1921 through 2001.

Membership and Giving, 1921-2001. Membership was changing for this group of 11 denominations during the 1921-2001 period as well. Figure 7 presents both per member giving as a percentage of income and membership as a percent of U.S. population, for the composite of eleven Protestant denominations, from 1921 through 2001.

Between 1921 and 1961, the portion of U.S. population that this group of 11 denominations represented grew from 16.1% of the U.S. population to 20%, or one-fifth of the United States. In that same year of 1961, the first decline in giving as a percentage of income occurred since 1952.

In 1962, a decline in membership as a percent of U.S. population occurred for this group that would continue through the year 2001. While this group of denominations continued to increase in membership until 1968, U.S. population grew at a faster rate. Therefore, while this group represented 20% of U.S. population in 1961, by the year 2001, this group represented 12.6% of U.S. population.

During this 1961-2001 period, the Southern Baptist Convention grew from 9,792,426 to 16,052,920. Meanwhile, the other ten denominations, all of which might be termed mainline Protestant, declined in membership, from 26,683,648 to 19,959,612.

The growth in the number of members in the Southern Baptist Con-vention offset the mainline Protestant membership loss, so that as a whole, the group's membership was fairly static, measuring 36,661,788 in 1961 and 36,012,532 in 2001. However, U.S. population increased from 183,742,000 in 1961, when the group of 11 denominations repre-sented 20% of the U.S. population, to 282,822,000, when the 11 denominations represented 12.6% of the U.S. population.

It is interesting to note that giving as a percentage of income declined the year before membership as a percent of U.S. population began its decline, and nine years before the 11 denominations experienced a decline in absolute membership, from 37,785,048 in 1968 to 37,382,659 in 1969.

Although giving as a percent of income decreased to 2.3% in 1979 and 1980, it recovered to 2.42% in 1983 and was again at that level in 1986. It declined to 2.30% in 1990 and 1992, but as of 2001 had recovered to 2.55%.

In contrast, membership as a percent of population for the 11 denominations as a group began a decline in 1962

Figure 7: Per Member Giving as a Percent of Income and Membership as % of U.S. Population, 11 Denominations, 1921-2001

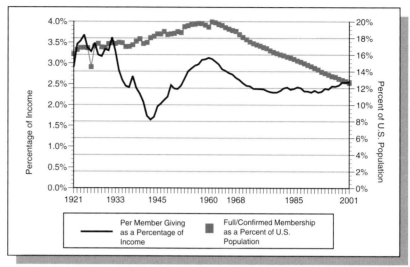

Source: empty tomb analysis; *YACC* adjusted series; U.S. BEA

empty tomb, inc. 2003

that continued uninterrupted through the year 2001.

Change in Per Member Giving and U.S. Per Capita Disposable Personal Income, in Inflation-adjusted 1996 Dollars. For this group of 11 communions, per member giving in inflation-adjusted 1996 dollars increased half the time during the 1921-1947 period. Per member giving in inflation-adjusted dollars decreased from 1924 to 1925. While it increased from 1925 to 1926 and again in 1927, giving began a seven-year decline in 1928. This seven-year period, from 1928 to 1934, included some of the worst years of the Great Depression. Giving increased again in 1935. Declines in 1939, 1940, 1942, 1946 and 1947 alternated with increases in the other years.

Then, from 1948 through 1968,[2] the members in these 11 communions increased per member giving in inflation-adjusted 1996 dollars each year. During the 1948-1960 interval of 12 years, per member giving averaged an increase of $9.97 a year. Although giving continued to increase for the next few years, it was at the slower rate of $3.56 per year. Overall, in inflation-adjusted 1996 dollars, income grew 57% from 1948 to 1968, while per member giving increased 89%.

Per member giving in inflation-adjusted dollars declined in 1969, 1970 and 1971, followed by two years of increase and two of decline.

The longest sustained period of average annual increases in per member giving in inflation-adjusted dollars during the 90-year period occurred during the most recent 25-year interval, from 1976 to 2001. During this time, income increased an average of $402.65 annually in inflation-adjusted 1996 dollars. Meanwhile, per member giving increased $10.18 on average each year, a higher overall rate than during the 20-year interval of 1948-1968, when the annual increase was $7.41. Giving increased 81% from 1976 to 2001, while income increased 68%. Therefore, giving as a percentage of income was 2.38% in 1976 and 2.55% in 2001.

---

[2]For the years 1965 through 1967, estimated data is used. See first footnote in this chapter.

Table 15: Average Annual Increase in U.S. Per Capita Disposable Personal Income and Per Member Giving, Inflation-Adjusted 1996 $, and Average Per Member Giving as a Percent of Income, in 11 Denominations, 1950-2001

Time Period	U.S. Per Capita Income			Per Member Giving			Avg. Ann. Chg. Giv. as % Avg. Annual Chg. in Income	Avg. Per Member Giving as % of Income
	First Year in Period	Last Year in Period	Average Annual Change	First Year in Period	Last Year in Period	Average Annual Change		
1950-1955	$7,954	$8,675	$144.12	$190.09	$249.39	$11.86	8.23%	2.59%
1955-1960	$8,675	$9,134	$91.92	$249.39	$285.64	$7.25	7.89%	3.01%
1960-1964 [3]	$9,134	$10,334	$299.96	$285.64	$295.16	$2.38	0.79%	3.02%
1964-1970 [3]	$10,334	$12,361	$337.88	$295.16	$311.42	$2.71	0.80%	2.70%
1970-1975	$12,361	$13,665	$260.66	$311.42	$325.40	$2.80	1.07%	2.43%
1975-1980	$13,665	$15,546	$376.25	$325.40	$357.57	$6.44	1.71%	2.33%
1980-1985	$15,546	$17,559	$402.60	$357.57	$419.30	$12.34	3.07%	2.37%
1985-1990	$17,559	$19,850	$458.15	$419.30	$456.77	$7.49	1.64%	2.36%
1990-1995	$19,850	$20,753	$180.69	$456.77	$492.94	$7.23	4.00%	2.34%
1995-2000	$20,753	$23,617	$595.56	$492.94	$599.81	$21.37	3.59%	2.47%
2000-2001	$23,617	$23,731	$114.15	$599.81	$604.86	$5.05	4.43%	2.54%

Details in the above table may not compute to the numbers shown due to rounding.

By reviewing this data in smaller increments of years from 1950 to 2001, as presented in Table 15, the time period in which giving began to decline markedly can be identified. In Table 15, data for the first and last year in each period is presented. The difference between these two years was calculated and then divided by the number of annual intervals in the period. The Average Annual Change in Giving as a Percent of the Average Annual Change in Income column presents the Per Member Giving Average Annual Change divided by the U.S. Per Capita Income Average Annual Change. The last column, titled Average Per Member Giving as a Percent of Income, is the average of giving as a percentage of income for all the years noted in each Time Period.

As indicated in Table 15, during the 1950 to 2001 period, the highest annual increase in per member giving in inflation-adjusted 1996 dollars occurred from 1995-2000. However, the highest annual increase in giving considered as a portion of the annual change in U.S. per capita income occurred in 1950-1955, followed by 1955-1960. In 1995-2000, the annual dollar increase in giving of $26.72 represented 4% of the average annual increase in U.S. per capita income, compared to the 8% represented by the increased dollars given during 1950-1955 and 1955-1960. Although not enough data to provide a meaningful comparison with the earlier segments, it is of interest to note that the one-year change from 2000-2001 was 5%.

Average annual change in per member giving declined markedly between 1960 and 1964 in these communions. While income was increasing at an annual rate of $299.96 in this four-year period, 226% greater than in the 1955-1960 period, the average annual increase in per member contributions in inflation-adjusted 1996 dollars was $2.38 in 1960-1964, only a third of the $7.25 annual rate of increase in the 1955-1960 period.

The 1960-1964 period predates many of the controversial issues often cited as reasons for declining giving as a percent of income. Also, it was at the end of the 1960-1964 period

---

[3]Use of the intervals of 1960-1964 and 1964-1970 allows for the use of years for which there is known data, avoiding the use of the 1965 through 1967 years for which estimated data is used in this chapter.

when membership began to decrease in mainline denominations, ten of which are included in this group. Therefore, additional exploration of that period of time might be merited.

Increases in per member giving were consistently low from 1960-1975. The annual rates of increase of $2.38 per year from 1960 to 1964, $2.71 from 1964 to 1970, and $2.80 from 1970 to 1975, were the lowest in the 1950 to 2001 period. From 1960 to 1970, the increase in dollars given represented less than one percent of the average annual increase in per capita income, while from 1970-1975, it was 1.07%.

In the 1975-1980 period, the average annual increase in giving grew to $6.44, representing 1.71% of the average annual increase in per capita income.

From 1980 to 1985, the average annual increase in giving of $12.34 represented 3.07% of the average annual increase in income during the 1980-1985 period. As a portion of the increase in per capita income, the 3.07% of the 1980 to 1985 period ranked fifth among the ten five-year periods from 1950 to 2001, not including the one-year period from 2000-2001.

The annual average change in giving as a percent of the average annual income increase during 1985 to 1990 fell from the 1980 to 1985 period. The 1990-1995 average change in giving as a percent of the average annual income increase represented more than double the 1985-1990 figure.

In the 1995-2000 period, the average annual change in contributions as a percentage of change in income decreased from the 1990-1995 period, even though the average annual change in per member contributions was almost triple that of the previous period. During the 1995-2000 segment, income was increasing at the fastest rate in the 1950-2001 period. Thus the larger increased number of dollars given were nevertheless a smaller portion of the income increases during the same period. This period of growth was less than half of the 1950-1960 period, when considered as a portion of the income increases.

Change in Per Member as a Portion of Income. In Table 16, giving as a percent of U.S. per capita disposable personal income is presented for the first and last year in the period noted.

The difference between giving in these two years was calculated and then divided by the number of annual intervals in the period to produce the Average Annual Change. Again, the Average Per Member Giving as a Percent of Income column is the average for all the years in each Time Period.

Table 16: Average Annual Increase in Per Member Giving as % of U.S. Disposable Personal Income, and Average Per Member Giving as % of Income, in 11 Denominations, 1950-2001

Time Period	Per Member Giving			Avg. Per Member Giving as % of Income
	First Year in Period	Last Year in Period	Average Annual Change	
1950-1955	2.39%	2.87%	0.10%	2.59%
1955-1960	2.87%	3.13%	0.05%	3.01%
1960-1964 [3]	3.13%	2.86%	-0.07%	3.02%
1964-1970 [3]	2.86%	2.52%	-0.06%	2.70%
1970-1975	2.52%	2.38%	-0.03%	2.43%
1975-1980	2.38%	2.30%	-0.02%	2.33%
1980-1985	2.30%	2.39%	0.02%	2.37%
1985-1990	2.39%	2.30%	-0.02%	2.36%
1990-1995	2.30%	2.38%	0.01%	2.34%
1995-2000	2.38%	2.54%	0.03%	2.47%
2000-2001	2.54%	2.55%	0.01%	2.54%

Details in the above table may not compute to the numbers shown due to rounding.

When considered as a portion of income in Table16, the period of 1960-1964 posted the highest Average Per Member Giving as a Percent of Income. Beginning in 1952, giving experienced the postwar and post-Depression increase as a percentage of income. Growing to 3% in 1958, this level was maintained through 1962. However, the 1960-1964 period also was the period within which giving as a portion of income began to decline. Even after giving began to decline in 1962, it was still at 2.97% in 1963. It is clear from the Average Annual Change column that giving as a portion of income had begun a downward trend. During 1990-1995, this trend began to reverse, but did not recover to the 1950-1960 Average Annual Change levels.

Per Member Giving as Percentage of Income, 1921, 1933 and 2001. By 2001, U.S. per capita disposable (after-tax) personal income had increased 404% since 1921 in inflation-adjusted 1996 dollars, and 508% since 1933—the depth of the Great Depression.

Meanwhile, by 2001, per member giving in inflation-adjusted 1996 dollars had increased 343% since 1921, and 373% since the depth of the Great Depression.

Consequently, per member giving as a percentage of income was lower in 2001 than in either 1921 or 1933. In 1921, per member giving as a percentage of income was 2.9%. In 1933, it was 3.3%. In 2001, per member giving as a percentage of income was 2.6% for the composite of the eleven denominations considered in this section. The percent change in the per member portion of income donated to the church had declined by 12% from the 1921 base, from 2.9% in 1921 to 2.6% in 2001, and by 22% from the 1933 base, from 3.3% in 1933 to 2.6% in 2001.

Appendix A contains a listing of the denominations contained in this analysis.

chapter 5

Church Member Giving and Membership Trends Based on 1968-2001 Data

HIGHLIGHTS

- Between 1992 and 2001, giving to Congregational Finances as a portion of income increased, in contrast to the decline suggested by an exponential projection based on 1968-1985 data.

- The relationship of actual 1986-2001 data to the projections based on 1968-1985 data suggest that, by the middle of this century, giving to Benevolences may represent a reduced portion of income.

- The composite data set communions analyzed in earlier chapters of this volume measured 14.1% of U.S. population in 1968 and 10.8% in 2001, down 23% as a portion of U.S. population from the 1968 base.

- Membership in a set of 37 Protestant denominations and the Roman Catholic Church represented 45% of U.S. population in 1968, and 38% in 2001, a decline of 15% from the 1968 base.

- Eleven mainline Protestant denominations represented 13.2% of the population in 1968, and 7.1% in 2001, a decline of 46% from the 1968 base.

- A set of fifteen evangelical denominations grew 46% as a portion of U.S. population between 1968 and 2001. However, the growth as a portion of population for this group peaked in the mid-1980s, and then began a slow decline through 2001.

- When considered as a portion of income, spending on new construction of religious buildings was higher in 1965 than in 2001, although the aggregate billions spent in 2001 was the highest annual amount spent in the 1964-2001 period.

NARRATIVE

Information as a Tool. The rich historical data series in the *Yearbook of American and Canadian Churches* has, in this volume, been supplemented with and revised by additional denominational data for the 1968-2001 period.

Analysis of this data has been presented in the *State of Church Giving*°series since the early 1990s. When first published, the finding that giving as a portion of income was shrinking was received with surprise and intense interest in many quarters.

Now, the data in chapter 1 of the present volume indicates that, since 1994, giving as a portion of income to Congregational Finances has made what begins to look like a recovery. The upward direction is in contrast to the fairly consistent decline in this category between 1968 and 1993.

It is generally acknowledged that most individuals do not decide how much to give based on academic information such as that contained in these analyses. However, is it possible that institutional leaders at all levels, particularly at the congregational level, are able to make use of trend information to formulate strategies in response to the findings? If so, the data indicating increased giving to Congregational Finances as a portion of income may be reflecting, in part, leadership recognizing a negative trend and taking steps to address it. The fact that the upturn in large part has been for local expenses, with only a slight slowing of the decline to Benevolences, indicates that church leadership may yet be operating with a limited vision of whole-life stewardship.

Nevertheless, facts and figures may be useful to those responsible for promoting the health of the church. The analyses in this chapter are presented in an effort to expand the available information base.

The Meaning of Trends. Statistical regression models are a tool to help leaders plan in response to reported data. Communities use them to know whether to build schools and roads. Hospitals consider trends to know the direction of health care several decades in the future. On a more alarming note, experts warn now of water shortages globally that could lead to conflict in fifty years if the situation is not soon redressed.

Statistical techniques can also be used to suggest both consequences and possibilities regarding church giving and membership patterns as well. Of course, trend data only indicates future directions. Data does not dictate what will happen. Available information, including trend analysis, can help formulate intelligent responses to current analysis. Church leaders and members can help decide, through action or inaction, what the future will look like.

Trend analysis was first included in this series partly in response to developments in national church offices. After talking with a number of denominational officials who were making painful decisions about which programs to cut, in light of decreased Benevolences dollars being received, it seemed useful to see where the present patterns of giving might lead if effective means were not found to alter present behavior. Were current patterns likely to prove a temporary setback, or did the data suggest longer-term implications?

The Current Trend in Church Giving. The first chapter in this report indicates that per member giving as a percentage of income decreased between 1968 and 2001. Further, contributions to the category of Benevolences have been declining proportionately faster than those to Congregational Finances between 1968 and 2001.

The data for the composite denominations analyzed for 1968 through 2001 has been projected in *The State of Church Giving* series, beginning with the edition that included 1991 data.[1] The most recent projection is based on data from 1968 through 2001.

The data for both Benevolences and Congregational Finances can be projected using linear and exponential regression analysis. To determine which type of analysis more accurately describes the data in a category's giving pattern, the data for 1968-1985 was projected using both techniques. Then, the actual data for 1986 through 2001 was plotted.

The more accurate projection was judged to be the procedure that produced the trend line most closely resembling the actual 1986-2001 data.

The Trend in Congregational Finances. The 1968-2001 church giving data contained in this report indicates that giving as a percentage of income for Congregational Finances declined from 2.45% in 1968, to 2.26% in 2001, a decline of 8%.

Both linear and exponential regression were used to analyze the data for giving as a percentage of income to Congregational Finances for the 17-year interval of 1968 through 1985. Then the actual data for 1986 through 2001 was plotted. The actual data for 1986-1992 followed the exponential curve, and then began to increase. In 2001, the giving level was higher rather than lower than the 1992 base. The results are shown in Figure 8.

Since data for the most recent years have differed markedly from the previous trend, long-term projections may not be meaningful. The upturn over the last nine years merits continuing observation.

The Trend in Benevolences. Per member contributions to Benevolences as a percentage of income decreased from 0.66% in 1968 to 0.40% in 2001, a percent change in giving as a percentage of income

Figure 8: Projected Trends for Composite Denominations, Giving as a Percentage of Income to Congregational Finances, Using Linear and Exponential Regression Based on Data for 1968-1985, with Actual Data for 1986-2001

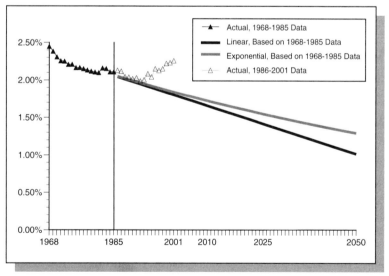

Sources: *YACC*, adjusted series; U.S. BEA   empty tomb, inc. 2003

---

[1]John Ronsvalle and Sylvia Ronsvalle, *The State of Church Giving through 1991* (Champaign, IL: empty tomb, inc., 1993), and subsequent editions in the series. The edition with data through 1991 provides a discussion of the choice to use giving as a percentage of income as a basis for considering future giving patterns.

of 39% from the 1968 base.

The data for giving as a percentage of income to Benevolences for the 17-year interval of 1968 through 1985 was also projected using both linear and exponential regression. The actual data for 1986 through 2001 was then plotted. The results are shown in Figure 9.

Reported per member giving as a percentage of income to Benevolences was above the projected value of

Figure 9: **Projected Trends for Composite Denominations, Giving as a Percentage of Income to Benevolences, Using Linear and Exponential Regression Based on Data for 1968-1985, with Actual Data for 1986-2001**

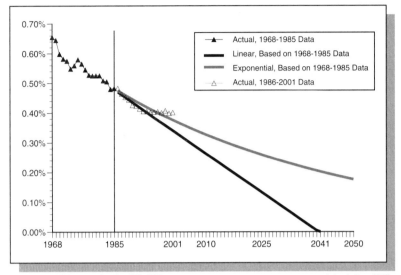

Sources: *YACC*, adjusted series; U.S. BEA   empty tomb, inc. 2003

the linear and exponential regressions for 1986. For 1988-1996, the reported data was close to or below the linear trend data. Although giving was at a relative plateau from 1997-2001, it reached the lowest point in the 1968-2001 period in 2000. Nevertheless, the 1997-2001 levels were higher than either the linear or exponential trends lines, suggesting a slowing in the rate of decline.

The linear trend based on 1968-2001 data indicated that per member giving as a portion of income to the category of Benevolences will reach 0% of income in the year A.D. 2050. The exponential curve based on 1968-2001 data indicated that giving in 2050 would be 0.18%, down 52% from the 0.40% level in 2001.[2] In both trend lines, by 2050 the amount of income going to support Benevolences, including denominational structures, would be either negligible or severely reduced, if the overall pattern of the last 34 years continues.

---

[2]In the linear regression, the value for the correlation coefficient, or r_{XY}, for the Benevolences data is -.97. The strength of the linear relationship in the present set of 1968-2001 data, that is, the proportion of variance accounted for by linear regression, is represented by the coefficient of determination, or r^2_{XY}, of .95 for Benevolences. In the exponential regression, the value for r_{XY}, for the Benevolences data is -.98, while the strength of the exponential relationship is .96. The Benevolences *F*-observed values of 585.24 for the linear, and 774.81 for the curvilinear, regression are substantially greater than the *F*-critical value of 7.5 for 1 and 32 degrees of freedom for a single-tailed test with an Alpha value of 0.01. Therefore, the regression equation is useful at the level suggested by the r^2_{XY} figure in predicting giving as a percentage of income.

[3]The denominations analyzed in this section include the composite data set whose financial patterns were analyzed in earlier chapters. The data for the composite communions is supplemented by the data of eight denominations included in an analysis of church membership and U.S. population by Roozen and Hadaway in David A. Roozen and Kirk C. Hadaway, eds., *Church and Denominational Growth* (Nashville: Abingdon Press, 1993), 393-395.

Trends in Church Membership as a Percentage of U.S. Population, 1968-2001.[3] Membership data for various church groupings is available for review for the years 1968 through 2001. When the reported data is considered as a percent of U.S. population, the membership data is placed in the larger context of the changing environment in which the church exists. This measurement is similar to giving as a percentage of income that reflects how much a financial donation represents of the resources available to the donor. In the same way, measuring membership as a percentage of U.S. population takes into account the changes in total population as well as in membership.

The State of Church Giving through 1993 included a chapter entitled, "A Unified Theory of Giving and Membership."[4] The hypothesis explored in that discussion is that there is a relationship between a decline in church member giving and membership patterns. One proposal considered in that chapter is that a denomination which is able to involve its members in a larger vision as evidenced in giving patterns will also be attracting additional members.

In the present edition, discussion will be limited to patterns and trends in membership as a percentage of U.S. population.

Membership in the Composite Denominations, 1968-2001. Figure 10 presents membership as a percent of U.S. population, and giving as a percentage of income, for the composite denominations, 1968-2001.

The composite denominations, which span the theological spectrum, included 28,256,265 Full or Confirmed Members in 1968.

Figure 10: Membership as a Percent of U.S. Population and Giving as a Percent of U.S. Per Capita Disposable Personal Income, Composite Denominations, 1968-2001

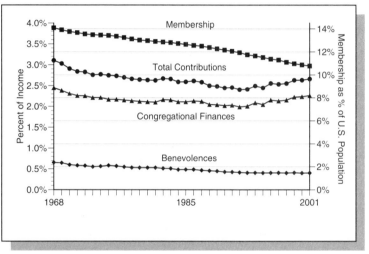

Source: empty tomb analysis; *YACC* adjusted series; U.S. BEA   empty tomb, inc. 2003

By 2001, these communions included 30,689,003 members, an increase of 9%.[5] However, during the same 33-year interval, U.S. population increased from 200,745,000 to 284,822,000, an increase of 42%. Therefore, while this church member grouping represented 14.1% of the U.S. population in 1968, it included 10.8% in 2001, a decline of 23% from the 1968 base.

---

[4] This article is available on the Internet at: <http://www.emptytomb.org/UnifiedTheory.pdf>.

[5] See Appendix B-1 for details of the composite denomination data included in these analyses. Consult Appendix B-4 for the total Full or Confirmed Membership numbers used for the American Baptist Churches in the U.S.A. See Appendix B-3.3 and Appendix B-4 for the membership data of the other denominations included in subsequent analyses in this chapter that are not one of the composite denominations.

percent of U.S. population, and giving as a percentage of income, for the composite denominations, 1968-2001.

Data Trends in Three Church Groups. Membership data for three subgroups within the historically Christian church in the U.S. is available. Data was analyzed for eleven mainline denominations, fifteen evangelical denominations, and the Roman Catholic Church. Figure 11 presents the membership data for these groups of communions.

Eleven Mainline Denominations. The declining membership trends have been noticed most markedly in the mainline Protestant communions. Full or Confirmed Membership in eleven mainline Protestant denominations affiliated with the National Council of the Churches of Christ in the U.S.A.[6] decreased as a percentage of U.S. population by 46% between 1968 and 2001, from the 1968 base. In 1968, this group included 26,508,288, or 13.2% of U. S. population. In 2001, the 11 denominations included 20,173,272, or 7.1% of U.S. population, a decline of 46% in the portion of U.S. population with membership in these groups.

Fifteen Evangelical Denominations. Data is also available for a group of fifteen denominations that might be classified on the evangelical end of the theological spectrum.[7] Although one or more of the communions in this grouping might prefer the term "conservative" to "evangelical" as a description, the latter term in its current sociological usage may be useful. These communions included some of the fastest growing denominations in the United States. This group grew 46% in membership, from 15,101,542 in 1968 to 22,074,816, in 2001, while U.S. population grew 42%. As a result, this group measured 7.5% of U.S. population in 1968, and 7.8% in 2001. In the mid-1980s, the group peaked at 8.23% as a portion of U.S. population peaked, and then declined to 7.75% by 2001, a decline of 6% as a portion of U.S. population from the 1986 peak. In 1993, these fifteen evangelical communions surpassed the 11 mainline communions in the portion of U.S. population that they represented.

Figure 11: Membership as a Percent of U.S. Population, 15 Evangelical Denominations, 11 Mainline Denominations, and the Roman Catholic Church, 1968-2001

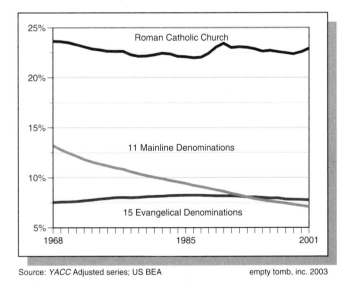

Source: *YACC* Adjusted series; US BEA   empty tomb, inc. 2003

The Roman Catholic Church. The Roman Catholic Church included 47,468,333 members in 1968, or 24% of U.S. population. Although the church's membership grew 38%, to 65,270,444 in 2001, it decreased to 23% as a portion of the faster-growing U.S. population, a decline of 3%.

---

[6]These eleven denominations include nine of the communions in the composite set of denominations as well as The Episcopal Church and The United Methodist Church.

[7]A list of the communions in this set is presented in Appendix A.

Membership in 38 Communions. In 1968, a set of 37 Protestant denominations and the Roman Catholic Church included a total of 90,252,533 members. With the U.S. population at 200,745,000, these Christians constituted 45% of the 1968 U.S. population. By 2001, the group had grown to 109,399,116 members. However, with U.S. population having grown to 284,822,000 in 2001, these Christians comprised 38% of the American population, a percent change of -15% from the 1968 base.

Projected Membership Trends in Eleven Mainline Denominations. As with giving as a percentage of income to Congregational Finances and Benevolences, trend lines using both linear and exponential regression were developed for the eleven mainline Protestant communions discussed above, using their 1968-1985 membership data. The actual 1986 through 2001 data was also plotted. As shown in Figure 12, the actual 1986-2001 data was slightly above the exponential curve for these denominations. An exponential curve based on the entire 1968-2001 reported data series suggested that these denominations would represent 2.8% of the U.S. population in 2050.

Figure 12: Trend in Membership as a Percent of U.S. Population, Eleven Mainline Protestant Denominations, Linear and Exponential Regression Based on Data for 1968-1985, with Actual Data 1986-2001

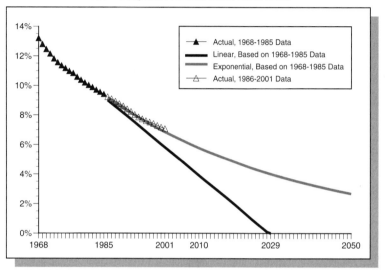

Sources: *YACC*, adjusted series; U.S. BEA

empty tomb, inc. 2003

Projected Membership Trends in the Composite Denominations. Nine of the eleven mainline Protestant denominations discussed above are included in the composite set of denominations that have been considered in earlier chapters of this report. Regression analysis was carried out on the 1968-1985 membership data for the composite denominations to determine if the trends in the larger grouping differed from the mainline denomination subset. The results were then compared to the actual 1986 through 2001 membership data for the composite data set.

The composite denominations represented 14.1% of the U.S. population in 1968, and 12.6% in 1985. Linear trend analysis suggests that this grouping would have represented 11.4% of U.S. population in 2001, while exponential regression suggests it would have been 11.5%. In fact, this composite grouping of communions represented 10.8% of the U.S. population in 2001, a smaller figure than that indicated by linear regression, suggesting the trend is closer to that predicted by linear regression than the exponential curve.

Figure 13: Trend in Membership as a Percent of U.S. Population, Composite Denominations, Linear and Exponential Regression Based on Data for 1968-1985, with Actual Data 1986-2001

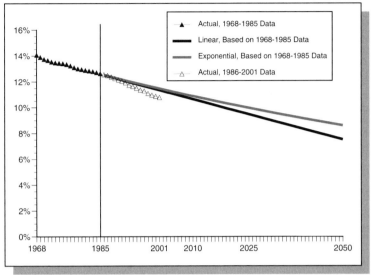

Source: *YACC* adjusted series; U.S. BEA   empty tomb, inc. 2003

If the linear trend continues uninterrupted into the future, these composite denominations would represent 7.5% of the U.S. population in the year 2050. Figure 13 presents this information in graphic form.

Buildings. The current level of building activity among churches in the U.S. has attracted attention in various quarters. Once again, data helps evaluate whether the present level of church construction is part of an ongoing trend or varies from past behavior.

Census Bureau data provides information on the new construction of religious buildings. For a series beginning in 1964, the Census Bureau defined its Religious category as follows: "*Religious* includes houses of worship and other religious buildings. Certain buildings, although owned by religious organizations, are not included in this category. These include education or charitable institutions, hospitals, and publishing houses."[8] A 2003 revision of this series presented the definitions as follows:

"Religious
    "Certain buildings, although owned by religious organizations, are not included in this category. These include educational or charitable institutions, hospitals, and publishing houses.
"House of worship
    " Includes churches, chapels, mosques, synagogues, tabernacles, and temples.
"Other religious
    "In addition to the types of facilities listed below, it also includes sanctuaries, abbeys, convents, novitiates, rectories, monasteries, missions, seminaries, and parish houses.
    "Auxiliary building—includes fellowship halls, life centers, camps and retreats, and Sunday schools."[9]

---

[8]U.S. Census Bureau, Current Construction Reports, C30/01-5, *Value of Construction Put in Place*: May 2001, U.S. Government Printing Office, Washington, DC 20402, Appendix A, "Definitions," p. A-2.

[9] U.S. Census Bureau; "Definitions of Construction"; July 30, 2003; <http://www.census.gov/const/C30/Definitions.pdf>; 8/17/2003 PM printout.

Although documentation for the revised series stated that the 1993 through 2001 data was not comparable to the earlier 1964-2000 data, a comparison of the two series found that there was an average of 0.1% difference between the estimated millions of dollars spent on construction of religious buildings from 1993-2000. For the purposes of the present discussion, the difference in the two series was not deemed sufficient to impact the multi-decade review to the degree that discussion would not be useful.

According to the data, current dollar aggregate construction of religious buildings was $1.04 billion dollars in 1964, compared to $8.4 billion in 2001. On a current-dollar aggregate level, more building was going on in 2001 than in the mid-1960s.

However, as has been emphasized in previous chapters of this volume, aggregate numbers considered apart from inflation, as well as changes in population and income, do not give a complete picture.

When inflation was taken into account, the data indicated that the total aggregate $36.2 billion cost of new religious building construction, summed for the 1997-2001 period, was higher than the 1964-1968 period cost of $23.5 billion. At $7.7 billion, building in 2001 was highest in the 1964-2001 period. The 1965 level of $5.3 billion had been the highest amount of aggregate, inflation-adjusted dollars spent on the construction of new religious buildings from 1964 through 1996. In 1997, aggregate inflation-adjusted spending passed the 1965 level and continued to increase through 2001.

Yet, to obtain the most realistic picture about giving patterns, changes in population and income also need to be factored into the evaluation. For example, taking population changes into account, in 1965 the per capita expenditure in the U.S. on religious buildings was $27 dollars per person in inflation-adjusted 1996 dollars. In 2001, it was also $27 dollars.

The period 1964 through 1968 posted an average per capita expenditure on new religious buildings of $24. The period 1999-2001 was higher at $26, suggesting that construction of new religious buildings was only slightly higher in the latter period than in the mid-1960s.

Of course, a smaller portion of the entire U.S. population may have been investing in religious buildings in the late 1990s through 2001 than in the mid-1960s. To have the most meaningful comparison, changes in membership as a portion of population would have to be taken into account. Data considered above suggests that membership in historically Christian churches declined as a portion of the U.S. population between 1964 and 2001. However, other religions were added to the religious milieu of the United States during this period. The Census data includes all religious construction, not just Christian churches. So the rough estimate may be fairly useful as a first approximation.

Even comparing per capita inflation-adjusted dollars spent is of limited use because it does not account for the difference in incomes in the two periods. Again, the $27 per capita spent on religious buildings in 1965 represented a different portion of income than the $27 spent in 2001. In fact, as a portion of income, Americans spent 0.25% on the construction of new religious buildings in 1965, compared to 0.11% in 2001.

Figure 14: Construction of Religious Buildings in the U.S., 1964-2001, Aggregate Inflation-Adjusted 1996 Dollars, and Percent of U.S. Per Capita Disposable Personal Income

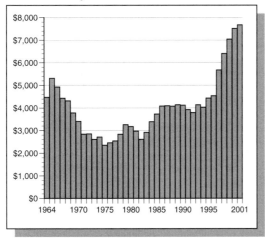

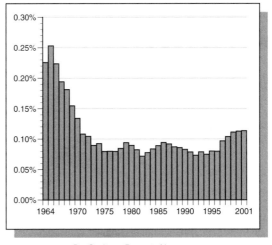

Aggregate Billions of Inflation-Adjusted Dollars

Source: U.S. Census Bureau; empty tomb analysis

Per Capita as Percent of Income

empty tomb, inc. 2003

One must conclude, therefore, that the population was investing a higher portion of available resources in religious buildings in the mid-1960s than at the turn of this century. The building activity occurring in the late 1990s through 2001 has to be evaluated in the context of the general affluence produced by decades of economic expansion in the U.S. in order to make an intelligent evaluation of whether religious construction has in fact increased over the mid-1960s level. This fact is clear from the two charts in Figure 14. These charts contrast the annual aggregate dollar value of new religious building construction with the per capita expenditure as a portion of U.S. per capita income for the 1964-2001 period.

The Response to the Trends. As in other sectors, trend lines in church giving and membership are designed to provide an additional source of information. Planning, evaluation and creative thinking are some of the types of constructive responses which can be made in light of projections. The information on church member giving and membership trends is offered as a possible planning tool.[10] The trend lines are not considered to be dictating what must happen, but rather as providing important indicators of what might happen if present conditions continue in an uninterrupted fashion. Trends in church giving and membership, if used wisely, may be of assistance in addressing conditions present in the body of Christ in the United States.

---

[10]For additional discussion of the implications of the trends, see Ronsvalle and Ronsvalle, *The State of Church Giving through 1991*, pp. 61-67.

chapter 6

The Potential of the Church

HIGHLIGHTS_____

- If members of historically Christian churches in the United States were giving an average of 10% of their incomes in 2001, there would have been an additional $143 billion a year going through church channels.

- If church members decided to spend most of this additional money on helping others, in keeping with the Great Commandment to love God and love neighbor, there would have been an additional $86.0 billion for international outreach, and $28.7 billion for domestic outreach, with another $28.7 billion available for related congregational activities.

- Four congregations demonstrate that it is possible to distribute 37% or more of their budgets to missions.

- Recent international studies suggest that it is possible to stop more global child deaths.

NARRATIVE_____

What difference does it make that church member giving as a portion of income was 2.66% in the year 2001, instead of at the classic tithe, or 10%?

Of course, it would not be reasonable to expect that every person in every congregation would give 10% of their incomes. But what difference would it make if congregation members, on a congregation-wide average, gave 10%? Some would always give less, and some already give more than that level. Would an average of 10% giving really be so very different than present levels?

These questions reflect the culturally invisible state of church giving. The role of religion in general, and the church in particular, is largely taken for granted in U.S. culture. While the media and the public avidly watch portions of points change on the stock market, church giving is not seen as having much significance in the culture.

Yet, as noted in the "Measurement of Charitable Giving" chapter in this volume, various sources agree that giving to religion is the single largest recipient category in charitable giving. One estimate is that three-quarters of every charitable dollar goes to a religious cause. Religious causes focus not only on worship, but also on social services and international activities, as well as education. The vast majority of the religious charitable dollars are donated to congregations, where some portion is then directed to charitable activity beyond the local congregation.

Further, the church in the U.S. has been, and continues to be, one of the main educators of philanthropic values in the United States. Not only is the church the seedbed of morality, but congregations also provide the grassroots promotion of charitable behavior that helps to define the quality of life in the United States.

Here is an exercise to try to make the impact of church giving more visible. Imagine U.S. and global society if private charitable activity were cut in half. Picture a massive decline in the ministries often undertaken by religious groups to assist: the homeless; the hungry; the elderly; orphans; refugees; youth; international relief and development. A bleak picture emerges of what society would be like without the activities often taken for granted.

Now imagine what that picture would look like if the present level of private charitable activity, both domestically and globally, were expanded many times. Can we picture a world where infant mortality was an exception in all countries: Where a parent could expect a child not only to live past age five, but also be healthy and educated to make a positive contribution to that country's society, and thereby also to the global community?

The difference between these two pictures, to a great degree, has to do with whether church member giving levels move towards or away from the religiously-recognized standard of giving 10% of one's income.

Potential Giving. Some religious leaders debate whether, in the affluent culture that describes the early twenty-first century U.S., the tithe is too low a standard. Others are concerned because it suggests legalism. However those who support the tithe note that it provides a biblically-based standard, against which church members can compare their own practice of their faith. Moreover, a congregation-wide average of ten percent giving would allow for a range in which some might give considerably more than ten percent, while some may not feel they can give, or refuse to consider giving, at that level.

If members of historically Christian churches in the U.S. had been giving at an average of 10% of income in 2001, they would have donated an additional $143.4 billion dollars to their churches.

One may continue this hypothetical discussion by supposing that these additional donations could have been directed not to the internal operations of the congregations, but rather to the broader mission of the church, as represented by Benevolences. Finally, one may suppose that denominations had adopted a proposed formula that 60% of this additional money be designated for international missions—where the greatest need is—and 20% be directed to domestic benevolences.[1]

The amount available for international ministries, had 60% of the $143.4 billion increase been directed to that category, would have been $86.03 billion shared in Jesus' name to provide word and deed witness to global neighbors in need. This amount is more than the $5 billion[2] additional that has been estimated could stop most of the 10.6 million, global under-five child deaths each year, or the $7 billion additional each year that could provide primary education enrollment for all children. Estimates are that $70 to $80 billion a year additional could ensure access to basic services for the world's population.[3]

Meanwhile, the 20% of the $143 billion additional giving that would be available for domestic benevolences, to help local neighbors in need, would have amounted to $28.68 billion.

After the 60% for international ministries, and 20% for domestic ministries, 20% of the increased giving would be a basic increase for related expenses. Part of this portion of the additional Benevolences money could be used for mission education activities within the congregation, including work project trips internationally—as well as to cover additional direct expenses related to raising and distributing the additional funds.[4]

---

[1]UNICEF estimates that approximately 29,600 children under the age of five die *daily* around the globe, mostly from preventable poverty conditions. UNICEF also estimates that 31,000 children under the age of five die *annually* in the United States (Carol Bellamy, *The State of the World's Children 2003* [New York: UNICEF, 2003], p. 87.) These statistics indicate that the great majority of need is in countries other than the U.S. The 60%/20% formula was used in the authors' work with congregations. For a discussion of their international and domestic strategy approaches, see John Ronsvalle and Sylvia Ronsvalle, *The Poor Have Faces* (Grand Rapids, MI: Baker Books, 1992).

[2] James P. Grant, *The State of the World's Children 1990* (New York: Oxford University Press, 1990), 16, estimated $2.5 additional each year could stop most of the under-five global child deaths occurring from preventable poverty conditions. This number has been increased by the authors to account for inflation and growth in the economy.

[3]Bellamy, *The State of the World's Children 2001*, 81; Carol Bellamy, *The State of the World's Children 1999* (New York: UNICEF, 1999), 85; and Bellamy, *The State of the World's Children 2000*, 37.

[4]*Basis for the Calculations.* In the chapter in this volume titled "Measuring Charitable Giving in the United States," a 2001 figure of total giving to religion is presented in the "Denomination-Based Series Keyed to 1974 Filer Estimate." That figure is $61.9 billion.

In 2001, if giving increased to an average of 10% giving, instead of $61.9 billion, an amount of $232.6 billion would have been donated to all religions in the U.S. The difference would have been an additional $170.7 billion (rounded) given to religion in the United States that year.

An analysis based on information in George H. Gallup, Jr., *Religion in America* [(Princeton, NJ: The Princeton Religion Research Center, 1996), p. 42] resulted in an estimate that 84% of the U.S. population identifies with the historically Christian church—those communions and traditions, such as Roman Catholic, Orthodox, mainline Protestant, Pentecostal, evangelical, and Anabaptist, that profess a commitment to the historic tenets of the faith. This figure of 84% can be applied to the additional $170.7 billion, to calculate the additional $143 billion giving activity of the historically Christian church, had giving been at the 10% level in 2001. This somewhat conservative estimate assumes that the religious giving was given by 100% of the U.S. population. If total religious giving comes only from the 91% of the U.S. population that claims a religious affiliation (see Gallup, p. 35), then the historically Christian component gave 92% of the total (84%/91%). In that case, rather than $143 billion, $157 billion of the total potential $170.7 billion additional would have been given by those who identify with the historically Christian church.

**Figure 15: Potential Additional Church Giving at a 2001
Average of 10%, and Illustrations of Global Need
That Could Be Addressed**

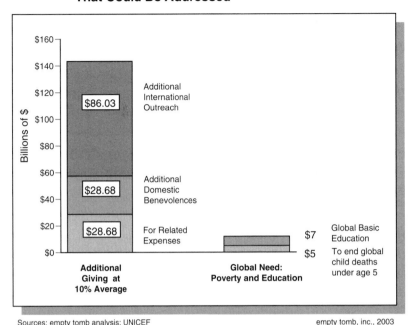

Sources: empty tomb analysis; UNICEF   empty tomb, inc., 2003

Figure 15 presents both the potential giving amounts, and two areas of global need that could be addressed.

Is Improvement Possible in Church Member Giving? If giving had increased to an average of 10%, and the additional funding had been directed to Benevolences, then giving would have increased from 0.40% of income to about 7.74%, with Congregational Finances staying at about the same level of 2.26%. That would mean that church budgets would be divided into 23% for Congregational Finances and 77% for Benevolences out of current income. That is a marked contrast to the present pattern of 85% for Congregational Finances and 15% for Benevolences evident in chapter 1 of this volume.

As of this writing, the authors did not know of any congregations practicing the theoretical level of 23% Congregational Finances and 77% Benevolences. Any information about historically Christian congregations that approach, or operate at, that level would be welcome.

The authors were aware of four churches that indicated they directed 37% or more of their budgets beyond their congregations.

•   The Memorial Drive Presbyterian Church in Houston, Texas, indicated a commitment to "Dollar for Dollar" giving. Their Web site read, "This means it is our goal to contribute a dollar to those in need for every dollar we spend on the operation of our church programs."[5]

---

[5] Memorial Drive Presbyterian Church; "Give"; <http://www.mdpc.org/cgi-bin/index.cgi?section=give>; p.1 of 9/2/03 1:29 PM printout.

• The Reston Bible Church of Reston, Virginia, indicated on its Web site that as of 1998, the congregation earmarked 40% for global missions. A September 2003 phone call to the church indicated that the information on the Web site was being updated, and that the 40% for missions figure was still practiced by the congregation at that time.[6]

• The Park Street Church in Boston budgeted 37% for global missions in 2003.[7]

• The Black Rock Congregational Church in Fairfield, Connecticut, noted on its Web site that in 2003 the congregation supported about 76 missionary families or singles, and that "more than 40% of our annual budget goes to these missionaries. Our current missions budget is $800,000 for 2003-04 fiscal year."[8]

These congregations indicate that it is possible to grow beyond the national average of 15% for Benevolences.

Is Progress Possible in Efforts to Stop Global Child Deaths? A June 27, 2003, *Washington Post* article highlighted a new series of studies about efforts to stop global child deaths.[9] The authors of the studies were affiliated with the Bloomberg School of Public Health at Johns Hopkins University, UNICEF, and the World Health Organization, among other entities. The studies were being published in a "child survival" series in *The Lancet*, a European medical journal.

The second paper in *The Lancet* series concluded, "Our findings show that about two-thirds of child deaths could be prevented by interventions that are available today and are feasible for implementation in low-income countries at high levels of population coverage."[10]

In *The Washington Post* article, Hans Troedsson, head of child and adolescent health at the World Health Organization in Geneva, was quoted as saying, "Our failures are that we have not been able to scale up the interventions that we know are effective . . . We all dropped the ball."[11]

The Implications of the Hypothetical Scenario of Tithing Church Members. The church giving analyses in this chapter indicate that church members could increase giving by billions of dollars if they chose to do so. The scientific analyses appearing in *The Lancet* ought to underscore for church members the implications of how they choose to spend their money. A lack of faithfulness in spending choices on the part of individual church members, and an inward-focused budget on the part of congregations, has real-world implications for the children who will not be helped, and therefore who will die this year and next from

---

[6]Reston Bible Church; "The History of Reston Bible Church"; <http://www.restonbible.org/administration/history.htm>; p. 8 of 12/17/02 4:57 PM printout.

[7] Park Street Church; "Park Street Church General Information, Park Street Finances"; <http://www.parkstreet.org/info/budget.shtml>; p. 1 of 9/2/2003 1:56 PM printout.

[8] Black Rock Congregational Church; "Missions at Black Rock"; <http://www.brcc.org/missions.asp>; p. 1 of 9/2/2003 2:07 PM printout.

[9] David Brown; "Studies: Child Deaths Avoidable"; *The Washington Post*; <http://www.washingtonpost.com/ac2/wp-dyn/A37367-2003Jun26?language=printer>; 9/2/03 6:57 AM printout.

[10] Gareth Jones, et al.; "How Many Child Deaths Can We Prevent This Year?"; *The Lancet*; <http://www.thelancet.com/journal/vol1362/iss9377/full/llan.362.9377.child_survival.26292.1>; p. 6 of 7/7/03 2:06 PM printout.

[11] David Brown, pp. 1, 2.

preventable causes. What is more, the good that could be done, and the witness that could be carried out, in Jesus' name will go undone.

The data indicates that, if giving had increased from the actual 2001 level to an average giving level of 10%, there could have been an additional $143 billion available to assist people through both word and deed witness. In theory, therefore, the church could have the resources necessary to impact domestic need, even while working at a significant level to alleviate global need in partnership with international sister churches.

However, it may also be noted that giving as a percentage of income did not increase at the rate that income did between 1968 and 2001, nor had it reached the 10% level by 2001. On the contrary, giving as a percentage of income declined by 14% between 1968 and 2001. More to the point, the portion of income going to Benevolences, the category that would take into account programs that address poverty conditions in the U.S. among other issues, declined by 39% in the 1968 to 2001 period. Further, the monetary potential of the church to address both domestic and global needs has remained culturally invisible in most church circles, as well as secular media discussions.

Any novel writer will confirm that bad characters are easy to make interesting and good characters always are difficult to make anything but boring.

In crafting our society, it seems that it is easier to complain about all that is wrong rather than have a vision for what is possible. Christianity is supposed to give church members the ability to see beyond themselves to a higher and better order of living. If faith in Jesus Christ is having a practical impact on those members, potential giving levels will move from an invisible option to a visible reality.

chapter 7

Measuring Charitable Giving in the United States

HIGHLIGHTS

- Current measurement of philanthropy efforts in the United States are inadequate to provide accurate information about charitable giving to a concerned public.

- The third annual Report Card on the Measurement of Philanthropy evaluates major entities involved in the reporting of charitable giving (see Fig. 16).

- Recommendations to improve the measurement of philanthropy include:

  - Reports of philanthropic giving need to be adjusted by population and income.

  - Changes are needed in the Internal Revenue Service Form 990 to provide information about contributions from living individuals as a distinct category. In order to assist this development, the Unified Chart of Accounts needs to provide a meaningful category dedicated to contributions from living individuals.

  - A policy decision is needed to change Form 990, so that a nonprofit may choose between the governance categories of either faith-based or secular. Groups also need to be able to define themselves through the use of a standard classification system, such as the National Taxonomy of Exempt Entities.

  - A policy decision is needed to measure contributions to recipient categories, by source of donations. Form 990 needs to be changed so that reporting recipient organizations define their contributions by source, choosing among individual, bequest, corporations (businesses), and foundations.

  - A permanent commission with a Presidentially-appointed and U.S. Senate-approved chair, similar to one recommended in the 1970s by the Filer Commission, is needed to establish and maintain consistent standards of philanthropy measurement.

  - A peer-reviewed Journal of Philanthropy Measurement would assist with developing and refining standards of philanthropy measurement.

- A validation comparison of AAFRC's widely quoted *Giving USA* series suggested that the estimate for religion, the single largest charitable category, is not accurate.

Figure 16: Report Card on the Measurement of Philanthropy, Twelve Entities

Evaluation Category	Providers of Public Estimates of Giving				
	Giving USA: AAFRC, Indiana Univ. Center on Phil.	Independent Sector Publications	Philanthropy 400: Chronicle of Philanthropy	NPT 100: NonProfit Times	Statistical Abstract of the United States
Addresses Annual Measurement	A	D	A	A	A
Adjusts for Population & Income	C	A	F	F	D
Report Available for Timely Review	D	F	A	A	A
Distance from For-Profit Counsel	D	A	F	F	A
Consistency over Time	D	F	D	D	A
Treatment of Religion	D	F	F	F	D
Provides Comparable Data	D	F	C	C	F
Revisits Major Questionable Findings	D	D	D	D	D
Availability of Information	D	C	B	A	A
Takes Steps to Maximize Validity	D	F	F	F	F
Summary Grade	**D+**	**D+**	**C-**	**C-**	**C+**

NARRATIVE

Current measurement of philanthropy efforts in the United States is inadequate to inform a concerned public. As Hayden W. Smith wrote in a 1993 article, "But we must face the truth: no one—repeat, no one—really knows how much money and other property is given to charity in any given year . . ."[1]

The media regularly reports one major professional organization's estimates as fact, other surveys cannot be externally validated, and the available tools to measure philanthropy neither provide nor emphasize a clear gauge of contributions from living individuals.

Yet, private contributions involve tens of billions of dollars each year. The nonprofit institutions that they support are estimated to constitute as much as six percent of the U.S. economy, when various sources of income including fees and government grants are taken into account.[2] In addition, the charitable activity that is widespread throughout American society provides assistance to segments of the population whose needs would otherwise be

---

[1]Hayden Smith, "Some Thoughts on the Validity of Estimates of Charitable Giving," *Voluntas*, Vol. 4, No. 2, August 1993, p. 251.

[2]"Nonprofit Information Center"; <http://www.independentsector.org/Nonprofit%20Information%20Center/ nonprofit_size_and_scope.htm>; p. 1 of 8/23/01 4:28 PM printout.

Additional Entities Involved in the Measurement of Philanthropy						
Advisory Committees, GUSA and GAVITUS	Foundations	Form 990 IRS Treasury Dept.	U.S. Government	National Bureau of Economic Research	Urban Institute	Universities (with Nonprofit Programs)
B	C	A	C	F	D	D
C	C	F	F	—	D	—
D	F	—	A	—	D	—
C	A	A	A	—	A	—
D	D	A	A	—	D	—
F	F	F	D	—	F	—
F	C	F	F	—	D	—
D	D	D	D	—	D	—
B	A	D	C	—	C	—
F	F	F	F	—	D	—
D+	**C-**	**C-**	**C-**	**F**	**D+**	**D**

severely, or in some cases completely, underserved. Whether the category is assistance to the poor or giving to the arts in the U.S., it is difficult to obtain a good measure of the condition of this society without an adequate measure of the charitable giving level.

As a first step toward changing this condition, an evaluation scale of those involved with measuring philanthropy was designed to provide an overview of the current situation. In this chapter, a third annual Report Card on the Measurement of Philanthropy evaluates twelve national entities involved in one or more aspects of the measurement of charitable giving.

The overall grade for the measurement of philanthropy in the United States is a C-. This grade combines the resulting numerical values from the 10 categories on which the twelve entities were evaluated.

These twelve groups can be generally divided into those that provide public estimates of giving, and the additional groups involved in one or more aspects of the measurement of philanthropy. The following list includes the entities and their overall grades. The details of the evaluation of each entity are presented in the last section of this chapter.

Providers of Public Estimates of Giving:

D+ The American Association of Fundraising Counsel Trust for Philanthropy's *Giving USA* reports, researched and written, under contract, at the Indiana University Center on Philanthropy

D+ Independent Sector's *Giving and Volunteering in the United States* series, *Balancing the Scales*, and *The New Nonprofit Almanac and Desk Reference*

C- *The Chronicle of Philanthropy* Philanthropy 400

C- *The NonProfit Times* NPT 100

C+ *The Statistical Abstract of the United States*

Additional Entities Involved in the Measurement of Philanthropy:

D+ Advisory Committees to the *Giving USA* and *Giving and Volunteering in the United States* publications

C- Foundation efforts in the area of the measurement of philanthropy

C- U.S. Government Internal Revenue Service Form 990

C- U.S. Government efforts to secure and disseminate philanthropy information

F National Bureau of Economic Research

D+ Urban Institute efforts, both in cooperation with the U.S. Government and independently

D Universities with philanthropy centers

Grades for each of the twelve groups were given in several categories. The categories and standards of evaluation were as follows.

Annual Measurement. Does the entity address issues related to, and provide regular information on, the annual measurement of philanthropy?

Adjustments for Population and Income. Does the entity address issues related to the adjustment of aggregate philanthropic figures for changes in U.S. population and income?

Report Available for Timely Review. If the entity issues a report, does it make that full report available for review by researchers at the same time that it makes news of the report available to the general public via press releases or other announcements?

Distance from For-Profit Counsel. Does the entity have sufficient independence and distance from the influence and agenda of groups involved in fundraising on a for-profit basis that therefore may have a vested interest in the results of any measurement analysis?

Consistency over Time. Does the entity approach its work with a reasonable degree of consistency over a period of years?

Treatment of Religion. Does the entity treat the category of religion, the single largest charitable category, in a reasonable and comprehensive fashion?

Comparable Data. Does the entity present data in ways that facilitate comparisons with other sources of information, or among its own categories?

Review of Major Questionable Findings. Does the entity review and reevaluate major findings in the entity's published reports that are questioned or challenged by others in the field?

Availability of Data. Does the entity publish or otherwise make its data available to researchers for independent analysis?

Validity of Data. Does the entity take comprehensive steps to insure and maximize the likelihood of valid, integrated data for its measurement of philanthropy?

Grade Standards. Each entity involved with the measurement of philanthropy that was evaluated was issued a grade in each of the relevant categories. The grades for each category were then averaged, and an overall grade issued. An "A" was measured at 95, a "B" at 85, a "C" at 75, a "D" at 65, and an "F" at 55.

RECOMMENDATIONS. Several steps could be taken to improve the reporting of philanthropy in the United States. Some are fairly simple to implement. Others would require more of an investment, both financial and academic.

Funding the Solutions. For these suggestions to be useful, the reader must be assured that they are feasible. To be feasible, these efforts will need to be funded. A budget could be available from either of two sources to underwrite efforts to improve the measurement of philanthropy in the United States.

The first option is the excise tax levied on foundations by the U.S. Government beginning in 1969. The purpose of this tax, according to Pablo Eisenberg of the Georgetown University Public Policy Institute, was "to use the income to regulate tax-exempt organizations and handle the myriad administrative tasks associated with them. But things didn't work out that way. That income has gone into the general treasury." Eisenberg argues that redirecting the tax to the Internal Revenue Service's oversight of nonprofits could not only provide for regulation and supervision, but also help to make the collected data available for purposes of public accountability.[3]

Another potential funding source would be pooled foundations funds for a "Foundation Research Service." A model can be found in the Congressional Research Service, which is designed to provide "comprehensive and reliable analysis, research and information services that are timely, objective, unbiased, and confidential."[4] Since 1987, at least 31 foundations have spent some unspecified millions of dollars on the measurement of philanthropy. Yet, there has been little to no evaluation or accountability that would improve the giving estimates produced by this funding. The Foundation Research Service could provide coordinated objective analysis of reports issued by grantees, including research on issues related to the measurement of philanthropy. The Foundation Research Service could provide evaluation of additional categories of research, particularly those that receive funding from multiple foundations. The Foundation Research Service could also keep track of whether reports funded by foundations were published in a timely fashion—or whether these reports were

---

[3]Pablo Eisenberg, "How to Help the IRS Improve Charity Oversight," *The Chronicle of Philanthropy*, October 18, 2001, p. 34.

[4]"CRS Employment Home Page — What's CRS: History and Mission;" <http://lcweb.loc.gov/crsinfo/whatscrs.html#org>; p. 1 of 10/4/01 12:10 PM printout.

published at all. It is important that foundations that facilitate the identification of, or help recruit, funding partners not use the multi-foundation nature of a project to diffuse and avoid clear lines of responsibility and accountability.

Adjustment for Population and Income for the General Public Audience. As discussed in chapter one of this volume, the type of measurement of charitable giving defines the type of information that results. If church member contributions are measured in dollars, then the figures provide a limited measure of how much church institutions had to spend. If the contributions are measured as a portion of income, then the figures indicate the value that the church member places on the contribution in the context of the resources available.

In the same way, whether philanthropy measures are reported in aggregate numbers or in per capita numbers defines the quality of information that is being conveyed.

To provide the best measure of charitable giving levels, data should be presented in per capita dollars, and as a portion of after-tax income. These standards account for changes in population and in income. A more accurate picture of the public's level of giving results.

Confusion exists in the measurement and reporting of philanthropy because the audience for the information is not well defined. The needs of the general public are different than the interests of those involved in the profession of fundraising. Consider that religion is the single largest charitable giving category, and attendance at houses of worship is highly correlated with charitable giving behavior.[5] A pastor or lay leader of a congregation will use individual giving levels as a portion of income to "see how they are doing" compared to average individual giving levels. Yet public discussion of philanthropy is routinely conducted in terms of the professional fundraisers' concerns about the aggregate billions of dollars raised.

The fact that the fundraising profession has different interests than the public was expressed by two experts in the field. Ann E. Kaplan, then editor of *Giving USA*, was asked about the value of waiting to issue giving estimates in order to provide more precise information when more reliable data became available. "Ms. Kaplan says that approach is not appealing. 'The longer you wait,' she says, 'the more accurate the data, but when you're fund raising and making public-policy decisions it's hard to wait.' "[6]

The Center on Philanthropy at Indiana University studies the area of philanthropy, and also offers courses to professional fundraisers. The Philanthropic Giving Index is produced by the Center on Philanthropy. This index is a nationwide survey of fundraisers and consultants. One aspect of the Index is to measure the optimism of fundraisers. The Center on Philanthropy has recently been researching, writing, and editing *Giving USA* under contract with the American Association of Fundraising Counsel. *The NonProfit Times* interviewed Eugene R. Tempel, executive director of the Center on Philanthropy. The interview referred to the *Giving USA* estimates as a validation of the optimism expressed in the Philanthropic Giving Index. "'Fundraisers may be optimistic people,' he said, noting that such an outlook helps them keep going after failed solicitations."[7]

---

[5] Arthur D. Kirsch, et al., *Giving and Volunteering in the United States 1999 Edition* (Washington, DC: Independent Sector, 2002), pp. 84-85.

[6] Harvy Lipman, "Report's Numbers Are No True Measure of Charity, Critics Say," *The Chronicle of Philanthropy*, June 3, 1999, p. 30.

[7] Matthew Sinclair, "Giving Attitudes: Survey Shows Drop in Optimism," *The NonProfit Times*, Feb. 2001, p. 32.

While the fundraiser is motivated by having an optimistic report of aggregate billions of dollars raised, unadjusted for population and income, the denominational leader or pastor needs to know if his people are being as faithful in giving as they could be.

Adjusting Media Reports for Population and the Economy. Trade estimates of fundraising may do their constituents a service by providing them with encouragement and overly positive information that fosters their optimism. However, the media reports the *Giving USA* series, funded by a professional trade group of for-profit fundraisers, the American Association of Fundraising Counsel, Inc. Trust for Philanthropy, to the general public as an objective measure of fundraising levels in the United States.

The headlines routinely reflect the upbeat tone of the *Giving USA* press releases. Consider both the 2002 and 2003 editions of *Giving USA*.

The headline on its *Giving USA 2002* press release read "Charitable Giving Reaches $212 Billion."[8] This headline was echoed in Stephanie Strom's *New York Times* story titled, "Charitable Contributions in 2001 Reached $212 Billion."[9] Matthew Sinclair of *The NonProfit Times* wrote, "Giving Hit $212 Billion; Individual Donors Led The Way."[10] The headline in the Associated Press story by Helena Payne declared, "2001 Charitable Giving Same As 2000."[11]

Only the headline in the story by Nicole Lewis of *The Chronicle of Philanthropy* reflected the entire AAFRC press release as it announced, "Charitable Giving Slides." [12]

The third paragraph on page one of the AAFRC press release read, "The 2001 total is an increase of one-half of one percent (0.5 percent) over the $210.89 billion now estimated for total giving in 2000. Adjusted for inflation, giving in 2001 is a decrease of 2.3 percent compared to the previous year."

A similar pattern was evident with the release of *Giving USA 2003*. The headline of the Association of Fundraising Counsel's (AAFRC) Indianapolis, IN press release read, "Charity Holds Its Own in Tough Times: Giving in 2002 Nears $241 billion, 1 Percent above New Figures for 2001."[13]

Of the major media that were reviewed, including trade magazines and newspapers with fulltime, dedicated philanthropy reporters, none bannered *Giving USA 2003* results adjusted for population and income. The headline of the Associated Press' article by Mark

---

[8] AAFRC, "Charitable Giving Reaches $212 Billion," <http://www.aafrc.com/press3.html>; 9/26/02 2:06 PM printout.

[9] Stephanie Strom; "Charitable Contributions in 2001 Reached $212 Billion;" *New York Times*; published June 21, 2002; <http://www.nytimes.com/2002/06/21/national/21CHAR.html?pagewanted=print&position=bottom>;

[10] Matthew Sinclair, "Giving Hit $212 Billion; Individual Donors Led The Way," *The NonProfit Times*, July 1, 2002, p. 1.

[11] Helena Payne, Associated Press Writer; "2001 Charitable Giving Same As 2000;" published June 20, 2002, <http://www.washingtonpost.com/ac2/wp-dyn/A17534-2002Jun20?language=printer>; 12:20 PM; p. 1 of 6/27/02 9:09 PM printout.

[12] Nicole Lewis, "Charitable Giving Slides," *Chronicle of Philanthropy*, June 27, 2002, p. 27.

[13] AAFRC Trust for Philanthropy, "Charity Holds Its Own in Tough Times: Giving in 2002 Nears $241 billion, 1 Percent above New Figures for 2001" (Indianapolis, IN: AAFRC Trust for Philanthropy, June 23, 2003), p. 1.

Jewell, datelined Indianapolis, announced, "Donations Held Steady in 2002."[14] *The New York Times* headline of a story by Stephanie Strom read, "Gifts to Charity in 2002 Stayed Unexpectedly High."[15]   In the *International Herald Tribune*, a version of the same *New York Times* story was headlined, "Americans Remain Generous: Sweet Charity,"[16]   *The NonProfit Times'* Matthew Sinclair wrote an article under the headline, "Giving Hits Record $240.9 Billion." [17] The *Mercury News'* headline of a story by John Boudreau stated, "Giving Increased Slightly in 2002."[18]   The Direct Marketing Association's June 23, 2003 article on *Giving USA* was headlined, "Charitable Giving Increases In 2002, 'Giving USA' Reports."[19] Not focusing on giving adjusted for population and income, the headline of a *Chronicle of Philanthropy* article by Harvy Lipman read, "Giving in 2002 Didn't Outpace Inflation, Report Says."[20]

The media in general has not done a critical review of AAFRC's public relations efforts that emphasize aggregate billions of dollars raised. For example, to its credit, AAFRC added a new table category in *Giving USA 2003*. On page 201, it listed Individual giving as a percent of both personal income and disposable (after-tax) personal income. This information indicated that Individual giving declined as a percent of both categories. The media could have calculated this number, or if the media had asked, AAFRC presumably would have told them that Individual giving as a portion of disposable personal income posted a −5 percent decrease from 2001 to 2002 from the 2001 base,[21] which may have been worth a headline.

Although the American public thinks of "giving" generally in terms of individual giving, the media does not make a distinction between AAFRC's total contributions numbers, that also include gifts from bequests, corporations and foundations, and individual-only numbers. Giving from Individuals was 76% of Total Contributions, according to *Giving USA 2003*. Giving from Individuals and Corporations are the two categories that track giving from living donors, making current decisions about their own resources. Of the combined billions given by Individuals and Corporations in 2002, donations from Individuals represented 94%.[22]

---

[14] Mark Jewell; "Donations Held Steady in 2002;" published June 23, 2003, 4:23 PM; <http://www.washingtonpost.com/wp-dyn/A23604-2003Jun23.html>; p. 1 of 6/26/03 8:49 AM printout.

[15] Stephanie Strom; "Gifts to Charity in 2002 Stayed Unexpectedly High;" *New York Times*; published June 23, 2002; <http://www.nytimes.com/2003/06/23/national/23CHAR.html?pagewanted=print&position=>; p. 1 of 6/26/03 11:00 AM printout.

[16] "Americans Remain Generous: Sweet Charity," *International Herald Tribune*; June 28, 2003; <http://www.iht.com/ihtsearch.php?id=101030&owner=(NYT)&date=2003060050958>; p. 1 of 6/30/03 8:12 AM printout.

[17] Matthew Sinclair, "Giving Hits Record $240.9 Billion," *NonProfit Times*, July 1, 2003, p. 1.

[18] John Boudreau; "Giving Increased Slightly in 2002;" *Mercury News*; published June 23, 2003; <http://www.bayarea.com/mld/mercurynews/business/6150439.htm>; p. 1 of 6/26/03 9:07 AM printout.

[19] "Charitable Giving Increases In 2002, 'Giving USA' Reports;" The Direct Marketing Association; published June 23, 2003; <http://www.the-dma.org/cgi/dispnewsstand?article=1267>; p. 1 of 6/26/03 8:53 AM printout.

[20] Harvy Lipman, "Giving in 2002 Didn't Outpace Inflation, Report Says," *Chronicle of Philanthropy*, June 26, 2003, p. 7.

[21] Center on Philanthropy at Indiana University, *Giving USA 2003* (New York: AAFRC Trust for Philanthropy, 2003), p. 201.

[22] empty tomb, inc. analysis of *Giving USA 2003*, p. 10 data.

To obtain a meaningful measure of the public's participation in philanthropy, population and economic factors need to be included and reported in more than a passing mention lost in the preoccupation with aggregate numbers that present an overly rosy picture. Since individual giving is estimated to constitute the bulk of all giving, an analysis of individual giving in light of these factors is very important. Although AAFRC used to provide a breakdown by source of donations (individual, bequest, corporation, foundation) for each recipient sector (such as religion, education, etc.), it has not done so for the past several years. It is not likely to do so again unless the public, likely through the media, holds it accountable.

Media could develop generally accepted standards for the reporting of philanthropy. Contacts with major newspapers, syndicated services and national newsweeklies found that six had designated philanthropy reporters: *The Atlanta Constitution-Journal*/Cox News Service; *The Dallas Morning News*; *The New York Times*; *The San Jose Mercury News*; *The Wall Street Journal*; and *The Washington Post*. Clear responsibility could be established for reporting in the area of philanthropy at other media. Reporters could be sensitized to the need for adjustments for changes in population and disposable personal income.

Media Holding Academia Accountable for the Measurement of Philanthropy. Given that academics have done a poor job of adequately measuring philanthropy, the media may step into the vacuum. The results, however, may be not only unusual, but may misguide the discussion of philanthropy measurement into specious arenas.

For example, *The Chronicle of Philanthropy* conducted a study of giving as a percent of income entitled "The State of Generosity," published in that periodical's May 1, 2003 issue. "The State of Generosity" perpetuates the tendency within professional fundraising and trade paper circles to report overly optimistic findings.

In the instance of "The State of Generosity," giving is reported as a percent of "discretionary" income, rather than as a percent of "disposable" (after-tax) income. While "giving as a percent of discretionary income" produces a higher percentage of giving, it also introduces serious problems into the definitions within the analysis to the degree that the resulting percentages are of questionable usefulness at best.

The *Chronicle*'s analysis was based on U.S. Bureau of Labor Statistics data. An effect of *The Chronicle* introducing "discretionary" income was to elevate giving as a percentage of income to the comparatively high level of 6.4% (p. 8), for the last three quarters of 2001 and the 1ˢᵗ quarter of 2002 (p. 13). That result is considerably more positive than the annual figure of 1.9% as a percent of disposable personal income, based on the last three quarters of 2001, that was extrapolated by empty tomb, inc., also from the Bureau of Labor Statistics, in this case, "Table 1800. Region of residence: Average annual expenditures and characteristics, Consumer Expenditure Survey, 2001" (p. 18).

Using its "discretionary income" methodology, *The Chronicle of Philanthropy* found that, "All giving" as a percentage of discretionary income, by region, was 4.2% in the East, 6.4% in the Midwest, 7.0% in the South, and 7.8% in the West. In contrast, using similar Bureau of Labor Statistics data, giving as a percentage of disposable (after-tax) income in the Northeast, Midwest, South and West was 1.3%, 2.1%, 2.2%, and 1.8%, respectively.

The Chronicle of Philanthropy analysis of "Religious giving" as a percentage of discretionary income by region found that giving in the East, Midwest, South, and West was 2.7%, 5.0%, 5.9%, and 5.7%, respectively, while giving as a percentage of disposable (after-tax) income in the Northeast, Midwest, South and West was 0.9%, 1.6%, 1.8%, and 1.3%, respectively.

The Chronicle of Philanthropy analysis did not have an estimate of giving for those with income below $30,000, and reported that those with income "Less than $15,000" and from "$15,000- $29,999" have -$7,232 and -$1,886 negative "discretionary income," respectively. The explanation for this finding was that, "Annual expenses exceed reported net income for these income levels; percentage cannot be calculated."

Yet, Eugene R. Tempel, in a *NonProfit Times* article that addressed questions regarding possible efficiencies stemming from consolidating small nonprofits, included comments that are applicable to measures of American giving patterns that focus disproportionately on those with greater "discretionary income." Tempel wrote, "Individual giving in relatively small amounts is the backbone of fundraising in America. Even though a small number of donors do account for a large percentage of philanthropic giving, small nonprofits depend heavily on small donors." Tempel continued, "If fundraisers focus solely on large donors, they will cut off a main source of the lifeblood of nonprofit fundraising and a source for the future."[23]

In a "How the Chronicle's Rankings of Generosity Were Compiled" section, Harvy Lipman explained the rationale for the use of "discretionary income." Lipman wrote, "One basic premise underlies *The Chronicle*'s analyses of charitable giving: Most previous analyses of individual philanthropy have ignored differences in the cost of living in various parts of the country. Simply put, a dollar in New York City does not have the same value as a dollar in Tuscaloosa, Alabama" (p. 13).

A shortcoming in this logic stems from the fact that consumers in New York City also have more dollars with which to purchase goods than do those in Tuscaloosa, Alabama. BEA data shows that in 2001 Tuscaloosa County had a per capita personal income of $25,041, while New York County had a per capita personal income of $92,984. Simple economics would suggest that any significant discrepancy between the cost of consumer goods and income level in a geographical area would generally be accompanied by migratory behavior within America with its permeable state and county borders. Just such a trend was seen, for example, in the fact that, "For the first time since the government started keeping track, more people are leaving California for other U.S. addresses than are moving in from other states." Higher prices and economic factors related to lowered income are seen as contributing factors to such migratory behavior. "Soaring housing prices and a slumping economy in Southern California during the 1990s may have prompted some residents to find new addresses, said Dowell Myers, professor of urban planning and demography at the University of Southern California."[24]

---

[23] Eugene R. Tempel, "Pluralism and Efficiency," *NonProfit Times*, August 1, 2003, p. 14.

[24] "Data: More Leaving California than Coming," an Associated Press (New Orleans) article appearing in *Champaign (Ill.) News-Gazette*, 6 August 2003, sec. A, p. 3.

In fact, both prices and incomes vary by region, making a category such as disposable (after-tax) personal income a useful national or regional standard.

The flaw in the "basic premise" underlying *The Chronicle of Philanthropy*'s analyses of giving using discretionary income can be further seen by substituting other study categories in the sentence from the *Chronicle* report that reads, "Simply put, a dollar in New York City does not have the same value as a dollar in Tuscaloosa, Alabama." *The Chronicle of Philanthropy*'s basic premise seems to assume that a dollar spent by those at a "$70,000 or more" income level, "does not have the same value as" a dollar spent by those at a "$15,000-$29,999" income level, respectively. In fact, geographical, race and ethnic, and income levels are automatically adjusted by calculating giving as a percent of disposable (after-tax) personal income because that category is an average that takes substantive variations into account.

Another shortcoming in the "discretionary income" approach utilized in *The Chronicle of Philanthropy* is that it inappropriately marginalizes the fungible nature of money in relationship to lifestyle choices. That is, by comparing the amount of giving as a percent of "discretionary income" left after subtracting living expenses, *The Chronicle of Philanthropy* ignores the reality that many people, in all racial and ethnic groups, and many of those earning at various income levels, do not routinely or necessarily choose to give out of cash that is left over after they determine their living expenses. Rather, for many, their living expenses, savings, and investments are curtailed through a thoughtful, disciplined effort that includes their philanthropic values. So, in that sense, their giving is donated from their total income as they use discretion to decide how to allocate their total resources. Their lifestyles choices take their practice of philanthropy into account.

Discretionary income is a concept of limited value precisely because there is so much individual discretion in its definition. There is a great deal of potential variability and choice involved for each category of expense including current living expenses, giving, saving, and investment. The foundations of philanthropy, in general, and certainly religious philanthropy, are ignored by suggesting that giving should be considered as being out of, or calculated as a percentage of, the funds remaining only after one has spent whatever the individual desires on living expenses.

The author of the *Chronicle* study, Harvy Lipman, did not fully define what were considered as the base living expenses beyond which "discretionary income" appears. Did the *Chronicle*'s base living expense definition include all or part of the "major components of spending—food, housing, apparel and services, transportation, health care, entertainment, and personal insurance and pensions" as defined by the Bureau of Labor Statistics? Additional categories in the Bureau's expense list, representing smaller spending levels, include, "alcoholic beverages, personal care products and services, reading, education, tobacco products and supplies, miscellaneous, and cash contributions."[25]

Further, a wealthy person could decide that a felt need for elaborate housing, savings designated for family inheritance, regular restaurant meals determined necessary because of long work days, and designer clothes eliminated the category of "discretionary income" from his or her budget altogether.

---

[25] U.S. Bureau of Labor Statistics; *Consumer Expenditures in 2001*, Report 966; published April 2003; <http://www.bls.gov/cex/csxann01.pdf>; pp. 1, 3.

For these and other reasons, the category of "discretionary income" is generally regarded as problematic.

Donna J. Owens, in a Spring 1991 *Perspectives on Labour and Income* article entitled, "Tracking Down Discretionary Income," wrote, "'Discretionary income,' 'unencumbered funds,' 'fun money,' or 'spare cash': call it whatever you like, no one ever thinks that they can have enough of it. Even economists are dissatisfied with the term 'discretionary income.' But theirs is a conceptual concern: what is discretionary income and how can it be measured?" Providing background information, Owens continued, "Little analytical work has been done on discretionary income (DI) but one of the few attempts in recent years was made in a joint study by the U.S. Consumer Research Centre, The (U.S.) Conference Board and the U.S. Bureau of the Census. The study avoided defining 'necessities' and instead used an income threshold as a measure. It defined DI as 'the amount of money which would permit a family to maintain a living standard comfortably higher than the average for similar families.'"[26]

A 2003 "Fast Facts" section published by The Conference Board's Consumer Research Center used a question and answer format. Question number five asked, "What percentage of the population has discretionary income?" The answer, with a source listed as "Discretionary Income, 1999," was, "53% of U.S. households have discretionary income."[27]

A Marketer's Guide to Discretionary Income published by The Conference Board notes in a discussion of its methodology, "The methodology described here is arbitrary—there is no precise definition of discretionary income." [28] *A Marketer's Guide to Discretionary Income* also observed, "Discretionary income, as expected, is concentrated in the upper income brackets. While households with annual earnings in excess of $100,000 account for less than 10 percent of all households in the United States, they account for more than 70 percent of aggregate discretionary income."[29]

Discretionary income seems to be a concept useful for marketing analysis, given its promotion by The Conference Board. It seems to have been imported into the field of philanthropy measurement by *The Chronicle of Philanthropy*. In this context, the concept of discretionary income may be useful for general marketing analyses, including for for-profit and other professional fundraisers and philanthropic trade magazines, with their emphases on identifying likely prospects. Discretionary income, however, is not generally

---

[26] Donna J. Owens; "Tracking Down Discretionary Income;" Spring 1991 (Vo. 3, No. 1) Article No. 3, pp. 1-2; <http://216.239.33.104/search?q=cache:COqzmYQctDoJ:www.statcan.ca/english/indepth/75-001/archive/1991/pear1991003001s1a03.pdf+%22discretionary+income%22&hl=en&ie=UTF-8>; pp. 1-2 of 8/6/2003 4:57 PM printout.

[27] "Fast Facts;" The Conference Board, Inc.; copyright 2003; <http://www.crc-conquest.org/fast_facts/index.htm>; p. 1 of 8/7/2003 3:05 PM printout.

[28] Lynn Franco; *A Marketer's Guide to Discretionary Income*; published 1999; The Conference Board; p. 23; <http://216.239.33.104/search?q=cache:gfMdCV3mtd4J:www.crc-conquest.org/members/profiles/DiscretionaryIncome.pdf+%22discretionary+income%22&hl=en&ie=UTF-8>; p. 23 of 8/7/2003 3:14 PM printout.

[29] Lynn Franco; *A Marketer's Guide to Discretionary Income*; published 1999; The Conference Board; p. 4; <http://216.239.33.104/search?q=cache:gfMdCV3mtd4J:www.crc-conquest.org/members/profiles/DiscretionaryIncome.pdf+%22discretionary+income%22&hl=en&ie=UTF-8>; p. 4 of 8/7/2003 3:14 PM printout.

useful for scholarly analyses of the American public's giving patterns. *The Chronicle of Philanthropy* article, "The State of Generosity," and its table, "How Americans Give," may be misleading in regard to the American public's understanding of its giving patterns.

Rather, the media would do well to hold academia accountable for the improvement of the measurement of philanthropy.

Changes in Form 990. The Internal Revenue Service requires any tax-exempt group registered as a 501(c)(3) charitable organization that normally has more than $25,000 in annual income, and is not an exception under defined criteria, to file a Form 990 each year. Three changes in the information requested by the Internal Revenue Service's Form 990 would assist in improving the measurement of philanthropy in the United States. The recommendations about contributions from living donors, and the self-definition of organizations, are developed more fully under the section on recommendations related to the Urban Institute that follows.

Contributions from Living Donors. Theoretically, the most accurate measure of individual giving possible is from receipts by nonprofit organizations via a revised Form 990, rather than from IRS itemizer returns and estimates of nonitemizer amounts. A policy decision needs to be made that it is important to obtain a sound Form 990 measure of individual giving by living donors. Individual giving, in addition to bequests, corporations (businesses), and foundations, the four categories tracked in the *Giving USA* series, could be one of four options for the organization to choose when reporting contributions by source.

Self-Definition of Purpose and Governance Type. Form 990 needs to be changed so that reporting, recipient organizations define themselves through the use of a numerical system based on a standard classification such as the National Taxonomy of Exempt Entities.

Another change in Form 990 would be the implementation of a self-definition category describing the governance of the organization as either faith-based or secular. Currently, no such self-description is systematically requested. The result is the undercounting of the role of religion in the philanthropic sector, and consequently, in American society as a whole. An organization that is faith-based and provides, for example, human services is offered only the choice of being categorized as "human services" with the religious component ignored.

Contributions by Source. Form 990 does not now, but should, request that organizations provide donation information based on source of contributions. A policy decision is needed to measure contributions to recipient categories (religion, education, etc.) by source of donations. Currently, the standard source categories reported by *Giving USA* are individuals, bequests, corporations (businesses), and foundations. If the 990 were to collect this information from organizations defined by standard recipient categories, the information could serve as a validation test for the *Giving USA* series and other survey-based giving data.

Recommendations Related to the Urban Institute. The Urban Institute is involved in a variety of ways in the measurement of philanthropy. Several actions could be taken by this group to improve the national collection of giving data.

Changes in the Urban Institute's Unified Chart of Accounts to Account for Donations by Living Individuals. The Urban Institute provides a permanent home for the Unified Chart of Accounts (UCOA),[30] "designed so that nonprofits can...**quickly and reliably translate their financial statements into the categories required by the IRS Form 990**, the federal Office of Management and Budget, and into other standard reporting formats. UCOA also seeks to...promote uniform accounting practices throughout the nonprofit sector" (bold emphasis in original).[31]

1. A critical weakness in the UCOA is its treatment of individual giving. This category is combined with "small businesses" in category "4010-xxx," to be reported on Form 990 Line Number 1a. The UCOA provides that gifts from individuals, whether designated, pledged or undesignated, be included on the same line as gifts from small businesses, including commercial co-ventures. In order to obtain a clear measure of individual giving, Account Number 4010-xxx should be reserved for individuals. "Small businesses" should be moved either to a new or some existing account series, such as "4210-xxx, Corporate and other business grants."

Part of the rationale for this separation in the reporting of individuals and small businesses is the definition of "small business." Contributions from small businesses are often not the type that can be compared with the IRS *Statistics of Income Bulletin*'s Table 1:—Individual Income Tax Returns "Itemized deductions" for "Charitable contributions." The Small Business Administration indicates that "Approximately 95% of all businesses are eligible for SBA [Small Business Administration] assistance."[32] The Small Business Administration has size standards that include: 500 employees for most manufacturing and mining industries; 100 employees for all wholesale trade industries; $5 million for most retail and service industries;[33] 4 million megawatt hours for energy producing companies; and $100 million in assets for banks or similar institutions.[34]

If the Form 990 is ever going to provide a clear set of data on giving by living individuals, then the data must be separated from this wide spectrum of additional sources of business donations. To assist organizations in classifying donations, incorporated businesses that make deductible charitable contributions could be required to identify in a clear, standardized and regulated fashion that the gift comes from an incorporated business. In this way, the organization can easily attribute the gift to the appropriate bookkeeping/accounting category, which will subsequently be used for Form 990 reporting purposes.

2. Form 1040 (Individual Return) Schedules A and C and Form 1065 (Partnership Return) should also be changed. Currently contributions made through certain businesses,

---

[30]Russy D. Sumariwalla and Wilson C. Levis, Unified *Financial Reporting System for Not-for-Profit Organizations: A Comprehensive Guide to Unifying GAAP, IRS Form 990, and Other Financial Reports Using a Unified Chart of Accounts* (San Francisco: Jossey-Bass, 2000), p. 211, Note.

[31]"The Unified Chart of Accounts;" National Center for Charitable Statistics, Urban Institute; <http://nccs.urban.org/ucoa/nccs-ucoa.htm>; p. 1 of 8/20/01 3:18 PM printout.

[32]U.S. Small Business Administration; "Small Business Resource Guide;" "startup pdf;" created Thu, Apr 6, 2000, 9:24 PM; downloaded from: <http://www.sba.gov/starting/startup.pdf>; p. 38.

[33]U.S. Small Business Administration, Office of Size Standards; "Frequently Asked Questions (FAQs);" <http://www.sba.gov/size/indexfaqs.html>; p. 1 of 9/13/01 8:00 AM printout.

[34]U.S. Small Business Administration; "Small Business Size Standards: Matched to North American Industry Classification System (NAICS) Codes Effective December 21, 2000;" <http://www.sba.gov/size/Table-of-Small-Business-Size-Standards-from-final-rule.html>; pp. 4 and 23 of 9/12/01 2:43 PM printout.

specifically sole proprietorships or partnerships, can be reported on Schedule A for Form 1040. Gifts from such businesses might best be deducted on the business's tax return on Form 1065 rather than the individual's return. A precedent for separating personal and business contributions is found in the treatment of "Car and Truck Expenses" in the "Tax Guide for Small Business." The Tax Guide reads "If you have an expense that is partly for business and partly personal, separate the personal part from the business part."[35] If not changed, then the individual donor should be required to indicate to the organization that the gift will be reported as an individual, rather than business, contribution so that the organization can attribute the gift accordingly.

3. "Contributions through commercial co-ventures" should be moved to the corporate/business UCOA account number. Income from such co-ventures cannot validly be compared with the IRS Statistics of Income Bulletin's Table 1:—Individual Income Tax Returns "Itemized deductions" for "Charitable contributions." Commercial co-ventures can involve millions of dollars to nonprofits in exchange for positive marketing results for the company. While the arrangement may be a legitimate symbiotic relationship, it cannot be compared with the type of philanthropy normally assumed to be defined by the term "individual giving."

Any effort to change the Form 990 to yield an accurate measure of the level of giving from living individuals will be impeded to the extent that the Uniform Chart of Accounts, being championed by the Urban Institute for use by nonprofit organizations as a standard basis for bookkeeping categories, is structurally designed not to collect information specifically about giving by living individuals.

Categorization of organization by self-description of purpose and governance. The Urban Institute's National Center for Charitable Statistics has worked with the U.S. Internal Revenue Service to categorize nonprofit organizations that return Form 990. Further refinements could help to classify organizations using nationally-accepted standards.

In 1993, the National Center for Charitable Statistics was housed at Independent Sector. Virginia Hodgkinson authored a report calling for "a check-off list for charities based on the categories developed by Independent Sector for the National Taxonomy of Exempt Entities, an effort to classify all non-profit organizations registered with the IRS."[36] More specifically, the report recommended, "The Form 990 should be revised to allow for institutions of various functions to report their major purposes and programs, taking into account systems already in place to define such institutions."[37]

A precedent for this type of information gathering is Schedule C (Form 1040) that is used to report "Profit or Loss from Business (Sole Proprietorship)." This form requires a reporting business to select a category from the "Principal Business or Professional Activity

---

[35]Internal Revenue Service, "Tax Guide for Small Business (For Individuals Who Use Schedule C or C-EZ): For use in preparing 2000 Returns," Publication 334, Cat. No. 11063P, p. 26.

[36]Jennifer Moore, "Charity Group Backs Overhaul of Tax Form," *The Chronicle of Philanthropy*, November 30, 1993, pp. 34-35.

[37] Virginia Hodgkinson, et al., *A Portrait of the Independent Sector: The Activities and Finances of Charitable Organizations*, (Washington, DC: Independent Sector, 1993), p. 80.

Codes" that best describes the business. The codes provide 300 activities under 19 general categories.[38]

The National Taxonomy for Exempt Entities contains ten core categories from which a nonprofit organization could select to identify its main activity.

An important further refinement would provide a more complete picture of philanthropy in America. Before selecting one of the ten core categories, the nonprofit organization would first indicate its form of governance as either "faith-based" or "secular." This identification could provide valuable information to help clarify the role of religion in the area of giving. Form 990 could also require that the organization define itself, first by selecting either faith-based or secular as the category of governance, and then the specific activity described by one or more of the NTEE core codes.

In their book on the Unified Chart of Accounts, Russy D. Sumariwalla and Wilson C. Levis reproduced a graphic originally prepared by United Way of America that depicts how the account classification would appear in practical application.[39] For purposes of the present discussion, that graphic was adapted to include a statement about receipts classification, and to describe at what point the choice of faith-based or secular governance would be included in the accounting hierarchy (see Figure 17).

Do Not Count Donations from Private Foundations. This recommendation is made persuasively in a 1993 paper by Hayden Smith. He noted that it is understandable that AAFRC, in its *Giving USA* series, for example, would include contributions to private foundations as charitable giving. Yet he developed the position that it is a mistake to include the donations from foundations in a measure of the current flow of Total Contributions, writing in part:

> However, if we are thinking about the flow of contributions and bequests from outside the charitable community, it is a mistake to include private foundation grants in our measure of total philanthropy, for one simple reason: private foundations themselves are charitable organizations and they are the recipients of gifts and bequests from individuals and families as well as makers of grants to other charities. By including them, we double-count some of the dollars that flow from donors to ultimate donations. . . Perfect validity requests that grants made out of the income generated from the investment of foundation assets, or any transfers of those assets to other charities, should not be included as part of the current flow of charitable giving.[40]

A Commission on Private Philanthropy and Public Needs. A standing United States Commission on Private Philanthropy and Public needs was recommended in previous volumes of *The State of Church Giving* series. A recommendation for such a commission by Act of Congress was a finding of the original Commission on Private Philanthropy and Public Needs, also known as the Filer Commission. Details of that proposal are outlined in the Commission's report.[41] Among the recommendations were that the Commission's chair and 12 additional members would be appointed by the President of the United States, all

---

[38]Internal Revenue Service, "Profit or Loss From Business (Sole Proprietorship)," Schedule C (Form 1040) 2000, OMB No. 1545-0074, Cat. No. 11334P, and Internal Revenue Service, "2000 Instructions for Schedule C, Profit or Loss From Business," Cat. No. 24329W, pp. C-7 and C-8.

[39]Sumariwalla and Levis, p. 41.

[40] Hayden Smith, *Voluntas*, p. 253.

Figure 17: Account Classification Application with Faith-based/Secular Governance Option Included

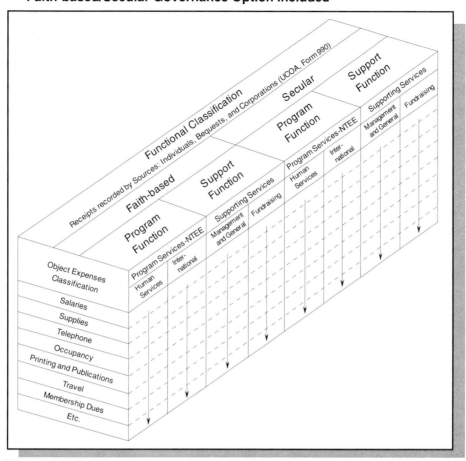

Source: Adaptation of graphic in Sumariwall and Levis   empty tomb graphic 2001

subject to senatorial confirmation. These 13 appointees would name an additional 12 members. The term of the Commission would be permanent. The focus of the Commission was described in the Filer Commission Report as follows.

> Among other purposes and roles of the commission would be continuous collection of data on the sources and uses of the resources of the nonprofit sector; exploring and proposing ways of strengthening private giving and nonprofit activity; providing a forum for public discussion of issues affecting, and for commentary concerning, the nonprofit sector; studying the existing relationships between government and the nonprofit sector and acting as an ombudsman in protecting the interests of the sector as affected by government.[42]

The Commission could also assist in developing standards for the reporting of philanthropy data, facilitating changes in Form 990 to yield giving data by living individuals, and assisting in the dissemination of Form 990 data in an effort to increase the public accountability of nonprofit organizations. The Commission ought to involve academic

---

[41]Commission on Private Philanthropy and Public Needs, *Giving in America: Toward a Stronger Voluntary Sector: Report of the Commission on Private Philanthropy and Public Needs* (n.p.: Commission on Private Philanthropy and Public Needs, 1975), pp. 191-193.

[42]Commission on Private Philanthropy and Public Needs, p. 27.

economists of the highest caliber, who are well versed in national economic accounting and the development of the National Income and Products Accounts of the United States, including those who would have a link to the Council of Economic Advisors, and the Internal Revenue Service Form 990, as well as those who could influence the National Bureau of Economic Research to assist with the improvement of the measure of philanthropy.

Journal of Philanthropy Measurement. A peer-reviewed journal on the topic of philanthropy measurement is needed to raise the reporting standards in this field of study. The journal would be dedicated to obtaining sound annual estimates of philanthropy in the United States. The Hauser Center for Nonprofit Organizations housed at Harvard University's John F. Kennedy School of Government would be one logical place in which to house such a journal. The Hauser Center was designed to take a broader view of the field of philanthropy. As reported in the May 1, 1997 issue of *The Chronicle of Philanthropy*, "Harvard officials say that after they examined the existing academic centers in the field, they felt that many were parochial in their approach."[43]

NBER. The National Bureau of Economic Research needs to be encouraged to elevate the study of the nonprofit sector to a standing program, instead of only issuing occasional papers.

USBEA. The U.S. Department of Commerce, Bureau of Economic Analysis National Income and Product Accounts should expand its analysis of the nonprofit sector.

GIVING ESTIMATES BY GIVING USA. By far, the most commonly quoted estimates of giving are produced by the American Association of Fundraising Counsel Trust for Philanthropy and published in its *Giving USA* series. The general opinion seems to be that while the numbers may not be great, they're the best that's available.

Patrick Rooney, the Center on Philanthropy at Indiana University's director of research, oversees the production of *Giving USA* for the AAFRC Trust for Philanthropy. Noting the variety of estimates available, he concluded, "We think this is one of the best."[44]

"Best" appears to be a relative term. Peter Dobkin Hall, a Harvard University John F. Kennedy School of Government lecturer, noted that the projections in *Giving USA* produce "soft numbers at best. They're probably jumping the gun by releasing them in such a high-profile way before the final numbers are in." He went on, "We have neither solid data on giving or receiving," concluding that *Giving USA* "is the best we have, but far from perfect."[45]

Testing the validity of the most recent *Giving USA* projections is indeed difficult to do in a timely fashion. A July 2003 *NonProfit Times* article on the release of *Giving USA 2003* and its estimates for 2002 cited Steve Zekoff of The United Methodist Church, which received $5 billion in 2001, as saying that "because of reporting processes it was too early for a 2002 national tally of donations."[46]

---

[43]*The Chronicle of Philanthropy*, May 1, 1997, p. 10.

[44] Jeff Jones, "Giving to Religion Beats Inflation—Again," *The NonProfit Times*, July 1, 2003, p. 4.

[45] Harvy Lipman, "Giving in 2002 Didn't Outpace Inflation, Report Says," *The Chronicle of Philanthropy*, June 26, 2003, p. 18.

[46] Jeff Jones, p. 4.

Elizabeth Boris is the Urban Institute's Center on Nonprofits and Philanthropy executive director. She expressed the opinion that, "I don't think anyone associated with *Giving USA* would say these are real, true numbers, but they're the best we have."[47]

In the area of philanthropy measurement, there is a curious willingness to accept something less than academic excellence. In fact, several recommendations could improve the presentation of *Giving USA* as a nationally cited source of giving information.

Adjust for Population and Income. The *Giving USA* publications and press releases continue to emphasize the aggregate billions of dollars raised each year.

The publication has been presenting an increasingly nuanced analysis of giving, likely under the direction of the Center on Philanthropy staff who edit the volume. The press releases do contain information on giving adjusted for population and income. However, the resounding emphasis of *Giving USA*'s announcements and presentation is evident in media reports that tout the increased billions of dollars raised from one year to the next.

Giving USA is in a position to lead the national discussion in a more informative direction, that is, one that acknowledges that changes in population and income define changes in giving levels.

To continue to focus primarily on the aggregate billions raised is a serious flaw in the national dissemination to the public of philanthropy information. The problem can be illustrated by one example drawn from the *Giving USA 2003* presentation of "new church construction" data, unadjusted for population and income.

Giving USA 2003 (p. 108) states, "Construction of churches and cathedrals was at a 40-year high in 2002, according to a study by McGraw-Hill Construction Information Group that was reported in the *NonProfit Times*."

Continuing with the "new church construction" topic, and referencing material from *The State of Church Giving through 2000* (p. 48), *Giving USA 2003* (p. 109) states, "Similar findings came from a study by empty tomb, inc., a research organization focusing on church membership and finances. They reported that the $6.9 billion spent on church construction in 2000 was the highest, in inflation-adjusted dollars, in the 1964-2000 period they reviewed. The empty tomb study used data from the current construction reports compiled by the Census Bureau to compare the value of church construction in each year."

The problem was that *Giving USA 2003* did not heed *The State of Church Giving through 2000* (p. 48) caution in the paragraph preceding the inflation-adjusted, aggregate findings, that stated, "However, as has been emphasized in previous chapters of this volume, aggregate numbers considered apart from population, inflation, and changes in income, do not give a complete picture." More specifically, *Giving USA 2003* failed to report the data adjusted for both population and income. As *The State of Church Giving through 2000* (p. 49) found, "In fact, as a portion of income, Americans spent 0.25% on the construction of new religious buildings in 1965, compared to 0.11% in 2000." *The State of Church Giving through 2000* (p. 49) graphically compared the results of aggregate data, both unadjusted, and adjusted for population and income, in "Figure 14: Construction of Religious Buildings in the U.S.,

---

[47] Lipman, June 26, 2003, p. 18.

1964-2000, Aggregate Inflation-Adjusted 1996 Dollars, and Percent of U.S. Per Capita Disposable Personal Income."

Giving USA 2003's report of aggregate inflation-adjusted dollars only, and concomitant neglect in adjusting "new church construction" for changes in population and income over the period studied, ignores the reality that United States population grew from 194,347,000 in 1965 to 282,489,000 in 2000. It also ignores the fact that inflation-adjusted United States Per Capita Disposable Personal Income increased from $10,799 in 1965 to $23,587 in the year 2000.

Systemic distortions are produced by *Giving USA*'s charting, and press release headline, and initial sentence and paragraph, emphases on aggregate data. The results serve not to advance the scientific measurement of philanthropy so much as to provide overly optimistic measures of philanthropy. That overly optimistic measures of philanthropy are useful to motivate professional fundraisers does not justify the lack of additional information designed to inform the general public through its news releases that are widely reported via the national media.

The field of philanthropy as a whole is faced with the decision as to whether it cherishes a motivational tool with a patina of scientific respectability that helps keep professional fundraisers optimistic, or whether it values an in-depth, scientifically sound measurement of philanthropy that accurately informs the American public about their giving patterns. Adjusting for population and income, combined with efforts to obtain accurate data, move in the direction of the second option.

Define *Giving USA* Methodology. The specific methodology and formulae for estimating giving by "Individuals" was not available at the time of publication of *Giving USA 2003*, according to its "Methodology" section. The significance of the methodology for estimating individual giving is seen from the fact that individual giving is estimated to comprise 76.3% of all giving in the *Giving USA 2003* Annual Report. A generic "Methodology" statement of factors utilized in estimating individual giving refers the reader to Note 3 on page 222 of the *Giving USA 2003* Annual Report, which reads, "Partha Deb, Mark Wilhelm, Patrick Rooney and Melissa Brown, Estimating charitable deductions in Giving USA, Nonprofit and Voluntary Sector Quarterly, forthcoming. Working paper version at web site listed in Note 1." Note 1 reads, "Technical papers will be available in Fall 2003 at www.philanthropy.iupui.edu, under the heading for Research, then Research Studies, then Giving USA." It may be noted that one would reasonably assume that methodology, having been clearly thought out and articulated prior to the investigation and publication of findings, would be published contemporaneously with findings.

Such adherence to standard research protocol would contribute to helping build a reputation that overcomes that observed in an evaluation from one of The Commission on Private Philanthropy and Public Needs (Filer Commission) research papers published by the United States Treasury Department in 1977: "Our estimation method is described in Appendix D. In contrast to our systematic sampling procedure, the *Giving USA* total is based on a survey of major foundations. Their method of imputation for small foundations' grants is not specified in their published reports; however, it appears, from the language used, that the AAFRC uses some undescribed rules of thumb and intuition to make its estimates of total foundation activity from the surveys of a relatively small number of large foundations."[48]

It would also be useful if the complete *Giving USA 2003* Methodology and Technical Papers that are scheduled for Fall 2003 were to address the timing and the role of the Advisory Committee on Methodology's activities in establishing methodological policies prior to *Giving USA*'s securing, analysis, and review of the data itself. In addition, one would benefit from clarification regarding the timing and role of *Giving USA 2003*'s Editorial Review Board in relation to the work of the Advisory Committee on Methodology. This information would be of particular interest in light of the fact that, apart from the AAFRC Trust For Philanthropy Executive Director, the other seven members of the Editorial Review Board are from for-profit fundraising firms that are represented either on the AAFRC Trust for Philanthropy or AAFRC Board of Directors. Six of the eight members of the Editorial Review Board are direct funders of the AAFRC Trust for Philanthropy, two of whom are the Chair and the Vice Chair of the AAFRC Trust for Philanthropy.

The full Methodology and Technical Papers should be included with the *Giving USA* Annual Report itself.

A Comparison of Estimates for Aggregate Giving to Religion. The largest category in philanthropy, as measured in *Giving USA* and other information sources, is religion. In 2002, according to *Giving USA 2003*, religion received 35% of all contributions, with Education receiving the next largest amount at 13%.[49] Therefore, any estimate of giving would be affected by the quality of the measurement of giving to religion.

The watershed Commission on Private Philanthropy and Public Needs of the 1970s, commonly referred to as the Filer Commission, produced an estimate of giving to religion. That report estimated that in 1974, giving to religion was $11.7 billion.[50] This estimate was relatively close to the AAFRC estimate for 1974 of $11.84 billion.[51]

In theory, one could follow a methodology for religion similar to that AAFRC used for the categories of education and health, in this case keying 1974 data to the Filer Commission estimate, and then calculate estimates for the years 1968 to 1973, and 1975 to 2001, based on an external source of data. The external source of data could be the same that AAFRC used to revise its religion data for 1987 forward: a set of denominations that publish data in the *Yearbook of American and Canadian Churches* series. This revised approach would remedy the estimates for those years, presumably from about 1977 to 1985 based on the data patterns, when AAFRC did not calculate a figure for religion, but rather considered it a "residual" category, having the religion category absorb the difference between AAFRC's

---

[48] Burton A. Weisbrod and Stephen H. Long, "The Size of the Voluntary Nonprofit Sector: Concepts and Measures," *History, Trends, and Current Magnitudes*, Vol. 1 in the series, *Research Papers Sponsored by The Commission on Private Philanthropy and Public Needs* (Washington, DC: Department of Treasury, 1977), p. 360, n. 19.

[49] Center on Philanthropy at Indiana University, *Giving USA 2003* (New York: AAFRC Trust for Philanthropy, 2003), p. 10.

[50] Gabriel Rudney, "The Scope of the Private Voluntary Charitable Sector," Research Papers Sponsored by The Commission on Private Philanthropy and Public Needs, Vol. 1, History, Trends, and Current Magnitudes, (Washington, DC: Department of the Treasury, 1977), p. 136.

[51] *Giving USA 2003*, 196.

estimate of total contributions and the sum of AAFRC's estimates for the other recipient categories. [52]

The starting base in this approach would be the Filer Commission estimate of $11.7 billion for 1974. The amount of change from year to year, calculated for 1968 to 1973 and also 1975 to 2001, would be the annual percentage change in the composite denomination set analyzed in other chapters of this report.[53] This calculation yielded a total of $8.01 billion given to religion in 1968, and $61.89 billion in 2001. These figures contrast with the AAFRC estimate of $8.42 billion in 1968 and $80.34 billion in 2001. Table 17 presents this data.

Table 17: Giving to Religion, AAFRC Series[54] and Denomination-Based Series, 1968-2001, Aggregate Billions of Current Dollars and Percent Difference

Year	AAFRC Series (Billions $)	Denomination-Based Series Keyed to 1974 Filer Estimate (Billions $)	Percent Difference between AAFRC and Denomination-Based Series
1968	$8.42	$8.01	5%
1969	$9.02	$8.33	8%
1970	$9.34	$8.67	8%
1971	$10.07	$9.13	10%
1972	$10.10	$9.78	3%
1973	$10.53	$10.69	-2%
1974	$11.84	$11.70	1%
1975	$12.81	$12.74	1%
1976	$14.18	$13.87	2%
1977	$16.98	$15.02	13%
1978	$18.35	$16.41	12%
1979	$20.17	$18.15	11%
1980	$22.23	$20.08	11%
1981	$25.05	$22.14	13%
1982	$28.06	$24.00	17%
1983	$31.84	$25.61	24%
1984	$35.55	$27.71	28%
1985	$38.21	$29.40	30%
1986	$41.68	$31.09	34%
1987	$43.51	$32.42	34%
1988	$45.15	$33.68	34%
1989	$47.77	$35.46	35%
1990	$49.79	$36.98	35%
1991	$50.00	$38.37	30%
1992	$50.95	$39.43	29%
1993	$52.89	$40.50	31%
1994	$56.43	$43.37	30%
1995	$58.07	$44.19	31%
1996	$61.90	$47.70	30%
1997	$64.69	$49.42	31%
1998	$68.25	$52.28	31%
1999	$71.25	$55.10	29%
2000	$76.95	$59.36	30%
2001	$80.34	$61.89	30%

[52] Nathan Weber, *Giving USA 1990*, (New York: AAFRC Trust for Philanthropy, 1990), 187.

[53]For this comparison, the composite data set of denominations was adjusted for missing data.

[54]*Giving USA 2003*, p. 196.

Comparing these two estimate series, one may observe that the two series are within a few percentage points of each other for two years on either side of 1974, the year of the Filer estimate to which the denominational-based series is keyed. AAFRC methodology does not indicate when religion became a residual recipient category, although the differences in the data series suggests a major change in AAFRC methodology took place between 1976 and 1977.

In 1982, while the denominational-based estimate series continues to change at a consistent rate, the AAFRC estimate series begins to expand more rapidly from year to year. The percentage difference grew from 17% in 1982 to 35% in 1989-1990. In 2001, the difference was 30%. AAFRC updates the aggregate *Giving USA* numbers each year by a percent from the previous year, and thus the later years continue to build on the data years when religion was a residual category, absorbing that portion of the estimated Total Contributions amount that could not be placed in another category.

A Comparison of Per Capita Giving as a Percent of Income to Religion. The aggregate data in Table 16 was divided by U.S. population to produce a per capita figure for both the AAFRC giving to religion series and the denomination-based series keyed to the Filer estimate. The two series were then converted to giving as a percentage of U.S. disposable personal income. Figure 19 displays a decline and then upturn in the AAFRC series, while the denomination-based series reflects the pattern in the composite denomination set. When the denomination-based series is taken as a portion of disposable (after-tax) personal income, in 1968 charitable giving was 1.28%, while in 2001, it was 0.84%, a decline of 35% in the portion of U.S. per capita disposable personal income contributed to religion.

An analysis was developed by consultant Joseph Claude Harris.[55] Harris had taken a sample of Catholic parishes. Using that data in combination with denominational data from the *Yearbook of American and Canadian Churches*, he developed an estimate for "All Denominations and the Catholic Church" for 1991-1999. His individual contributions to religion data, adjusted for population and income, followed the Filer-Adjusted series, as shown in Figure 18.

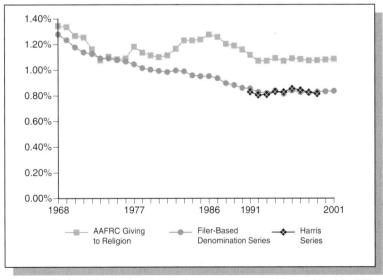

Figure 18: Giving to Religion as a Percent of U.S. Per Capita Disposable Personal Income, *Giving USA* and Filer-Adjusted Series, 1968-2001, and Harris Estimate, 1991-1999

Sources: AAFRC; *YACC* adjusted series; U.S. BEA   empty tomb, inc. 2003

---

[55]Joseph Claude Harris, "A Summary of Church Contributions.xls," Seattle, WA, Date Written March 7, 2001; Date Revised April 7, 2001. Letter and Spreadsheet to empty tomb, inc., July 10, 2001.

Comparison of Estimates of Giving to Religion and Individual Giving. A new development in the measurement of philanthropy has taken place in the U.S. Department of Labor Bureau of Labor Statistics. This agency's quarterly survey has begun to include philanthropy categories, including: "charities and other organization"; "church, religious organizations"; and "educational institutions." Based on the last three quarters of 2001, an annual figure was calculated for these categories. The result indicated that 76% of charitable contributions are perceived by the donors as going to "church, religious organizations."[56]

In contrast, "religion" represented only 44% of individual giving in 2001, based on *Giving USA 2003* numbers.[57] The difference may highlight the need described in Figure 17, "Account Classification Application with Faith-based/Secular Governance Option Included," presented earlier in this chapter. That is, many organizations included in the "human services," "international" and other categories by *Giving USA* are perceived by donors to actually represent religious organizations.

The disparity in these two estimates points to a lack of clear understanding of the connection between religion and the practice of philanthropy in the United States. To measure "religion" adequately, a governance classification of charitable organizations into "faith-based" and "secular" within recipient categories is needed.

Comparing the Bureau of Labor Statistics and *Giving USA 2003* estimates of 2001 individual giving also produced a gap between the two sources. Based on the three quarters of 2001 Bureau of Labor Statistics data, an approximation of $93.26 billion for individual giving was extrapolated for the year. That figure compared to the $182.47 billion figure presented in *Giving USA 2003* for individual giving.[58]

The wide variation in estimates of individual giving that exist also underscores the need for additional solid academic work in the area of measurement of philanthropy.

Per Capita Giving to Additional Recipient Categories, 1968-2001. Considering giving on a per capita basis as a percentage of income to various recipient categories in addition to religion may provide a different picture than presented by the aggregate AAFRC data for these categories. A comparison is presented in Table 18.

It should be noted that the recipient categories presented by AAFRC do not make a distinction by source of contribution. AAFRC does state that the majority of donations to religion comes from individuals. However, in recent years AAFRC does not provide figures within each of the various recipient categories as to the amount of donations from

---

[56] Individual Giving was calculated by multiplying "Number of consumer units" = 110,339,000, by the sum of consumer unit contributions for the last three quarters of 2001: $125.33 ("charities and other organizations") + $481.61 ("church religious organizations") + $26.95 ("educational institutions"). When the charitable contributions sum of $633.89 was multiplied by the Number of consumer units, the result was a total giving amount of $69,942,788,710. Divided by 75% to extrapolate to a full year, an annual amount of $93.26 billion resulted. Religion as a percent of the total was calculated by dividing $481.61 by $633.89, yielding 76%. Data source: "Table 1800. Region of Residence: Average annual expenditures and characteristics, Consumer Expenditure survey, 2001"; Region2001.pdf; Created 11/6/2002; (U.S. Department of Labor Bureau of Labor Statistics), pp. 1, 18.

[57] This figure was obtained by dividing the *Giving USA 2003* amount of giving to religion by individual giving. "Nearly all religious giving is from households" (*Giving USA 2003*, p. 106).

[58] *Giving USA 2003*, p. 194.

each source, the four being: individuals, bequests, corporations, and foundations. Therefore, the comparison in Table 18 is only approximate. The information does, however, suggest that population and income are important factors to be taken into consideration when discussing trends in charitable giving.

Table 18 presents the AAFRC published data for the recipient categories of: religion; education; health; human services; arts, culture, and humanities; and public/society benefit.[59] Since data for the recipient categories of environment/wildlife and international affairs is provided only for years beginning with 1987, these categories are not included. The category of giving to foundations has current dollar data only back to 1978, and likewise is not considered in this table. The category of unallocated is also not included.

From this table, it is apparent once again that giving to religion received the highest level of charitable giving support. Aggregate giving in both current and inflation-adjusted dollars increased. However, as a portion of U.S. per capita disposable personal income, the amount of giving to religion decreased by 19%. Table 18 uses AAFRC's *Giving 2003* estimate of giving to religion series.

All the categories in Table 18 showed an increase in terms of aggregate giving in both current and inflation-adjusted dollars. However, giving as a percentage of income provides additional information. Per capita giving as a portion of income to education increased by 14% during this period, compared to an increase of 164% in inflation-adjusted aggregate dollars. However, giving to health declined 21%, and giving to human services declined 24%, rather than an inflation-adjusted aggregate increase of 83% and 76% to health and human services, respectively.

Table 18: **AAFRC Giving to Recipient Categories, 1968 and 2001, Aggregate, Current and Inflation-Adjusted 2002 Dollars (Billions of Dollars), and Per Capita as a Percent of U.S. Disposable Personal Income, with Percent Change 1968-2001**

	Religion			Education		
	Aggregate (Billions $)		Per Capita	Aggregate (Billions $)		Per Capita
	Current $	Inf.-Adj. '02 $	% Income	Current $	Inf.-Adj. '02 $	% Income
1968	$8.42	$43.54	1.34%	$2.38	$12.31	0.38%
2001	$80.34	$81.61	1.09%	$31.98	$32.49	0.43%
% Change	854%	87%	-19%	1244%	164%	14%

	Health			Human Services		
	Aggregate (Billions $)		Per Capita	Aggregate (Billions $)		Per Capita
	Current $	Inf.-Adj. '02 $	% Income	Current $	Inf.-Adj. '02 $	% Income
1968	$2.08	$10.75	0.33%	$2.31	$11.94	0.37%
2001	$19.31	$19.62	0.26%	$20.71	$21.04	0.28%
% Change	828%	83%	-21%	797%	76%	-24%

	Arts, Culture and Humanities			Public/Society Benefit		
	Aggregate (Billions $)		Per Capita	Aggregate (Billions $)		Per Capita
	Current $	Inf.-Adj. '02 $	% Income	Current $	Inf.-Adj. '02 $	% Income
1968	$0.60	$3.10	0.10%	$0.43	$2.22	0.07%
2001	$12.14	$12.33	0.16%	$11.82	$12.01	0.16%
% Change	1923%	298%	71%	2649%	441%	133%

---

[59]*Giving USA 2003*, pp. 196-199.

Figure 19:   AAFRC Recipient Category Data, 1968-2001

Giving to Education

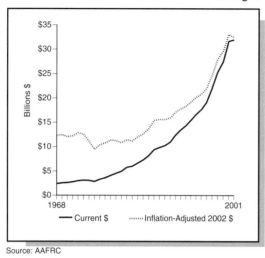

Source: AAFRC

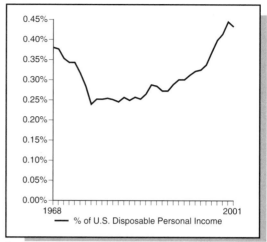

Source: empty tomb analysis, AAFRC data

Giving to Health

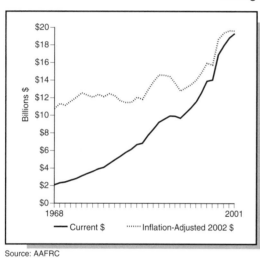

Source: AAFRC

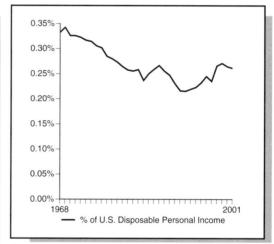

Source: empty tomb analysis, AAFRC data

Giving to Human Services

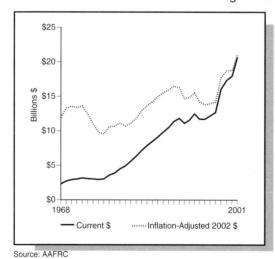

Source: AAFRC

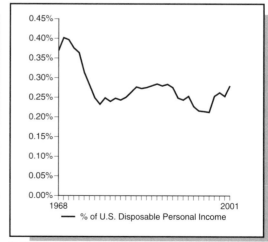

Source: empty tomb analysis, AAFRC data

Figure 19: AAFRC Recipient Category Data, 1968-2001, Continued

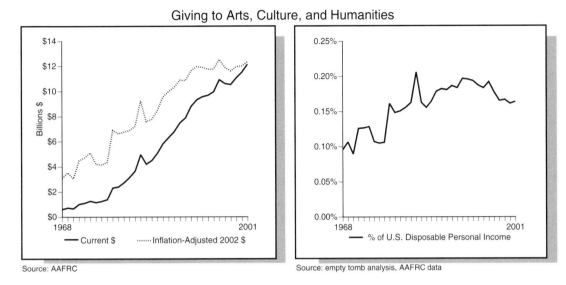

Source: AAFRC   Source: empty tomb analysis, AAFRC data

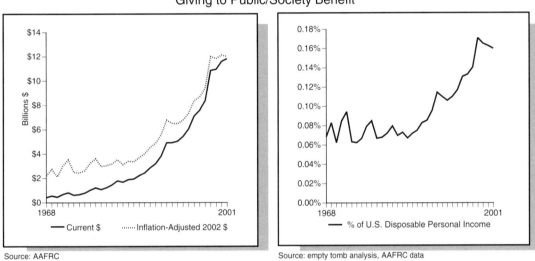

Source: AAFRC   Source: empty tomb analysis, AAFRC data

Two recipient categories that show an increase were arts, culture and humanities, and the category of public/society benefit. While neither group represented more than 0.2% of per capita giving as a portion of income in 2001, these two categories posted increases of 71% and 133% respectively, between 1968 and 2001, in contrast to the other categories in the table.

Figure 19 depicts two views of five recipient categories: education; health; human services; arts, culture, and humanities; and public/society benefit. The view in the left column presents the aggregate AAFRC data as it is presented in the *Giving USA* series, in both current and inflation-adjusted 2002 dollars. The view in the right column for each recipient category presents an additional view: the AAFRC data was converted to a per capita basis as a percentage of U.S. per capita disposable personal income. It may be observed that the two approaches present different pictures of charitable giving patterns.

GRADING SYSTEM METHODOLOGY AND DETAIL. The preceding discussion has considered various aspects of the measurement of philanthropy, and recommendations to improve it.

The Report Card on the Measurement of Philanthropy was designed to provide an overview of the quality of present efforts to measure charitable giving in the United States.

Each grade level from A to F was given a numerical value. Each of the twelve specific entities were graded in each relevant category. The numerical value of all the categories for which an entity was graded were then averaged to produce an overall grade for that entity.

For each of the twelve entities, Table 19 presents the Overall Grade, and lists the Evaluation Category, Grade, and Evaluation Comments that combined to provide the Overall Grade.

Table 19: Report Card on the Measurement of Philanthropy Detail

Providers of Public Estimates of Giving

AAFRC Trust for Philanthropy *Giving USA* series **Overall Grade: D+**		
Evaluation Category	Grade	Evaluation Comments
Annual Measurement	A	The American Association of Fundraising Counsel, Inc. Trust for Philanthropy (AAFRC) issues an annual *Giving USA* (*GUSA*) report.
Adjustments for Population and Income	C	The predominant emphasis in the *Giving USA* series' press release headline and text, and *Giving USA* tables, graphics, and text, is on aggregate dollar amounts and percent changes in aggregate dollar amounts, which do not account for changes in population and after-tax income. The result is an artificially optimistic estimate of changes in giving. *Giving USA 2003* did introduce a series of graphs that charted gross domestic product (GDP) and disposable personal income. Further, the supporting tables on pp. 200-201 of that volume provided giving as a percent of GDP, personal income, and disposable personal income. Adding disposable personal income contributed to an increase of this grade to a C from last year's D. It would be helpful to have the current dollar value of the GDP series, and not only the inflation-adjusted numbers. The essence and source of *Giving USA*'s artificially optimistic estimate of changes in giving is observed in the Foreword of *Giving USA 2003*. Referring to aggregate, current dollar giving, the lead sentence of the Foreword, coauthored by Leo P. Arnoult, CFRE, Chair, AAFRC Trust for Philanthropy, John J. Glier, Chair, AAFRC, and Eugene R. Tempel, Ed.D., CFRE, Executive Director, The Center on Philanthropy at Indiana University, reads, "Giving in 2002 is estimated to be $240.92 billion, growing one percent over the new estimate for 2001 of $238.46 billion" (pp. ii-iii). These leaders of *Giving USA* chose to focus on the growth in aggregate, current dollar giving, even though *Giving USA* elsewhere reported that total giving as a percentage of gross domestic product fell from 2.4% in 2001 to 2.3% in 2002 (pp. 23, 200), and individual giving as a percentage of disposable (after-tax) personal income fell from 2.47% in 2001 to 2.35% in 2002 (pp. 24, 201). This calculates to a –4% and a –5% decrease in giving as a percent of income from the 2000 base for total giving and individual giving, respectively. For further discussion, see the "Recommendations, Giving Estimates by *Giving USA*" section earlier in this chapter.
Report Available for Timely Review	D	A release titled "News" for the *Giving USA 2003* Annual Report was dated June 23, 2003. The *Giving USA 2003* press release was distributed in such a timely fashion that media as varied as The Associated Press, Business Wire, *Chicago Tribune*, The Direct Marketing Association, *The New York Times*, Newhouse News Service, and *San Jose Mercury News* (California) published stories on *Giving USA 2003* dated June 23, 2003.

		The fact that a preordered copy of *Giving USA 2003* was not shipped until July 18, 2003, would, in and of itself, have led to a lowered grade in 2003 of B from 2002's A. The lack of timely availability of the final print version of the *Giving USA 2003* Annual Report to interested scholars throughout the nation precludes considered evaluation of the Annual Report's findings in the national media. Media announcements of findings from serious academic papers and journals are standardly not released until the papers are available for peer review and comment.
		However, the evaluation for this category was further downgraded to a D due to a delay, referenced in the *Giving USA 2003* Annual Report "Methodology" section, in the availability of the specific methodology and formulae for estimating giving by "Individuals." For further discussion of this point, see the "Recommendations, Giving Estimates by *Giving USA*" section earlier in this chapter.
Distance from For-Profit Counsel	D	*Giving USA* is an industry publication. It may be a desirable professional fundraising tool. It is also generally quoted as an objective estimate of giving for use by the general public, even though the quality of the estimates do not qualify it for that purpose. The desire for latest year data has led to an emphasis on, and the development of, a series of models to produce estimates for the latest year. In the past, the result has frequently been both an annual estimate that is generally revised downward in subsequent years, and a lack of a comprehensive overview of philanthropy measurement. However, the revision for 1997-2000 data showed that the original estimates were lower than the revised estimates.
		In reference to the above discussion of the timing and role of the activities of *Giving USA 2003*'s Editorial Review Board in relation to the work of the Advisory Committee on Methodology, it would be interesting to understand precisely what the function is of an Editorial Review Board comprised of those fundraisers affiliated with AAFRC and AAFRC Trust for Philanthropy, in light of the fact that the AAFRC Trust for Philanthropy contracted with the Center on Philanthropy at Indiana University to research and write the *Giving USA* series. Such an arrangement raises a number of questions. Do academics at the Center on Philanthropy at Indiana University have full editorial control of their research and the dissemination of their findings? Does the AAFRC Trust for Philanthropy consider the Center on Philanthropy at Indiana University to be fully competent to research and write the *Giving USA* series? If the *Giving USA* series is purported to be the product of academia, what is the reason that a "News" release that focuses on aggregate dollar giving is released by the AAFRC Trust for Philanthropy? Would not a serious academic institution want to preserve its integrity by interpreting, writing, and distributing its news releases about its research findings—even if an industry group funds the research?

Consistency over Time	D	For an undisclosed period of time in the 1980s, Religion was a "residual category." More recently, Religion for the years 1987 through the most recent year has been adjusted, but earlier years, when Religion was the residual category, have not yet been.
		The emphasis on developing a latest year projection has led to the use of a changing mixture of variables with no published systematic basis for the revisions made on a frequent basis.
		The Chronicle of Philanthropy noted, "When the final IRS data are released, 'Giving USA' annually updates its estimates from the prior year's reports. Those updates can drastically change its findings..."
		" 'These are soft numbers at best,' says Peter Dobkin Hall, a lecturer on nonprofit organizations at Harvard University's John F. Kennedy School of Government. 'They're probably jumping the gun by releasing them in such a high-profile way before the final numbers are in.' "[60]
		While not sufficiently overcoming the above serious flaws to increase the 2002 evaluation a grade level, *Giving USA* is to be commended for reporting data from 1962 forward. This step, in keeping with a more scholarly approach, reverses the pattern, implemented in the 1993 edition of *Giving USA*, of including only the most recent 30 years of data. It may be hoped that, for the sake of increasing *Giving USA*'s scholarly credentials and usefulness, the series will be anchored to at least as far back as 1962 in coming editions of *Giving USA*.
Treatment of Religion	D	While *Giving USA* revised its Education and Health series, keying them to the Filer Commission estimates, it has not systematically treated the Religion series in a similarly thoughtful manner.
		Also, *Giving USA* does not take into account the fact that many groups included in other recipient categories are faith-based in governance. Therefore, the picture of giving to Religion is at the same time distorted and incomplete.
Comparable Data	D	*Giving USA* considers philanthropy by Source categories (e.g., corporations), and separately, by Recipient categories (e.g., education). Only rarely in the past has *Giving USA* provided a breakdown within Recipient categories by Source. It would be useful to know the sources of giving to each Recipient category.
		Further, September 11, 2001 giving to Human Services appears to be analyzed differently in *Giving USA 2002* as compared to in *Giving USA 2003*. Both *Giving USA 2002* (p. 171) and *Giving USA 2003* (p. 196) reported that, from 2000 to 2001, current dollar contributions to Human Services increased from $17.99 billion to $20.71 billion, an increase of $2.72 billion. However, *Giving USA 2002* (p. 124) highlights in the "Giving to Human

---

[60] Harvy Lipman, "Giving in 2002 Didn't Outpace Inflation, Report Says," *Chronicle of Philanthropy*, June 26, 2003, p. 18.

		Services" chapter, "The estimate of giving for human service organizations in 2001 includes an estimated $1.16 billion in contributions for relief and recovery after September 11, 2001." Curiously, *Giving USA 2003* "Giving to human services" chapter highlights (p. 133) omit any mention of temporary increased giving in response to September 11 as a possible contributing factor in the decline of giving to Human Services between 2001 and 2002. Rather, the emphasis in the GUSA 2003 analysis of the decrease in giving to Human Services from 2001 is associated primarily with "general economic weakness," as noted in the following quote. "Human services organizations reported increased need for food and shelter aid in 2002. Growing need occurred simultaneously with decreased philanthropic support and reduced government funding as state tax revenues fell because of the general economic weakness" (p. 133). This difference between the explanations for giving to Human Services from one edition to the next raises the question as to what portion of this analysis is scientific in nature and how much is related to public policy commentary.
Review of Major Questionable Findings	D	*Giving USA* has revised some of its historical series but has not reviewed others. The "residual category" years for Religion is one example. Another important example of questionable data that has not been adequately addressed is a 27% increase in Human Services from 1997 to 1998. In contrast to the GUSA series, data for the largest Human Services organizations in *The Chronicle of Philanthropy* 400 list indicated that these groups grew only 7% from 1997 to 1998. A request to review the data producing the *GUSA* estimate was denied by the editor of the 1997 and 1998 editions of *Giving USA* on the basis of confidentiality. Subsequent editions of *Giving USA* have not reported on a revisit of original *Giving USA* source data, or revised the 1998 giving to Human Services estimate in light of either *The Chronicle of Philanthropy* 400 list finding, or the finding of Paul Arnsberger, "an economist with the IRS" who, as reported in Table 4 of *Giving USA 2003* (p. 138), found that, using IRS data, charitable revenue to Human Service organizations increased 11.6% from 1997 to 1998. A "Charitable revenue" note in Table 4 presenting the Arnsberger data read, "Charitable revenue includes gift and foundation grants (which is comparable to what *Giving USA* tracks) as well as government grants and allocations from other nonprofit agencies such as United Way and United Jewish Communities (which are not included in *Giving USA* estimates for this subsector)."
Availability of Data	D	Each issue of *Giving USA* provides discussion and also a series of data tables based on the information in their study. However, as noted in the previous category comments, a request to the previous editor for the data that served as the basis for the 1997-1998 Human Services giving estimates was refused based on a stated need of AAFRC to keep the data confidential.
Validity of Data	D	*Giving USA* has not published an adequate validation comparison study between its estimates and other available information.

Independent Sector *Giving and Volunteering in the United States, Balancing the Scales*, and *The New Nonprofit Almanac and Desk Reference.*		
Overall Grade: D+		
Evaluation Category	Grade	Evaluation Comments
Annual Measurement	D	Independent Sector's *Giving and Volunteering in the United States* (*GAVITUS*) was published biannually from 1988 to 1996. A 1999 edition and a 2001 edition were published in 2002.
Adjustments for Population and Income	A	Independent Sector adjusts for population by using the number of households in the United States. It also adjusts for income.
Report Available for Timely Review	F	Independent Sector distributed a press release about *Giving and Volunteering in the United States, 1999 edition* in 1999. Media reports appeared that fall. The *Statistical Abstract of United States: 2000, The National Data Book*, listed a reference source indicating that the document, *Giving and Volunteering in the United States, 1999 edition*, was published in 2000 (p. 397). Yet, repeated contacts with Independent Sector resulted in varying publication due dates. The 1999 edition was finally available in May 2002.
		The Independent Sector Web site announced major findings in a November 4, 2001 release of its new "comprehensive study," measuring giving in 2000, the "comprehensive report" for which would "be available in the spring of 2002."[61] September 2002 correspondence indicated an October 2002 availability date. The report was finally available in October 2002, according to an Independent Sector "Newsroom" release dated October 18, 2002, that was headlined, "Independent Sector Releases Comprehensive Report on Giving and Volunteering in the United States," and stated, "*The Giving and Volunteering in the United States* 2001 survey is the seventh in a series of biennial national surveys by Independent Sector."
		There was also a delay between the announcement and the release of Independent Sector's publication, *Balancing the Scales: Measuring the Contributions of Nonprofit Organizations and Religious Congregations*. In another Independent Sector publication, *America's Religious Congregations: Measuring their Contribution to Society*, published in November 2000, six of the charts and tables each have a "Source" referring to the full report, *Balancing the Scales: Measuring the Contributions of Nonprofit Organizations and Religious Congregations*. The reference in the "Resources Section" list reads, "published by Independent Sector, Washington, DC, 2001." However, correspondence from February 2001 through May 2002 indicated *Balancing the Scales* had not yet been published. An Independent Sector "Newsroom" release dated October 8, 2002, was headlined, "Independent Sector Report Demonstrates Efforts of Nonprofits to Measure Effectiveness." The first sentence of the release stated, "...Independent Sector releases a comprehensive report on the state of nonprofits'

---

[61]"Independent Sector Survey Measures the Everyday Generosity of Americans;" Embargoed until November 4, 2001; <http://www.independentsector.org/media/GV01PR.html>; printed 11/25/01 2:30 PM.

		efforts to measure their organizational effectiveness." The first sentence of the second paragraph identified the report as, *"Balancing the Scales: Measuring the Roles and Contributions of Nonprofit Organizations and Religious Congregations..."* Although the title of this *"Balancing the Scales"* document includes the additional words, "Roles and," the October 8, 2002, "Newsroom" release identified this document as part of Independent Sector's Measures Project, and stated that, "Previous publications issued under the Measures Project Initiative include *America's Religious Congregations* and *Outcome Measurement in Nonprofit Organizations: Current Practices and Recommendations.*"
Distance from For-Profit Counsel	A	Independent Sector's "2000 Annual Report" described Independent Sector's membership as including "700 of the nation's leading foundations, prominent and far-reaching nonprofits of all sizes, and corporations with strong commitments to community involvement." The organization seems to have sufficient independence and distance from the influence and agenda of those who have a vested interest in the outcome of any measurement of philanthropy.
Consistency over Time	F	Independent Sector's *Giving and Volunteering in the United States* series has generally maintained a comparable series of data in its published editions—1988, 1990, 1992, 1994 and 1996. However, the *Giving and Volunteering in the United States 1999* edition available in 2002, for the first time in the series, did not include the category of "Religion," with its subcategories including Catholics, All Protestants, Baptists, Lutherans, Methodists, Presbyterians, Jewish, All Other Religions, in its table of "Demographic Characteristics of Volunteers and Contributing Households." Given the increasingly visible role of religion in America, this inconsistency, along with that noted in the following comment, led to the downgrade to F in 2002 from the 2001 rating of B. Independent Sector, referring to the then-forthcoming *Giving and Volunteering in the United States 2001* edition, reported that, due to a "change in methodology," it will be "difficult to compare these new findings to our earlier studies."[62] *Giving and Volunteering in the United State 2001*, in a 2002 Appendix A "Methodological Statement," stated, "The above changes, taken in total, mean comparisons to prior *Giving and Volunteering* studies cannot easily be made" (p. 141). The editors of the series have not adequately justified why they have dissociated from a decade of surveys, or made no effort through statistical or sampling methods to develop a consistent comparison.

---

[62]The press release for the new Independent Sector survey, *Giving and Volunteering in the United States 2001*, presenting figures for reporting households that are 51% higher than two years earlier, includes a change in methodology that will make "it difficult to compare these new findings to our earlier studies," [a series beginning in 1988] according to Dr. Sara E. Melendez, President and CEO of Independent Sector. "Independent Sector Survey Measures the Everyday Generosity of Americans;" <http://www.independentsector.org/media/GV01PR.html>; embargoed until November 4, 2001; printed 11/25/01 2:30 PM.

Treatment of Religion	F	The *Giving and Volunteering in the United States* (*GAVITUS*) survey instrument has, for the most part, provided for the measurement of several significant issues regarding religion, such as the relationship between membership/worship attendance and charitable giving and volunteering. However, in terms of actual giving estimates, the *GAVITUS* survey could be improved.
		For example, the 1990, 1992, 1994 and 1996 *GAVITUS* "Type of Organization" Attachment used by the interviewers provided the option for a breakdown between "Nonprofit, Religious" and "Nonprofit, Nonsectarian" in the types of organizations. However, the report does not provide a table that breaks down Use categories, such as International or Human Services, into these two categories. A detailed analysis of the potential distortion of not including such a distinction in such areas as International and Human Services was provided in *The State of Church Giving through 1991* (*SCG91*). Also in *SCG91*, the recommendation was made to include the option of distinguishing between gifts to "church, synagogue or mosque" and other religious organizations. This distinction would provide the basis for external validation of the survey instrument by enabling the comparison of survey responses with available church giving data.
		In contrast, the *GAVITUS 1999* failure to include Religion in its table of "Demographic Characteristics of Volunteers and Contributing Households" led to a 2002 grade of F in comparison to the 2001 rating of D.
		In 2002, Independent Sector published *Faith and Philanthropy: The Connection Between Charitable Behavior and Giving to Religion* that was "based on analysis from Independent Sector's *Giving and Volunteering in the United States* 2001 national survey" (p.4). Neither *Faith and Philanthropy* nor *GAVITUS 2001* provide a breakdown by various major denominations or denominational families as has been the case in the 1990, 1992, 1994 and 1996 *GAVITUS* series. Reported gifts to denominations provide one of the better opportunities for validation studies of giving survey data because (1) of the relatively large size of some denominational memberships, and (2) denominations annually compile and publish their congregations' giving reports.
Comparable Data	F	While Independent Sector uses household contributions as a standard, AAFRC's *Giving USA* uses aggregate. When the Independent Sector data is multiplied by the number of households in the United States to obtain an aggregate number to compare with *Giving USA*, the difference between the two estimates was $56 billion for 1998 data.
		That the Independent Sector household data represented the United States was stated in its own press releases. Further, its methodology, while acknowledging that the sample did not target the wealthy, states, "Weighting procedures were used to ensure that the final sample was representative of the adult population in the United States in terms of age, race/ethnicity, education, marital status, size of household, region of country

and household income."[63] One may assume, therefore, that multiplying its average household contribution by the number of households in the United States would yield an aggregate estimate for contributions in the United States. This calculation yielded an estimate of $78.3 billion, compared to a *Giving USA* estimate of $134.1 billion in 1998.[64]

An unexplained development in Independent Sector's process was a 2001 comment on the Independent Sector Web site. While the Key Findings section reproduced the Key Findings section of the *GAVITUS* 1999 edition, another sentence was added that stated, "from 1995 to 1998, after inflation, the average household contribution decreased by 1.2%.*" The note to the asterisk stated, "At present both Independent Sector and AAFRC's *Giving USA* 1999 estimate $135 billion in total individual giving for 1997."[65] No basis for Independent Sector's estimate was provided.

The *GAVITUS 2001* edition seems, on the face of it, to make two mutually exclusive assertions, namely that (1) weighting procedures were used to ensure that the sample is representative, and (2) the weighted sample is not representative due to an undersampling of those with incomes over $200,000.

On the one hand, *GAVITUS 2001* stated, "This survey included an oversampling of Hispanics, blacks, and affluent Americans with household incomes of $100,000 or higher in order to increase the sample sizes of these groups for statistical analysis purposes...Household income and respondent age were the only variables for which values were imputed because it was necessary for weighting. Weighting procedures were used to ensure that the final sample of respondents was representative of all noninstitutionalized adults 21 years of age or older."[66]

On the other hand, *GAVITUS 2001* stated, "Readers are cautioned because of survey limitations not to use the giving data to estimate total contributions, i.e., multiplying average household contributions by the number of households. If they do so, they will obtain total amounts that are considerably below amounts derived based largely on Internal Revenue Service data. One crucial reason is that high-income households, those with incomes of $200,000 or more, are few in number and not generally available to be interviewed. Such households give a disproportionate share of total contributions relative to their presence among households."[67] It is interesting to observe that no similar caveat is given about all the giving-related tables and charts in *GAVITUS 2001*, due to the presumed, potential distortion occurring in giving-related findings as a function of the disproportionate effect of donors with incomes of $200,000 or more.

---

[63]Susan K.E. Saxon-Harrold et al., "Methodology and How to Interpret Survey Data," *Giving and Volunteering in the United States: Executive Summary*, (Washington, DC: Independent Sector, 1999), p. 16.

[64]For a detailed comparison of the two estimates, see John Ronsvalle and Sylvia Ronsvalle, *The State of Church Giving through 1998* (Champaign, IL: empty tomb, inc., 2000), pp. 61-68.

[65]"Household Giving in America;" "Giving and Volunteering in the United States: Findings from a National Survey;" published 1999; <http://www.independentsector.org/GandV/s_keyf.htm>; p. 2 of 1/26/01 9:41 AM printout.

[66] Christopher M. Toppe, Arthur D. Kirsch, and Jocabel Michel, *Giving and Volunteering in the United States 2001: Findings from a National Survey* (Washington, DC: Independent Sector, 2002), p. 140.

[67] Christopher M. Toppe, Arthur D. Kirsch, and Jocabel Michel, *Giving and Volunteering in the United States 2001: Findings from a National Survey* (Washington, DC: Independent Sector, 2002), p. 15.

Review of Major Questionable Findings	D	External validation tests of Independent Sector data suggest a great volatility in the level of contributions from one survey to another, compared to the relatively stable trends of other data.[68] These findings have not been adequately acknowledged or addressed in subsequent surveys. To date, the revised 2001 edition survey series does not provide enough of a base to determine if this volatility has been eliminated.
Availability of Data	C	Independent Sector has the *GAVITUS* data set available for purchase. While Independent Sector was rated A in 2001 for the availability of its data to researchers for independent analysis, its rating was downgraded to C in 2002 as a function of inadequate specificity in its documentation and/or publication of source data for some of the tables and technical notes in *The New Nonprofit Almanac and Desk Reference* (Jossey-Bass, 2002) which Independent Sector co-published with the Urban Institute in 2002. This weakness is observed in relation to the critically important area of giving by individuals. *The New Nonprofit Almanac* Table 3.3 and Sources notes on page 59, Table 3.6 on page 64, with the accompanying technical note on pages 218-219, neither list methodological or formulaic detail, nor provide or reference documentation and rationale for *The New Nonprofit Almanac's* shift from the AAFRC's *Giving USA* individual giving series for the 1986-1998 period, while following the *Giving USA* series from 1964-1985. Both *The New Nonprofit Almanac* and the AFFRC *Giving USA*[69] series adjust for non-itemizer giving. *The New Nonprofit Almanac* Table 3.2, "Distribution of Private Contributions by Recipient Area: AAFRC Trust for Philanthropy Estimates, 1968-1998," compares eight "Recipient" areas. A Note states, "Giving to some categories prior to 1985 cannot be compared to giving since 1985 because of different statistical tabulation and analysis procedures."[70] This lack of specificity renders major portions of the Table unintelligible. The last column of the same Table 3.2 is labeled "Unclassified" and is referenced to "AAFRC Trust for Philanthropy, 1999." Yet, AAFRC's *Giving USA 1999* has the Recipient category of "Unallocated" for 1968-1998 along with the Recipient category of "Gifts to Foundations" for the years 1978-1998.
Validity of Data	F	As noted above, external validation tests, comparing Independent Sector *GAVITUS* data with other sources indicated a volatility in the Independent Sector data that was not present in the other sources. Steps to reduce this variation were not taken as of the 1999 edition, and the 2001 edition indicated that the revised data is not comparable.

---

[68]Ronsvalle, *The State of Church Giving through 1998*, pp. 68-73.

[69] Ann Kaplan, ed., *Giving USA 1999* (New York: AAFRC Trust for Philanthropy, 1999), pp. 148-149.

[70] Murray S. Weitzman, Nadine T. Jalandoni, Independent Sector, and Linda M. Lampkin, Thomas H. Pollak, Urban Institute, *The New Nonprofit Almanac and Desk Reference* (New York: John Wiley & Sons/Jossey-Bass, 2002), p. 57.

The Chronicle of Philanthropy Philanthropy 400		
Overall Grade: C-		
Evaluation Category	Grade	Evaluation Comments
Annual Measurement	A	This report is issued annually.
Adjustments for Population and Income	F	The Philanthropy 400 does not address issues related to the adjustment of philanthropic giving in U.S. population and income. In an expansion of its giving analysis, *The Chronicle of Philanthropy* also published a study, "The State of Generosity" in 2003. The introduction of the highly subjective "discretionary income" category did nothing to improve this grade. For a discussion of this additional study, see the "Recommendations, Media Holding Academia Accountable for the Measurement of Philanthropy" section earlier in this chapter.
Report Available for Timely Review	A	The report is published in full in *The Chronicle of Philanthropy*.
Distance from For-Profit Counsel	F	*The Chronicle of Philanthropy* is supported directly by advertising from for-profit fundraising groups.
Consistency over Time	D	The report is published annually using the same categories. However, the report is fundamentally flawed in that it presents a changing list of organizations from one year to the next as a basis for determining any change in giving patterns.
Treatment of Religion	F	The Philanthropy 400 does not treat religion in a reasonable and comprehensive way. For example, Americans' philanthropic contributions to houses of worship, which are compiled annually by religious denominations and published annually in the New York-based National Council of the Churches of Christ in the U.S.A.'s *Yearbook of American & Canadian Churches*, are excluded. Among other societal contributions, houses of worship have long served as primary educators of philanthropic values in American culture. A special cover story report, entitled, "The State of Generosity," in the May 1, 2003 issue of *The Chronicle of Philanthropy* was, after The Philanthropy 400, one of the more ambitious analyses of giving that *The Chronicle of Philanthropy* has undertaken. On the one hand, "The State of Generosity" provided a valuable service in publicizing the fact that the U.S. Bureau of Labor Statistics began to ask in the 2nd quarter of 2001 questions about "charitable giving to…religious organizations…secular charities, and …educational institutions" (p. 13). "The State of Generosity" is illuminating in that it finds that Religious giving as a percent of income constitutes over 75% of individual giving. Other demographic and geographic findings are instructive. On the other hand, the treatment of religion in "The State of Generosity" continues the systemic bias against religious denominations—in particular, large, historically Christian denominations—found in The Philanthropy 400. The fairly extensive report on Americans' giving patterns, extending over pages six through twenty-five, states, "More than $3 of every $4 donated to charity is given to houses of worship or other religious causes, the *Chronicle* study found" (p. 7). Coverage is given to "Baptists," the Salvation Army, and one mention is made of "Catholic Charities of Brooklyn and Queens." Nevertheless, a computer "text search" of the articles, with "Match Case" unchecked, for each of the terms, "lutheran,

		elca, episcopal, presbyterian, adventist, southern baptist, and methodist" found no entries. Such a search indicated that none of the seven denominations—that the National Council of the Churches of Christ in the U.S.A.'s *Yearbook of American & Canadian Churches 2003* reported each had total contributions of over $1 billion for the years 2000 or 2001—were institutionally identified at either the congregational or denominational level in the report of the study. The seven denominations with total contributions of over $1 billion listed in the *Yearbook of American & Canadian Churches 2003* were the Episcopal Church, Evangelical Lutheran Church in America, The Lutheran Church Missouri Synod (LCMS), Presbyterian Church (USA), Seventh-day Adventist, Southern Baptist Convention, and The United Methodist Church. While *The Chronicle of Philanthropy* has covered various religious stories including an annual "Contributions to U.S. Protestant Churches" series that summarizes denominational information from the *Yearbook of American & Canadian Churches*, the Philanthropy 400 excludes this data set in a systematic way. The consequence is an inaccurate, distorted view of the practice of philanthropy in the United States.
Comparable Data	C	The Philanthropy 400 uses publicly available reports. However, it does not present data that facilitates comparisons either internally (using faith-based/secular categories) or externally (using standardized recipient or source categories).
Review of Major Questionable Findings	D	Although concerns about not using a consistent set of organizations for year-to-year comparisons have been published,[71] the Philanthropy 400 has not adequately addressed the issue.
Availability of Data	B	The Philanthropy 400 data is published and available for independent analysis. *The Chronicle of Philanthropy* expanded its giving analysis in 2003 with the publication of "The State of Generosity," affecting its grade in this category. The rating was downgraded in 2003 to B from the A grade in 2002 as a function of a lack of fully defined methodology or terms in that analysis.
Validity of Data	F	The Philanthropy 400 does not take comprehensive steps to maximize the likelihood of the valid, integrated measurement of philanthropy. Further, the Philanthropy 400 sits in the larger context of a lack of an integrated critical analysis by *The Chronicle of Philanthropy* of the overall measurement of giving among the various available estimates. The introduction of discretionary income in "The State of Generosity" analysis by the *Chronicle of Philanthropy* impacted this grade. In addition, "The State of Generosity" studied giving, for tax year 1997, from "taxpayers earning $50,000 or more annually who itemize deductions on their federal tax returns," and giving, for the last three quarters of 2001 and the first quarter of 2002, based on U.S. Bureau of

---

[71] John Ronsvalle and Sylvia Ronsvalle, *The State of Church Giving through 1997* (Champaign, IL: empty tomb, inc., 1999), pp. 62-63, and Ronsvalle, *The State of Church Giving through 1998*, pp. 73-74.

		Labor Statistics (BLS) survey data. *The Chronicle of Philanthropy* reported BLS giving data for the income categories of "$50,000-$69,999" and "70,000 or more," and provided an "Average Annual Charitable Giving by Blacks and Whites," graphic, which included the category, "People with incomes of $50,000 or more." However, even though different years' data was used by the IRS and BLS, and although the U.S. Bureau of Labor Statistics survey data reports "Cash contributions," *The Chronicle of Philanthropy* provided no total giving numbers, or comparative analysis of the overall giving level, found in the IRS and BLS data for those with incomes of $50,000 or more. This lack of exploratory and preliminary comparison of the two sets of individual giving data utilized supported the 2003 grade of F compared to the 2002 grade of D.

The NonProfit Times NPT 100		
Overall Grade: C-		
Evaluation Category	Grade	Evaluation Comments
Annual Measurement	A	The report is published annually in *The NonProfit Times*.
Adjustments for Population and Income	F	*The NonProfit Times* (NPT)100 does not address issues related to the adjustment of philanthropic giving for changes in U.S. population and income.
Report Available for Timely Review	A	The report is published in full in *The NonProfit Times*.
Distance from For-Profit Counsel	F	*The NonProfit Times* is supported directly by advertising from for-profit fundraising groups.
Consistency over Time	D	The report is published annually using the same categories. However, the report is fundamentally flawed in that it presents a changing list of organizations from one year to the next as a basis for determining any change in giving patterns.
Treatment of Religion	F	The NPT 100 does not treat religion in a reasonable and comprehensive way. For example, religious denominations are excluded.
Comparable Data	C	The NPT 100 uses publicly available reports. However, it does not present data that facilitates comparisons either internally (using faith-based/secular categories) or externally (using standardized recipient or source categories).
Review of Major Questionable Findings	D	Although concerns about not using a consistent set of organizations for year-to-year comparisons have been published,[72] The NPT 100 has not adequately addressed the issue.
Availability of Data	A	The NPT 100 data is published and available for independent analysis.
Validity of Data	F	The NPT 100 does not take comprehensive steps to maximize the likelihood of the valid, integrated measurement of philanthropy. Further, the NPT 100 sits in the larger context of a lack of an integrated critical analysis by *The NonProfit Times* of the overall measurement of giving among the various available estimates.

---

[72]Ronsvalle, *The State of Church Giving through 1997*, pp. 62-63, and Ronsvalle, *The State of Church Giving through 1998*, pp. 73-74.

The Statistical Abstract of the United States		
Overall Grade: C+		
Evaluation Category	Grade	Evaluation Comments
Annual Measurement	A	*The Statistical Abstract of the United States* annually presents tables containing data for the measurement of philanthropy.
Adjustments for Population and Income	D	Philanthropic data is not presented in a way that adjusts for changes in total U.S. population and income.
Report Available for Timely Review	A	The tables in the *Statistical Abstract* present complete data with references.
Distance from For-Profit Counsel	A	The *Statistical Abstract* has sufficient independence and distance from the influence and agenda of those who have a vested interest in the outcome of any measurement of philanthropy.
Consistency over Time	A	The *Statistical Abstract* approaches its work with a reasonable degree of consistency over the years.
Treatment of Religion	D	The *Statistical Abstract* does not treat religion in a reasonable and comprehensive fashion, primarily due to weaknesses in its source materials.
Comparable Data	F	The *Statistical Abstract* does not adequately present philanthropic data in a way that facilitates comparisons between the data sources it presents. *GAVITUS* data for households reporting charitable contributions is used, rather than all households; the reported data cannot be aggregated by using the number of households in the U.S. available elsewhere in the *Statistical Abstract*.
Review of Major Questionable Findings	D	The *Statistical Abstract* presents philanthropic data that is questionable primarily due to weaknesses in its source materials.
Availability of Data	A	The *Statistical Abstract* tables reproduces data from other sources that is then available for independent analysis.
Validity of Data	F	The *Statistical Abstract* does not take comprehensive steps to maximize the likelihood of valid, integrated measurement of philanthropy.

Additional Entities Involved in the Measurement of Philanthropy

Advisory Committees to the *Giving USA* and *Giving and Volunteering in the United States*[73]
Overall Grade: D+

Evaluation Category	Grade	Evaluation Comments
Annual Measurement	B	The advisory committees are related to the annual *Giving USA* publication and the occasional *Giving and Volunteering in the United States* (*GAVITUS*) publications.
Adjustments for Population and Income	C	*Giving USA* emphasizes aggregate data while *GAVITUS* does adjust for population and income.
Report Available for Timely Review	D	As of 2003, neither advisory committee had successfully influenced the respective publications to release the report in a coordinated fashion with the publication of press announcements. Independent Sector's *Giving and Volunteering in the United States 2001* report was available as of October 18, 2002, although press information was released on November 4, 2001. The *Giving USA 2003* Annual Report was not shipped until July 18, 2003, after the June 23, 2003 date the AAFRC Trust for Philanthropy release was published by press. Thus, the grade for this category declined to D in 2003 from 2002's C.
Distance from For-Profit Counsel	C	The *Giving USA* committee does not have distance from for-profit counsel. The *GAVITUS* committee does have distance from for-profit counsel.
Consistency over Time	D	While the advisory committee has not assisted *Giving USA* to produce consistent data over the years, the *GAVITUS* committee's failure to provide *GAVITUS 1999* consistency in Religion led to a 2002 grade of D in comparison to the 2001 rating of C.

---

[73]The *Giving USA* 1987-2003 advisory committees included, for one or more years, representatives of: the American Association of Fundraising Counsel (AAFRC) Trust for Philanthropy, Arnoult & Associates Inc., The Aspen Institute, Association for Healthcare Philanthropy, Boston College Social Welfare Research Institute, The Brookings Institution, Center for Responsive Governance, City University of New York, Committee to Encourage Corporate Philanthropy, The Conference Board, Council for Advancement and Support of Education, Council for Aid to Education, Council on Foundations, ePhilanthropy Foundation, The Ford Foundation, The Foundation Center, Georgetown University Center for the Study of Voluntary Organizations and Service, Independent Sector, Indiana University, Indiana University Center on Philanthropy, Indiana University/ Purdue University-Indianapolis, Johns Hopkins University, Marts & Lundy, Inc., National Bureau of Economic Research, National Council of the Churches of Christ in the U.S.A., The Nonprofit Sector Research Fund, Princeton Survey Research Associates, Raybin Associates, Inc., Ruotolo Associates, Inc., U.S. Treasury Department, United Way of America/International, University of Michigan Institute for Social Research, The Urban Institute, Yale University.

The Independent Sector *Giving and Volunteering in the United States* advisory committees for one or more years of the 1990-2001 editions or the Executive Summary for 1999 had representatives from: the American Association of Fund-Raising Counsel (AAFRC) Trust for Philanthropy, The Aspen Institute, Boston College, Canadian Centre for Philanthropy, College of St. Catherine, Council for Aid to Education, Council on Foundations, The Ford Foundation, The Gallup Organization, George Washington University, Georgetown University, Independent Sector, J. A. Couch Consultants, Johns Hopkins University, London School of Economics, The Minneapolis Foundation, the National Alliance of Business, The National Volunteer Center, *The NonProfit Times*, Northwestern University, Princeton University, Rockefeller Brothers Fund, United Way of America, University of Maryland, College Park, University of Massachusetts at Amherst, University of Minnesota, The Urban Institute, Volunteers of America, Weber Reports, and Westat, Inc.

Treatment of Religion	F	Neither advisory committee has successfully pressed to solve the long-standing problems in estimating giving to religion.
		The *GAVITUS 1999* failure to include Religion in its table of "Demographic Characteristics of Volunteers and Contributing Households" led to a 2002 grade of F in comparison to the 2001 rating of D.
Comparable Data	F	Neither advisory committee has successfully pressed to solve the long-standing problems in providing comparable data between the estimates.
Review of Major Questionable Findings	D	Neither advisory committee has successfully pressed to address major questions about the findings of the respective publications.
Availability of Data	B	The *Giving USA* committee has not insured that data is available for review. The *GAVITUS* committee has carried out its work in such a way that the data is available for independent analysis.
Validity of Data	F	Neither committee has successfully pressed to implement comprehensive steps that would help to maximize the likelihood of valid, integrated measurement of philanthropy.

Foundation Efforts in the Area of Measurement of Philanthropy[74]		
Overall Grade: C-		
Evaluation Category	Grade	Evaluation Comments
Annual Measurement	C	Foundations are involved in funding reports through other entities. However, foundations have not systematically addressed issues related to the annual measurement of philanthropy.
Adjustments for Population and Income	C	Foundations have not worked to insure that all major measures of philanthropy adjust for population and income.

---

[74]Foundations that have funded the *Giving and Volunteering the United States* series (edition year in parentheses) include The Atlantic Philanthropies (1999, 2001), The Chevron Companies (1994), The Ford Foundation (1990, 1992, 1994, 1996, 1999 Executive Summary, 1999, 2001), GE Foundation (1994), William Randolph Hearst Foundation (1990), IBM Corporation (1990), Robert Wood Johnson Foundation (2001), W.K. Kellogg Foundation (1992, 1994, 1996, 1999 Executive Summary, 1999, 2001), Knight Foundation (1990), Lilly Endowment Inc. (1990, 1992, 1999 Executive Summary, 1999, 2001), Robert McCormick Charitable Trust (1990), Metropolitan Life Foundation (1996, 1999 Executive Summary, 1999, 2001, Faith and Philanthropy 2002, Charles Stewart Mott Foundation (1992, 1994, 1996, 1999 Executive Summary, 1999, 2001), Rockefeller Brothers Fund (1992), Dr. Scholl Foundation (1992).

The Ford Foundation and Lilly Endowment Inc. funded the Independent Sector Measures Survey, published as *America's Religious Congregations: Measuring Their Contribution to Society* (Washington, DC: Independent Sector, November 2000), funded by the Lilly Endowment Inc., and *Balancing the Scales* (2002), which indicated the "Measures Project was funded by The Atlantic Philanthropies, The Ford Foundation, the W. K. Kellogg Foundation, The Lilly Endowment, and other donors… (p. 2).

Foundations that have funded the *Nonprofit Almanac* most recent series (publication year in parentheses) include The Atlantic Philanthropies (2002), The Chevron Companies (1996), The Ford Foundation (1996, 2001 In Brief, 2002), Robert Wood Johnson Foundation (2002), Ewing Marion Kauffman Foundation (2002), W.K. Kellogg Foundation (1996, 2002), Lilly Endowment (2001 In Brief, 2002), Andrew W. Mellon Foundation (1996), Charles Stewart Mott Foundation (1996, 2002), "Anonymous donors" (1996), "corporate, foundation, and nonprofit members of Independent Sector" (2002).

The Lilly Endowment, Charles Stewart Mott Foundation, Rockefeller Brothers Fund, and William Randolph Hearst Foundation funded the Russy D. Sumariwalla, Wilson C. Levis, *Unified Financial Reporting System for Not-for-Profit Organizations: A Comprehensive Guide to Unifying GAAP, IRS Form 990, and Other Financial Reports Using a Unified Chart of Accounts* (San Francisco: Jossey-Bass, 2000).

In addition, representatives of the Council on Foundations and The Foundation Center have been Advisory Council members of AAFRC's *Giving USA* series.

Report Available for Timely Review	F	Major reports that receive foundation funding are not available for researchers at the same time press releases are issued.
		The *Giving USA 2003* Annual Report was not shipped until July 18, 2003, after the June 23, 2003 date the AAFRC Trust for Philanthropy release was published by press.
		Independent Sector's *Giving and Volunteering in the United States 2001* report was available as of October 18, 2002, although press information was released on November 4, 2001.
		Independent Sector's *Balancing the Scales: Measuring the Contributions of Nonprofit Organizations and Religious* Congregations, is quoted in an Independent Sector November 2000 publication, and is elsewhere referenced by Independent Sector as having been published in 2001. Independent Sector announced that Independent Sector released a publication, with a slightly different title, *Balancing the Scales: Measuring the Roles and Contributions of Nonprofit Organizations and Religious Congregations*, on October 8, 2002.
		Thus, the grade for this category declined to F in 2003 from 2002's D.
Distance from For-Profit Counsel	A	Foundations appear to have sufficient independence and distance from the influence and agenda of those who have a vested interest in the results of any measurement of philanthropy.
Consistency over Time	D	While some aspects of reports funded by foundations provide a level of consistent categories over time, foundations on the whole do not approach this area with attention to consistency.
		GAVITUS 1999's omission of the Religion category and subcategories led to a 2002 grade of D in comparison to the 2001 rating of C.
Treatment of Religion	F	Foundations have not worked to insure that the annual measurement of religion is conducted in a reasonable and comprehensive fashion.
		Giving USA has not developed a reasonable series review, including the period when religion was a residual category.
		GAVITUS 1999's omission of the Religion category and subcategories led to a 2002 grade of F in comparison to the 2001 rating of D.
		GAVITUS 2001 did not contain provide a breakdown by various major denominations or denominational families as has been the case in the 1990, 1992, 1994 and 1996 *GAVITUS* series. Reported gifts to denominations provide one of the better opportunities for validation studies of giving survey data because (1) of the relatively large size of some denominational memberships, and (2) denominations annually compile and publish their congregations' giving reports.
Comparable Data	C	The funding of research produces data. However, foundations have not funded the presentation of data in ways that sufficiently facilitate comparisons, either between sources or within the same source.
Review of Major Questionable Findings	D	Foundations have not funded efforts that have adequately reviewed and addressed major questionable findings in national philanthropy estimates.
Availability of Data	A	Foundations generally emphasize the need for dissemination and making data available.

Validity of Data	F	Foundations have not taken comprehensive steps to maximize the likelihood of valid, integrated measurement of philanthropy. There are not adequate mechanisms in place to follow up on the coordinated implementation of, and comprehension of, the various streams of research that have been funded.

U.S. Government Internal Revenue Service Form 990

Overall Grade: C-

Evaluation Category	Grade	Evaluation Comments
Annual Measurement	A	Form 990 annually addresses issues related to the measurement of philanthropy.
Adjustments for Population and Income	F	The IRS Form 990 does not request a breakout of giving by living donors such that a measurement could be more precisely adjusted for population and income.
Report Available for Timely Review	—	
Distance from For-Profit Counsel	A	The IRS Form 990 has sufficient independence and distance from the influence and agenda of those who have a vested interest in the outcome of any measurement of philanthropy.
Consistency over Time	A	Form 990 provides a reasonable degree of consistency over time.
Treatment of Religion	F	Form 990 does not ask whether an organization is constituted as, governed as, or defines itself as "faith-based" or "secular." As a result, para-denominational activity cannot be adequately evaluated. The result is an overly secularized view of nonprofit activity.
Comparable Data	F	Form 990 data collection is critically flawed in terms of providing comparable data, in that it does not request information about donations from living individuals, nor does it allow an organization to identify its governance as "faith-based" or "secular."
Review of Major Questionable Findings	D	Form 990 has not addressed the need for the implementation of a classification system that includes a clear determination of faith-based or secular organizations, or donations by living individuals.
Availability of Data	D	The IRS has not computerized Form 990 in a way that summary data is readily available to donors, researchers and the media for independent analysis. Such computerization has been discussed beginning with the Filer Commission papers published in 1977.[75]
Validity of Data	F	The IRS has not taken comprehensive steps to maximize the likelihood of valid, integrated measurement of philanthropy. The full commitment of the federal government, including the Internal Revenue Service and the Office of Management and Budget, as well as the American Institute of Certified Public Accountants, would need to be marshaled to revise Form 990 to yield a sound measure of individual giving by living donors.

---

[75]Burton A. Weisbrod and Stephen H. Long, "The Size of the Voluntary Nonprofit Sector: Concepts and Measures," *History, Trends, and Current Magnitudes*, Vol. 1 in the series, *Research Papers Sponsored by The Commission on Private Philanthropy and Public Needs*, (Washington, DC: Department of the Treasury, 1977), p. 360, n. 17.

U.S. Government Efforts to Secure and Disseminate Philanthropy Information Overall Grade: C-		
Evaluation Category	Grade	Evaluation Comments
Annual Measurement	C	The U.S. Government is involved in the annual Form 990 collection, and in the *Statistical Abstract* tables on philanthropy. However, the U.S. Government does not systematically address issues related to the annual measurement of philanthropy.
Adjustments for Population and Income	F	The U.S. Government does not adequately address issues of the measurement of philanthropy adjusted for population and income.
Report Available for Timely Review	A	Through the *Statistical Abstract*, the U.S. Government annually disseminates philanthropy data.
Distance from For-Profit Counsel	A	The U.S. Government has sufficient independence and distance from the influence and agenda of those who have a vested interest in the outcome of any measures of philanthropy.
Consiste..cy over Time	A	The U.S. Government approaches the area with a reasonable degree of consistency over the years.
Treatment of Religion	D	The U.S. Government has not encouraged the treatment of religion in a reasonable and comprehensive fashion. In the second quarter of 2001, the U.S. Bureau of Labor Statistics began collecting Consumer Expenditure Survey data on "Cash contributions to charities and other organizations; Cash contributions to church, religious organizations; and Cash contributions to educational institutions." Thus the 2002 evaluation of F was upgraded to D in 2003. The grade is not higher than a D because of the lack of action on other more far-reaching recommendations, such as improving Form 990.
Comparable Data	F	The U.S. Government has not facilitated or encouraged the development of comparable data.
Review of Major Questionable Findings	D	While the U.S. Government revises its publications, it has not addressed major questionable findings, such as the lack of data for contributions from living individuals, or the distinction between faith-based and secular organizations.
Availability of Data	C	The U.S. Government provides information to researchers but could improve.
Validity of Data	F	The U.S. Government has not taken comprehensive steps to maximize the likelihood of valid, integrated measurement of philanthropy. This fact is particularly true in the category of donations from living individuals.

National Bureau of Economic Research Overall Grade: F		
Evaluation Category	Grade	Evaluation Comments
Annual Measurement	F	The National Bureau of Economic Research does not address issues related to the annual measurement of philanthropy in a regular way through one of its standing programs.
Adjustments for Population and Income	—	
Report Available for Timely Review	—	

Distance from For-Profit Counsel	—	
Consistency over Time	—	
Treatment of Religion	—	
Comparable Data	—	
Review of Major Questionable Findings	—	
Availability of Data	—	
Validity of Data	—	

Urban Institute Efforts, Both in Cooperation with the U.S. Government and Independently

Overall Grade: D+

Evaluation Category	Grade	Evaluation Comment
Annual Measurement	D	In 2001, even though the Urban Institute did not publish an estimate of philanthropy, the Urban Institute received an A for this category because of its infrastructure work that could reasonably result in improved annual measures of philanthropy. That is, through its work with the U.S. Government and Form 990, as well as the Center's work with the Unified Chart of Accounts and its National Center for Charitable Statistics, the Urban Institute addresses issues related to the annual measurement of philanthropy. In 2002, the rating for this category was downgraded to a D because Urban Institute explicitly involved itself with the occasional publication of specific measures of philanthropy by virtue of co-publishing *The New Nonprofit Almanac and Desk Reference* (Jossey-Bass, 2002) with Independent Sector.
Adjustments for Population and Income	D	Rated in 2002 for the first time based on the co-publication of *The New Nonprofit Almanac and Desk Reference* (Jossey-Bass, 2002) with Independent Sector, Urban Institute's D rating reflects two countervailing realities as illustrated by the following examples. Individual giving data adjusts for changes in population and income in *The New Nonprofit Almanac* Table 3.4. However, the accompanying Figure 3.4 graphs per capita individual income only in the overly positive categories of constant 1997 dollars and current dollars, excluding individual giving as a percentage of personal income presented in Table 3.4. Chapter 3, "Trends in Private Giving" introductory remarks do not adjust for changes in population and income. Chapter 4 considers subsector performance, again without adjusting for population or income in graphics addressing change over time. A further contribution to the D grade comes from the March 12, 2002 press release for *The New Nonprofit Almanac*. The release states, "In addition to the growth in the number of organizations, the total annual revenue of the independent sector increased from $317 billion in 1987 to an estimated $665 billion in 1997."[76] Adjustment for population and income is neither included nor, as a result, emphasized in the press release.

---

[76] Independent Sector; "New Nonprofit Almanac Gives Detailed Information on Size and Scope of Sector: Joint Independent Sector and Urban Institute Resource Provides New Insights Into How Nonprofits Work;" published March 12, 2002; <http://www.independentsector.org/media/NA01PR.html>; p. 1 of 9/26/02 5:09 PM printout.

Report Available for Timely Review	D	Rated in 2002 for the first time based on the co-publication of *The New Nonprofit Almanac and Desk Reference*[77] with Independent Sector, Urban Institute's D rating stems from Independent Sector's release of *The New Nonprofit Almanac In Brief—2001*[78] on July 18, 2001[79] and Independent Sector and Urban Institute releasing *The New Nonprofit Almanac and Desk Reference* on March 12, 2002.[80]
Distance from For-Profit Counsel	A	The Urban Institute seems to have sufficient independence and distance from the influence and agenda of those who have a vested interest in the outcome of any measurement of philanthropy.
Consistency over Time	D	Rated in 2002 for the first time based on the co-publication of *The New Nonprofit Almanac and Desk* Reference[81] with Independent Sector, Urban Institute's D rating is based on the shift from an emerging focus on a Form 990-based measure of individual giving to the lending of its organization's reputation to the promulgation and furtherance of a number of well-entrenched shortcomings in the measurement of philanthropy.
Treatment of Religion	F	The Urban Institute does not treat religion in a reasonable and comprehensive fashion, primarily due to weaknesses in the classification system for which it carries major responsibility.
Comparable Data	D	Rated in 2002 for the first time based on the co-publication of *The New Nonprofit Almanac and Desk Reference* (Jossey-Bass, 2002) with Independent Sector, Urban Institute's D rating reflects the fact that considerably more intentional and higher quality work is necessary to address the need for a critical approach to the limitations in comparability between data from Independent Sector, the American Association of Fund-Raising Counsel's (AAFRC) *Giving USA*, and U.S. IRS Form 990—employing standardized National Taxonomy of Exempt Entities major group categories.

---

[77] Murray S. Weitzman, Nadine T. Jalandoni, Independent Sector, and Linda M. Lampkin, Thomas H. Pollak, Urban Institute, *The New Nonprofit Almanac and Desk Reference* (New York: John Wiley & Sons/Jossey-Bass, 2002).

[78] *The Nonprofit Almanac in Brief—2001: Facts and figures from the forthcoming New Nonprofit Almanac and Desk Reference* and *Giving and Volunteering in the United States*, 1999, (Washington, DC: Independent Sector, 2001).

[79] Independent Sector; "Number of Charities Grows 74% in Just Over Decade: New Independent Sector Report Counts 1.6 Million Nonprofit Organizations, Including 734,000 Charities;" published July 18, 2001; <http://www.independentsector.org/media/InBriefPR.html>; p. 1 of 8/14/01 10:37 AM printout.

[80] Independent Sector; "New Nonprofit Almanac Gives Detailed Information on Size and Scope of Sector: Joint Independent Sector and Urban Institute Resource Provides New Insights Into How Nonprofits Work;" published March 12, 2002; <http://www.independentsector.org/media/NA01PR.html>; p. 1 of 9/26/02 5:09 PM printout.

[81] Murray S. Weitzman, Nadine T. Jalandoni, Independent Sector, and Linda M. Lampkin, Thomas H. Pollak, Urban Institute, *The New Nonprofit Almanac and Desk Reference* (New York: John Wiley & Sons/Jossey-Bass, 2002).

Review of Major Questionable Findings	D	Rated in 2002 for the first time based on the co-publication of *The New Nonprofit Almanac and Desk Reference* (Jossey-Bass, 2002) with Independent Sector, Urban Institute's D rating reflects the fact that the Urban Institute has not reviewed the questionable American Association of Fund-Raising Counsel's *Giving USA* finding that there was a 27% increase in Human Services from 1997 to 1998.
Availability of Data	C	While the Urban Institute was rated A in 2001 for publishing the data it has so that it is available to researchers for independent analysis, its rating was downgraded to C in 2002 as a function of inadequate specificity in its documentation and/or publication of source data for some of the tables and technical notes in *The New Nonprofit Almanac and Desk Reference* (Jossey-Bass, 2002) which the Urban Institute co-published with Independent Sector in 2002. This weakness is observed in relation to the critically important area of giving by individuals. *The New Nonprofit Almanac* Table 3.3 and Sources notes on page 59, Table 3.6 on page 64, with the accompanying technical note on pages 218-219, neither list methodological or formulaic detail, nor provide or reference documentation and rationale for *The New Nonprofit Almanac's* shift from the AAFRC's *Giving USA* individual giving series for the 1986-1998 period, while following the *Giving USA* series from 1964-1985. Both *The New Nonprofit Almanac* and the AFFRC *Giving USA*[82] series adjust for non-itemizer giving.
		The New Nonprofit Almanac Table 3.2, "Distribution of Private Contributions by Recipient Area: AAFRC Trust for Philanthropy Estimates, 1968-1998," compares eight "Recipient" areas. A Note states, "Giving to some categories prior to 1985 cannot be compared to giving since 1985 because of different statistical tabulation and analysis procedures."[83] This lack of specificity renders major portions of the Table unintelligible.
		The last column of the same Table 3.2 is labeled "Unclassified" and is referenced to "AAFRC Trust for Philanthropy, 1999." Yet, AAFRC's *Giving USA 1999* has the Recipient category of "Unallocated" for 1968-1998 along with the Recipient category of "Gifts to Foundations" for the years 1978-1998.
Validity of Data	D	A fundamental flaw in the Urban Institute's Unified Chart of Accounts (UCOA) is that it does not provide a measure of individual giving distinct from business giving. Urban Institute has also not acknowledged and provided for the distinction between faith-based and secular governance categories within recipient categories to provide for an accurate measure of religion. Urban Institute would need to make a policy decision to seek cooperation between the U.S. Government and the American Institute of Public Accountants to revise both Form 990 and the UCOA to make the necessary changes to produce a sound measurement of philanthropy by source and recipient categories.

---

[82] Ann Kaplan, ed., *Giving USA 1999* (New York: AAFRC Trust for Philanthropy, 1999), pp. 148-149.

[83] Murray S. Weitzman, Nadine T. Jalandoni, Independent Sector, and Linda M. Lampkin, Thomas H. Pollak, Urban Institute, *The New Nonprofit Almanac and Desk Reference* (New York: John Wiley & Sons/Jossey-Bass, 2002), p. 57.

Universities with Philanthropy Centers[84]		
Overall Grade: D		
Evaluation Category	Grade	Evaluation Comments
Annual Measurement	D	Universities do not systematically address issues related to the annual measurement of philanthropic giving. This is seen in part by the fact that published material suggests that academics enlisted to assist with the American Association of Fundraising Counsel's *Giving USA* annual reports have focused unduly on the for-profit fundraising industry's agenda of providing most recent year estimates through *Giving USA*, rather than the type of comprehensive, in-depth, scholarly analysis of philanthropy engaged in by academics enlisted by the Commission on Private Philanthropy and Public Needs in the mid-1970s.

However, two developments led to an improvement from an F to a D for this category in 2003. The Center on Philanthropy at Indiana University has contracted with the University of Michigan to add philanthropy questions to an ongoing study. Also, Georgetown University has added philanthropy questions to an ongoing study. These changes might suggest a growing awareness of the need for academic involvement in the measurement of philanthropy. |
Adjustments for Population and Income	—	
Report Available for Timely Review	—	
Distance from For-Profit Counsel	—	
Consistency over Time	—	
Treatment of Religion	—	
Comparable Data	—	
Review of Major Questionable Findings	—	
Availability of Data	—	
Validity of Data	—	

---

[84] At "Research: Academic Centers Focusing on the Study of Philanthropy;" Independent Sector; published 2000; <http://www.indepsec.org/programs/research/centers>; pp. 1-3 of 8/23/01 4:35 PM printout, 35 "Academic Centers Focusing on the Study of Philanthropy" were listed. These included: Boston College, Case Western University, [City] University of New York, Duke University, George Mason University, Harvard University, Indiana University/Purdue University, Loyola University, New York University, Northwestern University, Seton Hall University, Southern Methodist University, Texas Christian University, Tufts University, University of California-Berkeley, University of California-San Francisco, University of Maryland, University of Missouri-Kansas City, University of Pennsylvania, Virginia Polytechnic Institute and State University, and Yale University.

chapter 8

Reversing the Decline in Benevolences Giving: A Country-by-Country Needs Analysis

HIGHLIGHTS

A country-by-country analysis of global needs, with a reference point of stopping, in Jesus' name, global child deaths, is a key element of an effort to reverse negative Benevolences giving trends. This strategy addresses several factors that contribute to the decline in Benevolences giving as a portion of income that is detailed in earlier chapters of this volume.

NARRATIVE

A country-by-country analysis of global needs, with a reference point of stopping, in Jesus' name, global child deaths, is a key element of an effort to reverse negative Benevolences giving trends.

Such a strategy would address several factors that are contributing to the negative trend in giving to Benevolences as a percent of income that is detailed in earlier chapters of this volume. These factors include the need among congregation members to know "what their money is buying" when it leaves the congregation. Further, by providing a tool that leaders could use, this strategy would help to fill the current vacuum of church leadership that exists in the area of integrating faith and money. The strategy also complements several aspects of the "positive agenda for affluence" affirmed by national church leaders, and works in tandem with previously suggested strategies to improve giving to Benevolences.

Before reviewing the positive aspects of this strategy, it would be well to consider a few working assumptions that lay the foundation for this approach.

Underlying Assumptions. **Funding for missions should increase.** The most basic assumption supporting the suggestion for a country-by-country global needs analysis is that funding for missions should increase. While it may seem a foregone conclusion, the apparent lack of effective action among church leadership in the U.S. at the congregational, regional and national levels leaves the matter open to question. Therefore, a few observations about the role of mission in the church may be useful.

Missions has been seen as an integral reason for the existence of the church from the beginning. "The Great Commission," given by Jesus Christ in Matthew 28:19-20, was reaffirmed with Jesus' words at the ascension scene recorded in Acts 1. In the first instance, Jesus told the disciples to "make disciples of all nations" both baptizing them and "teaching them to obey everything" Jesus commanded (NIV). In Acts 1:8, Jesus promises power to the disciples so that they can be witnesses "in Jerusalem, and in all Judea and Samaria, and to the ends of the earth" (NIV).

This global reality continued through the centuries to the degree that Arthur Judson Brown wondered in 1902, "Does any sane man imagine that the Church could cease to be missionary and remain the Church?"[1]

Leaders throughout the two thousand years that the church has existed have affirmed missions—including good works in Jesus' name—as consistent with the theological conviction of salvation being a work of grace. A review of the writings of two of the best-known proponents of salvation by faith alone—*sola fide*—finds a strong affirmation for good works growing from faith. Both Martin Luther and John Calvin wrote about the natural fruit of a life saved by grace being good works that both glorify God and also demonstrate the effect of grace in one's life.[2]

The World Alliance of Reformed Churches took the position in 1997 that economic justice as well as ecological destruction are issues "at the very center of Christian faith." The Alliance decided that these issues were more than "moral and ethical questions" and "elevated" the issues to " 'the level of the faith' and the 'confession' of the church…a situation described as a processus confessionis (a Latin term referring to a 'committed process of progressive recognition, education and confession')."[3] From the Reformed point of view, not pursuing the good of the neighbor, which can be another definition of mission, becomes a denial of the demands of faith.

Increased Benevolences giving could make a positive impact. A second working assumption is that increased giving could make a difference. Chapter 6 in this volume explores the potential of church member giving at a congregation-wide average of ten percent (some members giving lower and some members giving higher than that level). Available

---

[1] R. Park Johnson, "Arthur Judson Brown, 1856-1963, Believing in the Power of the Sovereign Lord," in Gerald H. Anderson, et al., eds., *Mission Legacies* (Maryknoll, NY: Orbis Books, 1994), p. 556.

[2] John Ronsvalle and Sylvia Ronsvalle, "The Theological Implications of Church Member Giving Patterns," *The State of Church Giving through 1995* (empty tomb, inc., 1997), <http://www.emptytomb.org/implications.html>.

[3] Stephen Brown, "Reformed Group says 'Struggle for Economic Justice at Center of Faith,' " *The National Christian reporter*, August 29, 1997, 1, quoted in Ronsvalle, "The Theological Implications of Church Member Giving Patterns."

numbers indicate that church members could increase giving and make a major impact on global word and deed need.

Articles that appeared in the "Child Survival" series in the European medical journal, *The Lancet*, are a recent source of additional information about the difference that can be made. The authors in the series were affiliated with the Division of Policy and Planning, United Nation's Children's Fund (UNICEF); Division of International Health, Johns Hopkins Bloomberg School of Public Health; and the Public Health Nutrition Unit of the London School of Hygiene and Tropical Medicine, among others. The second paper in the series explored the topic, "How Many Child Deaths Can We Prevent This Year?" The study considered both specific strategies and the delivery systems available in low-income countries. The authors concluded, "Our findings show that about two-thirds of child deaths could be prevented by interventions that are available today and are feasible for implementation in low-income countries at high levels of population coverage." The authors found that "some of the most promising interventions may be delivered at the household level, with limited need for external material inputs."[4] The conclusion, therefore, is that the lives of as many as six million of the 10.8 million children who are dying this year could be preserved, if the public chose to do so.

The church is given the responsibility to do "mission" whether or not it is convenient or seemingly possible. However, these child survival studies suggest that word and deed mission through the established international network of denomination mission structures would not be a hopeless task, but rather could have a tremendous effect.

A consensus exists. The third assumption that lays the groundwork for increasing Benevolences giving is that there is a consensus among a broad spectrum of church leaders in the U.S. that it should happen. A survey of 202 leaders in historically Christian denominations based in the U.S. resulted in responses from 41% of those successfully contacted. Of those responding, 81% responded "Yes" to the assertion that church members in the United States should increase giving through their churches in an effort to stop, in Jesus' name, the millions of annual preventable global child deaths. The positive respondents represented African American, Anabaptist, Baptist, Evangelical, Fundamental, Mainline Protestant, Orthodox, Pentecostal, Roman Catholic and other Catholic communions.[5]

An earlier grouping of national church leaders concluded that "The church needs a positive agenda for the great affluence in our society."[6] Based on the broad support expressed in the more recent survey, it appears that the issue of preventing, in Jesus' name, global child deaths could serve as that agenda.

This broad consensus supports the active exploration of strategies to assist church leaders in moving from conviction to action regarding the need to increase giving for missions.

---

[4] Gareth Jones, et al.; "How Many Child Deaths Can We Prevent This Year?"; *The Lancet*; <http://www.thelancet.com/journal/vol362/iss9377/full/llan.362.9377.child_survival.26292.1>; p. 6 of 7/7/03 2:06 PM printout.

[5] John Ronsvalle and Sylvia Ronsvalle, "National Church Leaders Response Form," *The State of Church Giving through 1999* (empty tomb, inc., 2001), <http://www.emptytomb.org/ResponseForm.html>.

[6] John Ronsvalle and Sylvia Ronsvalle, *Behind the Stained Glass Windows: Money Dynamics in the Church* (Grand Rapids, MI: Baker Books, 1996), p. 293.

Country-by-Country Needs Analysis. From a practical point of view, the church in the U.S. is well suited to a country-by-country needs analysis. International denominational relationships link church structures in the U.S. with structures in every country of the globe. In many cases, denominations in the U.S. have frontline representatives, in the form of missionaries sent to serve in other countries. These missionaries are often dispersed throughout a nation's boundaries, serving in rural as well as urban areas. Church leaders of other countries also have working relationships with church leaders in the U.S. Thus, church leaders in the U.S. have a ready-made communications system on a country-by-country basis.

The value of looking at need by country was affirmed in the first of *The Lancet* "Child Survival" articles. In the summary findings, the authors state, "The causes of death differ substantially from one country to another, highlighting the need to expand understanding of child health epidemiology at a country level rather than in geopolitical regions."[7] Thus, an expansive network of frontline representatives from the U.S., and relationships with church leaders of those other countries, may suit the church in the U.S. well for servanthood leadership on this approach.

The church also has a largely untapped network of academic and practicing specialists who could assist with the development of the needs assessment under discussion. One church-related college president that the authors met at a presentation also had experience working in an international government organization and as a public university president. In a discussion of the country-by-country need analysis idea, he pointed out that church-related institutions that address international issues have not linked with people of like mind who are specialists in public institutions. For example, land-grant universities have many talented Christians on their faculties who are also very active in their churches. Many of these people would respond positively to an invitation to get involved in an effort to do a country-by-country needs analysis.

In a separate conversation, an economics professor at another church-related college noted that practical investigation of a strategy like a country-by-country global needs analysis could be conducted by interested members of a professional organization such as the Association of Christian Economists. He pointed out that the association membership encompasses both church-related colleges and land-grant, other public and private universities, as well as government agencies such as the International Trade Commission, the World Bank, and the U.S. Department of Agriculture. The association has regular national conferences and a publication called *Faith and Economics*. Topflight specialists could confer and apply their skills and knowledge to the challenge.

The information produced by a country-by-country global needs analysis would, of necessity, be designed to be accessible to church members in general. A great deal of knowledge about needs in various countries is already available. The problem with this information is that it is often geared to specialists. It is also not organized in a recoverable fashion, for example layered in priority of relevance for a church member who "wants to

---

[7] Robert E. Black, Saul S. Morris, Jennifer Bryce; "Where and Why Are 10 Million Children Dying Every Year?"; *The Lancet*; <http://www.thelancet.com/journal/vol361/iss9376/full/llan.361.9376.child_survival.26233.1>; p. 1 of 7/7/03 2:17 PM printout.

make a difference." It is very possible that the overlap between, for example, what the World Bank or multilateral government structures need and what is needed by laypeople in the pews would be as much as 75-90 percent. However, terminology and format for the layperson would have to be designed to make the information accessible. Further, in addition to the description of material needs, Christian economists would want to also provide church members with a description of the spiritual reality within the countries. An organizing principle of a country-by-country needs analysis could be that the information would be used as a tool to mobilize church members to act on the Great Commandment: to love God, and to love the neighbor as one's self. The itemization of global need, if targeted to be used by concerned congregation members, could work as part of an overall strategy to mobilize church member Benevolences giving as a logical consequence of the integration of faith and money, as discussed in the "mobilization and feedback" section below.

Factors Addressed by a Country-by-Country Needs Analysis. Giving to Benevolences as a percent of income has been declining among church members in the U.S. at least since the late 1960s. Unlike giving to Congregational Finances—the operations of the local congregation—which experienced a recovery in the mid-1990s, the decline in giving to Benevolences has been relatively uninterrupted. Analyses earlier in this volume have demonstrated that the trend is evident among evangelical as well as mainline Protestant church members. In chapter 3, Table 14 demonstrates that mainline Protestant denominations had fewer aggregate inflation-adjusted dollars in 2001 than in 1968. These are the dollars that not only pay for operations of regional and denominational structures, but also for domestic and international mission outreach.

In the same chapter, Table 12 indicates that Benevolences represented a smaller portion of per member donated dollars in 2001 than in 1968 among both evangelicals and mainline Protestants.

Table 1 in chapter 1 indicates that, in 1968, Benevolences represented 21¢ of each donated dollar in the composite denomination data set, and only 15¢ in 2001.

The consequences of the long-term decline in Benevolences giving are evident at the national denominational level. For example, in 2002, both the Lutheran Church-Missouri Synod and The United Methodist Church reduced the number of missionaries they were supporting.[8] Declines in investment income were cited as causes. However, the long-term decline in the amount of money being sent beyond the local congregation was a factor in the denominations' increased dependence on investment income.

It is proposed that a country-by-country global needs analysis, in combination with a broad mobilization strategy, could address the following factors that contribute to the decline in Benevolences giving.

People like to know what their money is buying. In a conversation with an economic historian, the question was posed as to why church members had not spontaneously responded to global need—specifically by stopping, in Jesus' name, preventable global child deaths— out of the increasing affluence they had experienced since 1950. Tremendous amounts of

---

[8] A Religion News Service article appeared as "Economic Doldrums Affecting Churches," *The Christian Century*, February 22, 2003, p. 17.

resources became available, as well as improved communications systems that documented the number of children dying. Yet, why have church members not responded generously to alleviate the tremendous suffering reported both in the news as well as through church publications? The economic historian's response was that what would be helpful to encourage such a response would be a specification of how much money it would take to accomplish needed projects in each country.

This suggestion independently reflected a strong finding about a dynamic that affects congregational operations. In a survey of pastors in 14 denominations across the theological spectrum of the Protestant church in the U.S., 89% affirmed the statement that "Most church members want to know 'what their money is buying' when sent out of the congregation."[9]

This survey finding correlates with an earlier observation in a Roman Catholic doctoral thesis about an adaptation of the tithing system in the early decades of the twentieth century. The author concluded, "The success of these tentative trials would seem to indicate that the people are as generous as they ever were, provided they understand the needs of the Church and feel that they are not being imposed upon."[10]

One strong point of a country-by-country analysis of global needs would be the specific lists that could be provided to church members. Requests to support denominational mission outreach could be accompanied by general line-item budgets that provide church members with the details of how their money will be used in a particular country. For example, the second *Lancet* article mentioned specific strategies to eliminate child deaths. A list of measles vaccine, vitamin A, tetanus toxoid, water sanitation projects, antibiotics and insecticide-treated nets,[11] depending on need in a particular country—accompanied by the denomination's own inventory of the need for Bibles and other print documents as well as personnel required to distribute the items—could provide congregation members with a "shopping list" to fund.

The strength of this point is evident in church member financial response to nationally-televised tragedies. Whether it was Hurricane Andrew's devastation in Florida or the aftermath of the September 11, 2001 terrorist strikes in New York, church members responded generously to denominational requests for financial support of relief efforts. A country-by-country analysis could move the level of congregation member financial support from irregular spontaneous outpouring to a sustained enthusiasm for impacting global need through available church structures.

Denominations need to focus on the larger issues. Denominational structures expanded during the well-funded decade of the 1950s. Many structures took on a "corporate" model.[12]

What began to erode was the level of service that these highly organized and centralized national structures offered to the local congregation. Congregations, treated like franchises,

[9] Ronsvalle, *Behind the Stained Glass Windows: Money Dynamics in the Church*, p. 90.

[10] Michael N. Kremer, *Church Support in the United States* (Washington, DC: The Catholic University of America, 1930), p. 37.

[11] Jones, p. 3.

[12] Craig Dykstra and James Hudnut-Beumler, "The National Organizational Structures of Protestant Denominations: An Invitation to a Conversation," in Milton J Coalter, John M. Mulder, and Louis B. Weeks, eds., *The Organizational Revolution*. (Louisville: Westminster/John Knox Press, 1992), p. 317.

were expected to provide certain levels of support to the larger central organization. Pastors often refer to denominational askings—whether titled "per capita" or "assessments" or "apportionments"—as taxes.

Further, national denominational officials appear to be preoccupied with the subsystems that support institutional maintenance. A vacuum of leadership exists in the overall system of discipleship and transformation of congregation members, accompanied by the atrophying of giving to Benevolences.[13]

A country-by-country analysis of global needs would provide a service-oriented communication tool that denominational leaders could provide to local congregation members. In essence, congregations would once again have a reason to support the large denominational structures that were helping them make sense of an otherwise overwhelming amount of input about the global neighbors for whom congregation members are supposed to be caring

A country-by-country global needs analysis complements mobilization and feedback efforts. In *The State of Church Giving through 2000*, two additional strategies were proposed to reverse the decline in giving to Benevolences.[14]

The first was a blue-ribbon commission of national church leaders in the U.S. This broadly representative commission could be formed to implement a national policy calling on church members to mobilize on behalf of dying children around the globe.

The second blue-ribbon commission could develop software for a generic and dynamic Web-based feedback system for use by denominations within their independent and unique structures. The feedback system would provide church members with the information about what their money was accomplishing when it left the congregation.

The proposed country-by-country global needs analysis would be a vital component of the mobilization effort. It could also give focus to the feedback system, providing denominations a reason to ask congregation members for specific support, combined then with timely, project-specific feedback through a dynamic Web-based system.

The Need for a Strategy to Win the Hearts and Minds of Congregation Members. The proposed country-by-country analysis of global needs could help congregation members understand the needs of their neighbors around the world. Through this understanding, church leadership could help members integrate their faith and money, a stated if generally unimplemented goal in the current practice of historic Christianity.

When church leaders do not provide church members with a positive agenda for their affluence, the church member is left to cope alone. There are strong alternative monetary agendas assaulting the member. Without spiritual guidance, how is the member to choose?

---

[13] John Ronsvalle and Sylvia Ronsvalle, "System and Subsystems: A Case Study," *The State of Church Giving through 1998* (empty tomb, inc., 2000), <http://www.emptytomb.org/SystemsSubsystems.pdf>.
[14] John Ronsvalle and Sylvia Ronsvalle, *The State of Church Giving through 2000* (Champaign, IL: empty tomb, inc., 2002), pp. 91-107.

To illustrate this point, the authors developed Figure 20.

The top box is labeled "Stored Time and Talent." This box represents what money actually is. Money, in a very real sense, is what the Person has invested his or her time and talent in. The money represents how the Person's time has been invested in a job or other income-producing activity. That time and talent is now in a form that can be stored up and exchanged—money.

The bottom box is labeled "Current Time and Talent." The box represents the present time and talent that the Person has available to spend, not only on a job but also at leisure.

It is important to realize that the Person, whose head (mind) and heart are in the middle of the figure, is only one person, encompassing both stored time and talent and current time and talent.

The vertical line in the figure represents church giving. Note that there are two parts to the line. The lighter gray line on the left represents the 2.7% of income that it presently takes to run the church at a maintenance level. The darker gray line is the additional 7.3% of the tithe, which is a standard measure of faithful stewardship. When the full 10% or more of income is not given, the un-given portion can serve as a resistance barrier to breaking through to living for others. Until a compelling vision for stored time and talent is promoted by church leaders in ways that engage, and deeply involve, church members, the full ten percent of giving won't be activated.

What is the church's vision? The words on the left of the chart represent that message: the gray, smaller letters say, "Live for Others." When Jesus was asked what was the greatest commandment, the response was: "Love God . . . and love your neighbor . . . There is no greater commandment than these" (Mark 12:29-31, NIV).

However, "Church Input" largely focuses on the current time and talent quadrant. Pastors have not been taught about the spiritual dynamics of church members' relationship to their stored time and talent (money). So most of the time church leadership avoids the topic and focuses on current time and talent activities: church attendance, volunteering, personal relationships, etc.

That leaves most people overwhelmed by the input of Money's agenda. When it is understood that money is stored time and talent, Jesus' statement in Matthew 6:24 takes on a new dynamic: "You can serve God or money [Mammon]." If money is the stored time and talent of the Person, then the statement can be taken to read, "You can serve God or self."

That's the very message that consumer advertising generally promotes. Ads focus on the Person's stored time and talent, and they have a clear field, since the church has so little to say about that area of the Person's life. However, ads also appeal to and encourage Live for Self with current time and talent, as well. Issues in the Culture Wars that some say are going on in today's society often are rooted in the issue of choice between self and Other.

In terms of figure-ground, the Live for Self message is being dynamically promoted. Live for Self is the figure in the foreground, even for church members. Live for Christ and others is in the dull background. What is necessary is for the church to develop an exciting

Figure 20: **Mind-Heart, Figure-Ground**

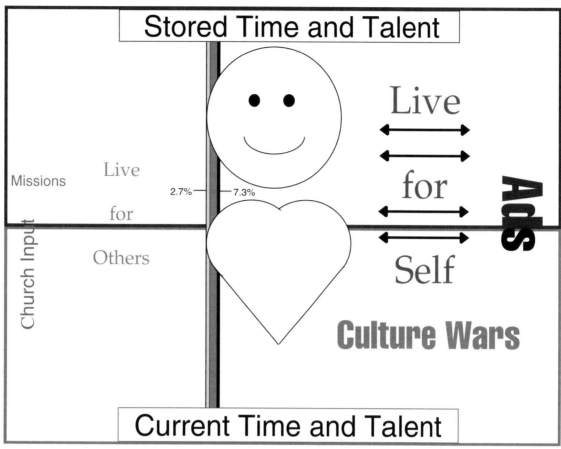

agenda for affluence that becomes the figure, with the Live for Self ads functioning as the ground.

To switch the figure and ground, the church needs to help each person integrate the different forces that are operating on each whole person. What help is there to offer?

In discussing the graphic and these related ideas at a presentation, the authors asked participants to develop strategies to counter these trends. One person talked about a "God-sized Vision" to challenge church members to live for the Other (God) and therefore others—neighbors in need.

A God-sized Vision. In the Great Commission and the Great Commandment, Jesus presented the newly-formed church with a God-sized global vision. In a world where 10.8 million children under five are expected to die this year, many in countries that do not have easy access to the Gospel, the Great Commission and the Great Commandment continue to be relevant.

Practical strategies, such as a commitment to mobilize church members to action, a feedback system, and a country-by-country analysis of global needs, can provide church leadership at all levels of the church with the tools to help church members act on their professed faith. Then giving patterns will take care of themselves.

APPENDIXES

APPENDIX A: *List of Denominations*

Church Member Giving, 1968-2001, Composite Set

American Baptist Churches in the U.S.A.
Associate Reformed Presbyterian Church
  (General Synod)
Brethren in Christ Church
Christian Church (Disciples of Christ)
Church of God (Anderson, Ind.) (through 1997)
Church of God General Conference (Oregon, IL and
  Morrow, GA.)
Church of the Brethren
Church of the Nazarene
Conservative Congregational Christian Conference
Cumberland Presbyterian Church
Evangelical Congregational Church
Evangelical Covenant Church
Evangelical Lutheran Church in America
  The American Lutheran Church (merged 1987)
  Lutheran Church in America (merged 1987)
Evangelical Lutheran Synod
Evangelical Mennonite Church
Fellowship of Evangelical Bible Churches
Free Methodist Church of North America
Friends United Meeting (through 1990)
General Association of General Baptists
Lutheran Church-Missouri Synod
Mennonite Church USA (1999)
  Mennonite Church (merged 1999)
  Mennonite Church, General Conference (merged
  1999)
Moravian Church in America, Northern Province
  (through 2000)
North American Baptist Conference
The Orthodox Presbyterian Church
Presbyterian Church (U.S.A.)
Reformed Church in America
Seventh-day Adventist Church, North American
  Division of
Southern Baptist Convention
United Church of Christ
Wisconsin Evangelical Lutheran Synod

Church Member Giving, 2000–2001

The Composite Set Denominations included in the
  1968-2001 analysis with data available for both
  years, plus the following:
Allegheny Wesleyan Methodist Connection (Original
  Allegheny Conference)

Apostolic Faith Mission Church of God
Bible Fellowship Church
Christian and Missionary Alliance
Church of Christ (Holiness)U.S.A.
Church of the Lutheran Brethren of America
Church of the Lutheran Confession
Churches of God General Conference
The Episcopal Church
Missionary Church
Presbyterian Church in America
Primitive Methodist Church in the U.S.A.
The Romano Byzantine Synod of the Orthodox
  Catholic Church
The United Methodist Church
The Wesleyan Church

By Organizational Affiliation: NAE, 1968-2001

Brethren in Christ Church
Church of the Nazarene
Conservative Congregational Christian Conference
Evangelical Congregational Church
Evangelical Mennonite Church
Fellowship of Evangelical Bible Churches
Free Methodist Church of North America
General Association of General Baptists

By Organizational Affiliation: NCC, 1968-2001

American Baptist Churches in the U.S.A.
Christian Church (Disciples of Christ)
Church of the Brethren
Evangelical Lutheran Church in America
Presbyterian Church (U.S.A.)
Reformed Church in America
United Church of Christ

Eleven Denominations, 1921-2001

American Baptist (Northern)
Christian Church (Disciples of Christ)
Church of the Brethren
The Episcopal Church
Evangelical Lutheran Church in America
  The American Lutheran Church
    American Lutheran Church
    The Evangelical Lutheran Church
    United Evangelical Lutheran Church

Lutheran Free Church
Evangelical Lutheran Churches, Assn. of
Lutheran Church in America
  United Lutheran Church
    General Council Evangelical Lutheran Ch.
    General Synod of Evangelical Lutheran Ch.
    United Synod Evangelical Lutheran South
  American Evangelical Lutheran Church
  Augustana Lutheran Church
  Finnish Lutheran Church (Suomi Synod)
Moravian Church in America, Northern Province
Presbyterian Church (U.S.A.)
  United Presbyterian Church in the U.S.A.
    Presbyterian Church in the U.S.A.
    United Presbyterian Church in North America
  Presbyterian Church in the U.S.
Reformed Church in America
Southern Baptist Convention
United Church of Christ
  Congregational Christian
    Congregational
  Evangelical and Reformed
    Evangelical Synod of North America/German
    Reformed Church in the U.S.
The United Methodist Church
  The Evangelical United Brethren
  The Methodist Church
    Methodist Episcopal Church
    Methodist Episcopal Church South
    Methodist Protestant Church

Trends in Membership, 11 Mainline Protestant Denominations, 1968-2001

American Baptist Churches in the U.S.A.
Christian Church (Disciples of Christ)
Church of the Brethren
The Episcopal Church
Evangelical Lutheran Church in America
Friends United Meeting
Moravian Church in America, Northern Prov.
Presbyterian Church (U.S.A.)
Reformed Church in America
United Church of Christ
The United Methodist Church

Trends in Membership, 15 Evangelical Denominations, 1968-2001

Assemblies of God
Baptist General Conference
Brethren in Christ Church
Christian and Missionary Alliance
Church of God (Cleveland, Tenn.)
Church of the Nazarene
Conservative Congregational Christian Conference
Evangelical Congregational Church
Evangelical Mennonite Church
Fellowship of Evangelical Bible Churches
Free Methodist Church of North America
General Association of General Baptists
Lutheran Church-Missouri Synod
Salvation Army
Southern Baptist Convention

Trends in Membership, 37 Denominations, 1968-2001

11 Mainline Protestant Denominations (above)
15 Evangelical Denominations (above)
11 Additional Composite Denominations:
Associate Reformed Presbyterian Church (General Synod)
Church of God (Anderson, Ind.)
Church of God General Conference (Oregon, Ill and Morrow, Ga..)
Cumberland Presbyterian Church
Evangelical Covenant Church
Evangelical Lutheran Synod
Mennonite Church USA
North American Baptist Conference
The Orthodox Presbyterian Church
Seventh-day Adventist Church, North American Division of
Wisconsin Evangelical Lutheran Synod

APPENDIX B SERIES: *Denominational Data Tables*

Introduction

The data in the following tables is from the *Yearbook of American and Canadian Churches* (*YACC*) series unless otherwise noted. Financial data is presented in current dollars.

Data in italics indicates a change from the previous edition in *The State of Church Giving* (*SCG*) series.

The Appendix B tables are described below.

Appendix B-1, Church Member Giving, 1968-2001: This table presents aggregate data for the denominations which comprise the data set analyzed for the 1968 through 2001 period.

Elements of this data are also used for the analyses in chapters two through seven.

In Appendix B-1, the data for the Presbyterian Church (U.S.A.) combined data for the United Presbyterian Church in the U.S.A. and the Presbyterian Church in the United States for the period 1968 through 1982. These two communions merged to become the Presbyterian Church (U.S.A.) in 1983, data for which is presented for 1983 through 2001.

Also in Appendix B-1, data for the Evangelical Lutheran Church in America (ELCA) appears beginning in 1987. Before that, the two major component communions that merged into the ELCA—the American Lutheran Church and the Lutheran Church in America—are listed as individual denominations from 1968 through 1986.

In the Appendix B series, the denomination listed as the Fellowship of Evangelical Bible Churches was named the Evangelical Mennonite Brethren Church prior to July 1987.

For 1999, the Mennonite Church (Elkhart, IN) provided information for the Mennonite Church USA. This communion is the result of a merger passed at a national convention in July 2001 between the Mennonite Church and the Mennonite Church, General Conference. The latter's 1968-1998 data has been added to the composite set series. The Mennonite Church USA dollar figures for 1999, and membership through 2001, combine data for the two predecessor communions.

The 1999, 2000, and 2001 data for the Southern Baptist Convention used in the 1968-2001 analysis includes data only for those State Conventions that provided a breakdown of total contributions between Congregational Finances and Benevolences for that year. For the Eleven Denominations 1921-2001 analysis, 1999, 2000, and 2001, Southern Baptist Convention Total Contributions is $7,772,452,961, $8,437,177,940, and $8,935,013,659, respectively. For the Eleven Denominations 1921-2001 analysis, and the Membership Trends analysis, 1999, 2000, and 2001, Southern Baptist Convention Membership is 15,581,756, 15,960,308, and 16,052,920, respectively.

Data for the American Baptist Churches in the U.S.A. has been obtained directly from the denominational office as follows. In discussions with the American Baptist Churches Office of Planning Resources, it became apparent that there had been no distinction made between the membership of congregations reporting financial data, and total membership for the denomination, when reporting data to the *Yearbook of American and Canadian Churches*. Records were obtained from the denomination for a smaller membership figure that reflected only those congregations reporting financial data. While this revised membership data provided a more useful per member giving figure for Congregational Finances, the total Benevolences figure reported to the *YACC*, while included in the present data set, does reflect contributions to some Benevolences categories from 100% of the American Baptist membership. The membership reported in Appendix B-1 for the American Baptist Churches is the membership for congregations reporting financial data, rather than the total membership figure provided in editions of the *YACC*. However, in the sections that consider membership as a percentage of population, the Total Membership figure for the American Baptist Churches is used.

Appendix B-2, Church Member Giving for 41 Denominations, 2000-2001: Appendix B-2 presents the Full or Confirmed Membership, Congregational Finances and Benevolences data for the fifteen additional denominations included in the 2000-2001 comparison.

Appendix B-3, Church Member Giving for Eleven Denominations, 1921-2001: This appendix presents additional data which is not included in Appendix B-1 for the Eleven Denominations.

The data from 1921 through 1928 in Appendix B-3.1 is taken from summary information contained in the *Yearbook of American Churches, 1949 Edition*, George F. Ketcham, ed. (Lebanon, PA: Sowers Printing Company, 1949, p. 162). The summary membership data provided is for Inclusive Membership. Therefore, giving as a percentage of income for the years 1921 through 1928 may have been somewhat higher had Full or Confirmed Membership been used. The list of denominations that are summarized for this period is presented in the *Yearbook of American Churches, 1953 Edition*, Benson Y. Landis, ed. (New York: National Council of the Churches of Christ in the U.S.A., 1953, p. 274).

The data from 1929 through 1952 is taken from summary information presented in the *Yearbook of American Churches, Edition for 1955*, Benson Y. Landis, ed. (New York: National Council of the Churches of Christ in the U.S.A., 1954, pp. 286-287). A description of the list of denominations included in the 1929 through 1952 data summary on page 275 of the *YACC Edition for 1955* indicated that the Moravian Church, Northern Province is not included in the 1929 through 1952 data.

The data in Appendix B-3.2 for 1953 through 1964 was obtained for the indicated denominations from the relevant edition of the *YACC* series. Giving as a percentage of income was derived for these years by dividing the published Total Contributions figure by the published Per Capita figure to produce a membership figure for each denomination. The Total Contributions figures for the denominations were added to produce an aggregated Total Contributions figure. The calculated membership figures were also added to produce an aggregated membership figure. The aggregated Total Contributions figure was then divided by the aggregated membership figure to yield a per member giving figure which was used in calculating giving as a percentage of income.

Data for the years 1965 through 1967 was not available in a form that could be readily analyzed for the present purposes, and therefore data for these three years was estimated by dividing the change in per capita Total Contributions from 1964 to 1968 by four, the number of years in this interval, and cumulatively adding the result to the base year of 1964 and the succeeding years of 1965 and 1966 to obtain estimates for the years 1965 through 1967.

In most cases, this procedure was also applied to individual denominations to avoid an artificially low total due to missing data. If data was not available for a specific year, the otherwise blank entry was filled in with a calculation based on surrounding years for the denomination. For example, this procedure was used for the American Baptist Churches for the years 1955 and 1996, the Christian Church (Disciples of Christ) for the years 1955 and 1959, and the Evangelical United Brethren, later to merge into The United Methodist Church, for the years 1957, 1958 and 1959. Data for the Methodist Church was changed for 1957 in a similar manner.

Available Total Contributions and Full or Confirmed Members data for The Episcopal Church and The United Methodist Church for 1969 through 2001 is presented in Appendix B-3.3. These two communions are included in the Eleven Denominations. The United Methodist Church was created in 1968 when the Methodist Church and the Evangelical United Brethren Church merged. While the Methodist Church filed summary data for the year 1968, the Evangelical United Brethren Church did not. Data for these denominations was calculated as noted in the appendix. However, since the 1968 data for The Methodist Church would not have been comparable to the 1985 and 2001 data for The United Methodist Church, this communion was not included in the more focused 1968-2001 analysis.

Appendix B-4, Trends in Giving and Membership: This appendix presents denominational membership data used in the membership analyses presented in chapter five that is not available in the other appendices. Unless otherwise indicated, the data is from the *YACC* series.

APPENDIX B-1: *Church Member Giving 1968-2001*

Key to Denominational Abbreviations: Data Years 1968-2001

Abbreviation	Denomination
abc	American Baptist Churches in the U.S.A.
alc	The American Lutheran Church
arp	Associate Reformed Presbyterian Church (General Synod)
bcc	Brethren in Christ Church
ccd	Christian Church (Disciples of Christ)
cga	Church of God (Anderson, IN)
cgg	Church of God General Conference (Oregon, IL and Morrow, GA)
chb	Church of the Brethren
chn	Church of the Nazarene
ccc	Conservative Congregational Christian Church
cpc	Cumberland Presbyterian Church
ecc	Evangelical Congregational Church
ecv	Evangelical Covenant Church
elc	Evangelical Lutheran Church in America
els	Evangelical Lutheran Synod
emc	Evangelical Mennonite Church
feb	Fellowship of Evangelical Bible Churches
fmc	Free Methodist Church of North America
fum	Friends United Meeting
ggb	General Association of General Baptists
lca	Lutheran Church in America
lms	Lutheran Church-Missouri Synod
mch	Mennonite Church
mgc	Mennonite Church, General Conference
mus	Mennonite Church USA
mca	Moravian Church in America, Northern Province
nab	North American Baptist Conference
opc	The Orthodox Presbyterian Church
pch	Presbyterian Church (U.S.A.)
rca	Reformed Church in America
sda	Seventh-day Adventist, North American Division of
sbc	Southern Baptist Convention
ucc	United Church of Christ
wel	Wisconsin Evangelical Lutheran Synod

Appendix B-1: Church Member Giving 1968-2001 (continued)

	Data Year 1968			Data Year 1969			Data Year 1970		
	Full/Confirmed Members	Congregational Finances	Benevolences	Full/Confirmed Members	Congregational Finances	Benevolences	Full/Confirmed Members	Congregational Finances	Benevolences
abc	1,179,848 [a]	95,878,267 [a]	21,674,924 [a]	1,153,785 [a]	104,084,322	21,111,333	1,231,944 [a]	112,668,310	19,655,391
alc	1,767,618	137,260,390	32,862,410	1,771,999	143,917,440	34,394,570	1,775,573	146,268,320	30,750,030
arp	28,312 [a]	2,211,002 [a]	898,430 [a]	28,273	2,436,936 [a]	824,628 [a]	28,427 [a]	2,585,974 [a]	806,071 [a]
bcc	8,954	1,645,256	633,200 [a]	9,145	1,795,859	817,445	9,300 [a]	2,037,330 [a]	771,940 [a]
ccd	994,683	105,803,222	21,703,947	936,931	91,169,842	18,946,815	911,964	98,671,692	17,386,032
cga	146,807	23,310,682	4,168,580	147,752	24,828,448	4,531,678	150,198	26,962,037	4,886,223
cgg	6,600	805,000	103,000	6,700	805,000	104,000	6,800	810,000	107,000
chb	187,957	12,975,829	4,889,727	185,198	13,964,158	4,921,991	182,614	14,327,896	4,891,618
chn	364,789	59,943,750 [a]	14,163,761 [a]	372,943	64,487,669 [a]	15,220,339 [a]	383,284	68,877,922 [a]	16,221,123 [a]
ccc	15,127	1,867,978	753,686	16,219	1,382,195	801,534	17,328	1,736,818	779,696
cpc	87,044 [a]	6,247,447 [a]	901,974 [a]	86,435 [a]	7,724,405 [a]	926,317 [a]	86,683 [a]	7,735,906 [a]	1,011,911 [a]
ecc	29,582 [a]	3,369,308 [a]	627,731 [a]	29,652 [a]	3,521,074 [a]	646,187 [a]	29,437 [a]	3,786,288 [a]	692,428 [a]
ecv	66,021	14,374,162 [a]	3,072,848	67,522	14,952,302 [a]	3,312,306	67,441	15,874,265 [a]	3,578,876
elc	ALC & LCA	ALC & LCA	ALC & LCA	ALC & LCA	ALC & LCA	ALC & LCA	ALC & LCA	ALC & LCA	ALC & LCA
els	10,886 [a]	844,235 [a]	241,949 [a]	11,079	1,003,746	315,325	11,030	969,625	242,831 [a]
emc	2,870 [a]	447,397	232,331	NA	NA	NA	NA	NA	NA
feb	1,712 [a]	156,789 [a]	129,818 [a]	3,324	389,000	328,000	3,698	381,877	706,398
fmc	47,831 [a]	12,032,016 [a]	2,269,677 [a]	47,954 [a]	13,187,506 [a]	2,438,351 [a]	64,901	9,641,202	7,985,264
fum	55,469	3,564,793	1,256,192	55,257	3,509,509	1,289,026	53,970	3,973,802	1,167,183
ggb	65,000	4,303,183 [a]	269,921 [a]	NA	NA	NA	NA	NA	NA
lca	2,279,383	166,337,149	39,981,858	2,193,321	161,958,669	46,902,225	2,187,015	169,795,380	42,118,870
lms	1,877,799	178,042,762	47,415,800	1,900,708	185,827,626	49,402,590	1,922,569	193,352,322	47,810,664
mch	85,682 [a]	7,078,164 [a]	5,576,305 [a]	85,343	7,398,182	6,038,730	83,747 [a]	7,980,917 [a]	6,519,476 [a]
mgc	36,337 [a]	2,859,340 [a]	2,668,138 [a]	35,613	2,860,555 [a]	2,587,079 [a]	35,536	3,091,670	2,550,208
mus	MCH & MGC	MCH & MGC	MCH & MGC	MCH & MGC	MCH & MGC	MCH & MGC	MCH & MGC	MCH & MGC	MCH & MGC
mca	27,772	2,583,354	444,910	27,617	2,642,529	456,182	27,173	2,704,105	463,219
nab	42,371 [a]	5,176,669 [a]	1,383,964 [a]	55,100	6,681,410	2,111,588	55,080	6,586,929	2,368,288
opc	9,197	1,638,437	418,102	9,276	1,761,242	464,660	9,401 [a]	1,853,627 [a]	503,572 [a]
pch	4,180,093	375,248,474	102,622,450	4,118,664	388,268,169	97,897,522	4,041,813	401,785,731	93,927,852
rca	226,819 [b]	25,410,489 [b]	9,197,642 [b]	224,992 [b]	27,139,579 [b]	9,173,312 [b]	223,353 [b]	29,421,849 [b]	9,479,503 [b]
sda	395,159 [a]	36,976,280	95,178,335	407,766	40,378,426	102,730,594	420,419	45,280,059	109,569,241
sbc	11,332,229 [a]	666,924,020 [a]	128,023,731 [a]	11,487,708	709,246,590	133,203,885	11,628,032	753,510,973	138,480,329
ucc	2,032,648 [a]	152,301,536	18,869,136	1,997,898	152,791,512	27,338,543	1,960,608	155,248,767	26,934,289
wel	259,954 [a]	19,000,023 [a]	6,574,308 [a]	265,069	20,786,613	6,417,042	271,117	22,582,545	6,810,612
Total	27,852,553	2,126,617,403	569,208,785	27,739,243	2,200,900,513	595,653,797	27,880,455	2,310,504,138	599,176,138

[a] Data obtained from denominational source.
[b] empty tomb review of RCA directory data.

Appendix B-1: Church Member Giving 1968-2001 (continued)

Appendix B-1.1: Church Member Giving 1968-2001

	Data Year 1971			Data Year 1972			Data Year 1973		
	Full/Confirmed Members	Congregational Finances	Benevolences	Full/Confirmed Members	Congregational Finances	Benevolences	Full/Confirmed Members	Congregational Finances	Benevolences
abc	1,223,735 a	114,673,805	18,878,769	1,176,092 a	118,446,573	18,993,440	1,190,455 a	139,357,611	20,537,388
alc	1,775,774	146,324,460	28,321,740	1,773,414	154,786,570	30,133,850	1,770,119	168,194,730	35,211,440
arp	28,443 a	2,942,577 a	814,703 a	28,711 a	3,329,446 a	847,665 a	28,763 a	3,742,773 a	750,387 a
bcc	9,550	2,357,786	851,725	9,730	2,440,400	978,957	9,877 a	2,894,622 a	1,089,879 a
ccd	884,929	94,091,862	17,770,799	881,467	105,763,511	18,323,685	868,895	112,526,538	19,800,843
cga	152,787	28,343,604	5,062,282	155,920	31,580,751	5,550,487	157,828	34,649,592	6,349,695
cgg	7,200	860,000	120,000	7,400	900,000	120,000	7,440	940,000	120,000
chb	181,183	14,535,274	5,184,768	179,641 c	14,622,319 c	5,337,277 c	179,333	16,474,758	6,868,927
chn	394,197	75,107,918 a	17,859,332 a	404,732	82,891,903 a	20,119,679 a	417,200	91,318,469 a	22,661,140 a
ccc	19,279 a	1,875,010 a	930,485 a	20,081 a	1,950,865 a	994,453 a	20,712 a	2,080,038 a	1,057,869 a
cpc	86,945 a	7,729,131 a	1,009,657 a	88,200 a	8,387,762 a	1,064,831 a	88,203 a	9,611,201 a	1,220,768 a
ecc	29,682 a	4,076,576 a	742,293 a	29,434 a	4,303,406 a	798,968 a	29,331 a	4,913,214 a	943,619 a
ecv	68,428	17,066,051 a	3,841,887	69,815	18,021,767 a	4,169,053	69,922	18,948,864 a	4,259,950
elc	ALC & LCA	ALC & LCA	ALC & LCA	ALC & LCA	ALC & LCA	ALC & LCA	ALC & LCA	ALC & LCA	ALC & LCA
els	11,426 a	1,067,650 a	314,335 a	11,532	1,138,953	295,941 a	12,525	1,296,326	330,052 a
emc	NA	NA	NA	NA	NA	NA	3,131	593,070	408,440
feb	NA	NA	NA	NA	NA	NA	NA	NA	NA
fmc	47,933 a	13,116,414 a	2,960,525 a	48,400 a	14,311,395 a	3,287,000 a	48,763 a	15,768,216 a	3,474,555 a
fum	54,522	3,888,064	1,208,062	54,927	4,515,463	1,297,088	57,690	5,037,848	1,327,439
ggb	NA	NA	NA	NA	NA	NA	NA	NA	NA
lca	2,175,378	179,570,467	43,599,913	2,165,591	188,387,949	45,587,481	2,169,341	200,278,486	34,627,978
lms	1,945,889	203,619,804	48,891,368	1,963,262	216,756,345	50,777,670	1,983,114	230,435,598	54,438,074
mch	88,522	8,171,316	7,035,750	89,505	9,913,176	7,168,664	90,967	9,072,858	6,159,740
mgc	36,314	3,368,100	2,833,491	36,129	3,378,372	3,219,439	36,483	3,635,418	3,392,844
mus	MCH & MGC	MCH & MGC	MCH & MGC	MCH & MGC	MCH & MGC	MCH & MGC	MCH & MGC	MCH & MGC	MCH & MGC
mca	26,101	2,576,172	459,447	25,500	2,909,252	465,316	25,468	3,020,667	512,424
nab	54,997	7,114,457	2,293,692	54,441	7,519,558	2,253,158	41,516	6,030,352	1,712,092
opc	9,536 a	2,054,448 a	533,324 a	9,741 a	2,248,969 a	602,328 a	9,940 a	2,364,079 a	658,534 a
pch	3,963,665	420,865,807	93,164,548	3,855,494	436,042,890	92,691,469	3,730,312 d	480,735,088 d	95,462,247 d
rca	219,915 b	32,217,319 b	9,449,655 b	217,583 b	34,569,874 b	9,508,818 b	212,906 b	39,524,443 b	10,388,619 b
sda	433,906	49,208,043	119,913,879	449,188	54,988,781	132,411,980	464,276	60,643,602	149,994,942
sbc	11,824,676	814,406,626	160,510,775	12,065,333	896,427,208	174,711,648	12,295,400	1,011,467,569	193,511,983
ucc	1,928,674	158,924,956	26,409,521	1,895,016	165,556,364	27,793,561	1,867,810	168,602,602	28,471,058
wel	275,500	24,365,692	7,481,644	278,442	26,649,585	8,232,320	283,130	29,450,094	8,650,699
Total	27,959,086	3,062,967,758	628,448,369	28,044,721	2,612,739,407	667,736,226	28,170,850	2,873,608,726	714,393,625

a Data obtained from denominational source.

b empty tomb review of RCA directory data.

c YACC Church of the Brethren figures reported for 15 months due to fiscal year change: adjusted here to 12/15ths.

d The Presbyterian Church (USA) data for 1973 combines United Presbyterian Church in the U.S.A. data for 1973 (see YACC 1975) and an average of Presbyterian Church in the United States data for 1972 and 1974, since 1973 data was not reported in the YACC series.

125

Appendix B-1: Church Member Giving 1968-2001 (continued)

	Data Year 1974			Data Year 1975			Data Year 1976		
	Full/Confirmed Members	Congregational Finances	Benevolences	Full/Confirmed Members	Congregational Finances	Benevolences	Full/Confirmed Members	Congregational Finances	Benevolences
abc	1,176,989 a	147,022,280	21,847,285	1,180,793 a	153,697,091	23,638,372	1,142,773 a	163,134,092	25,792,357
alc	1,764,186	173,318,574	38,921,546	1,764,810	198,863,519	75,666,809	1,768,758	215,527,544	76,478,278
arp	28,570	3,935,533 a	868,284 a	28,589	4,820,846 a	929,880 a	28,581	5,034,270 a	1,018,913 a
bcc	10,255	3,002,218	1,078,576 a	10,784	3,495,152	955,845	11,375	4,088,492	1,038,484
ccd	854,844	119,434,435	20,818,434	859,885	126,553,931	22,126,459	845,058	135,008,269	23,812,274
cga	161,401	39,189,287	7,343,123	166,259	42,077,029	7,880,559	170,285	47,191,302	8,854,295
cgg	7,455	975,000	105,000	7,485	990,000	105,000	7,620	1,100,000	105,000
chb	179,387	18,609,614	7,281,551	179,336	20,338,351	7,842,819	178,157	22,133,858	8,032,293
chn	430,128	104,774,391	25,534,267 a	441,093	115,400,881	28,186,392 a	448,658	128,294,499	32,278,187 a
ccc	21,661 a	2,452,254 a	1,181,655 a	22,065 a	2,639,472 a	1,750,364 a	21,703 a	3,073,413 a	1,494,355 a
cpc	87,875 a	9,830,198 a	1,336,847 a	86,903 a	11,268,297 a	1,445,793 a	85,541 a	10,735,854 a	1,540,692 a
ecc	29,636 a	4,901,100 a	1,009,726 a	28,886 a	5,503,484 a	1,068,134 a	28,840 a	6,006,621 a	1,139,209 a
ecv	69,960	21,235,204 a	5,131,124	71,808	23,440,265 a	6,353,422	73,458	25,686,916 a	6,898,871
elc	ALC & LCA	ALC & LCA	ALC & LCA	ALC & LCA	ALC & LCA	ALC & LCA	ALC & LCA	ALC & LCA	ALC & LCA
els	13,097	1,519,749	411,732 a	13,489 a	1,739,255	438,875 a	14,504	2,114,998	521,018 a
emc	3,123	644,548	548,000	NA	NA	NA	3,350	800,000	628,944
feb	NA	NA	NA	NA	NA	NA	NA	NA	NA
fmc	49,314 a	17,487,246 a	3,945,535 a	50,632	19,203,781 a	4,389,757 a	51,565	21,130,066 a	4,977,546 a
fum	NA	NA	NA	56,605	6,428,458	1,551,036	51,032	6,749,045	1,691,190
ggb	NA	NA	NA	NA	NA	NA	NA	NA	NA
lca	2,166,615	228,081,405	44,531,126	2,183,131	222,637,156	55,646,303	2,187,995	243,449,466	58,761,005
lms	2,010,456	249,150,470	55,076,955	2,018,530	266,546,758	55,896,061	2,026,336	287,098,403	56,831,860
mch	92,930 a	13,792,266	9,887,051	94,209	15,332,908	11,860,385	96,092 a	17,215,234	12,259,924
mgc	35,534	4,071,002 a	4,179,003 a	35,673 a	3,715,279 a	3,391,943 a	36,397	4,980,967	4,796,037 a
mus	MCH & MGC	MCH & MGC	MCH & MGC	MCH & MGC	MCH & MGC	MCH & MGC	MCH & MGC	MCH & MGC	MCH & MGC
mca	25,583	3,304,388	513,685	25,512	3,567,406	552,512	24,938	4,088,195	573,619
nab	41,437	6,604,693	2,142,148	42,122	7,781,298	2,470,317	42,277	8,902,540	3,302,348
opc	10,186 a	2,627,818 a	703,653 a	10,129 a	2,930,128 a	768,075 a	10,372	3,288,612 a	817,589 a
pch	3,619,768	502,237,350	100,966,089	3,535,825	529,327,006	111,027,318	3,484,985	563,106,353	125,035,379
rca	210,866 b	41,053,364 b	11,470,631 b	212,349 b	44,681,053 b	11,994,379 b	211,628 b	49,083,734 b	13,163,739 b
sda	479,799	67,241,956	166,166,766	495,699	72,060,121	184,689,250	509,792	81,577,130	184,648,454
sbc	12,513,378	1,123,264,849	219,214,770	12,733,124	1,237,594,037	237,452,055	12,917,992	1,382,794,494	262,144,889
ucc	1,841,312	184,292,017	30,243,223	1,818,762	193,524,114	32,125,332	1,801,241	207,486,324	33,862,658
wel	286,858	32,683,492	10,002,869	293,237	35,889,331	11,212,937	297,862	40,017,991	11,300,102
Total	28,222,603	3,126,736,701	792,460,654	28,467,724	3,372,046,407	903,416,383	28,579,165	3,690,898,682	963,799,509

a Data obtained from denominational source.

b empty tomb review of RCA directory data.

Appendix B-1: Church Member Giving 1968-2001 (continued)

	Data Year 1977			Data Year 1978			Data Year 1979		
	Full/Confirmed Members	Congregational Finances	Benevolences	Full/Confirmed Members	Congregational Finances	Benevolences	Full/Confirmed Members	Congregational Finances	Benevolences
abc	1,146,084 [a]	172,710,063	27,765,800	1,008,495 [a]	184,716,172	31,937,862	1,036,054 [a]	195,986,995	34,992,300
alc	1,772,227	231,960,304	54,085,201	1,773,179	256,371,804	57,145,861	1,768,071	284,019,905	63,903,906
arp	28,371 [a]	5,705,295 [a]	1,061,285 [a]	28,644	6,209,447 [a]	1,031,469 [a]	28,513	6,544,759 [a]	1,125,562 [a]
bcc	11,915 [a]	4,633,334 [a]	957,239 [a]	12,430 [a]	4,913,311 [a]	1,089,346 [a]	12,923	5,519,037	1,312,046
ccd	817,288	148,880,340	25,698,856	791,633	166,249,455	25,790,367	773,765	172,270,978	27,335,440
cga	171,947	51,969,150	10,001,062	173,753	57,630,848	11,214,530	175,113	65,974,517	12,434,621
cgg	7,595	1,130,000	110,000	7,550	1,135,000	110,000	7,620	1,170,000	105,000
chb	177,534	23,722,817	8,228,903	175,335	25,397,531	9,476,220	172,115	28,422,684	10,161,266
chn	455,100	141,807,024	34,895,751 [a]	462,124	153,943,138	38,300,431 [a]	473,726	170,515,940 [a]	42,087,862 [a]
ccc	21,897 [a]	3,916,248 [a]	1,554,143 [a]	22,364 [a]	4,271,435 [a]	1,630,565 [a]	23,481 [a]	4,969,610 [a]	1,871,754 [a]
cpc	85,227 [a]	11,384,825 [a]	1,760,117 [a]	84,956 [a]	13,359,375 [a]	1,995,388 [a]	85,932 [a]	13,928,957 [a]	2,192,562 [a]
ecc	28,712 [a]	6,356,730 [a]	1,271,310 [a]	28,459 [a]	6,890,381 [a]	1,454,826 [a]	27,995 [a]	7,552,495 [a]	1,547,857 [a]
ecv	74,060	28,758,357 [a]	7,240,548	74,678	32,606,550 [a]	8,017,623	76,092	37,118,906 [a]	9,400,074
elc	ALC & LCA	ALC & LCA	ALC & LCA	ALC & LCA	ALC & LCA	ALC & LCA	ALC & LCA	ALC & LCA	ALC & LCA
els	14,652	2,290,697	546,899 [a]	14,833	2,629,719	833,543 [a]	15,081	2,750,703	904,774 [a]
emc	NA	NA	NA	3,634	1,281,761	794,896	3,704	1,380,806	828,264
feb	NA	NA	NA	3,956	970,960	745,059	NA	NA	NA
fmc	52,563	23,303,722 [a]	5,505,538 [a]	52,698 [a]	25,505,294 [a]	5,869,970 [a]	52,900 [a]	27,516,302 [a]	6,614,732 [a]
fum	52,599	6,943,990	1,895,984	53,390	8,172,337	1,968,884	51,426	6,662,787	2,131,108
ggb	72,030	9,854,533	747,842	NA	NA	NA	73,046	13,131,345	1,218,763
lca	2,191,942	251,083,883	62,076,894	2,183,666	277,186,563	72,426,148	2,177,231	301,605,382	71,325,097
lms	1,991,408	301,064,630	57,077,162	1,969,279	329,134,237	59,030,753	1,965,422	360,989,735	63,530,596
mch	96,609	18,540,237	12,980,502	97,142	22,922,417	14,124,757	98,027	24,505,346	15,116,762
mgc	35,575 [a]	5,051,708 [a]	4,619,590 [a]	36,775 [a]	5,421,568 [a]	5,062,489 [a]	36,736 [a]	6,254,850 [a]	5,660,477 [a]
mus	MCH & MGC	MCH & MGC	MCH & MGC	MCH & MGC	MCH & MGC	MCH & MGC	MCH & MGC	MCH & MGC	MCH & MGC
mca	25,323	4,583,616	581,200	24,854	4,441,750	625,536	24,782	4,600,331	689,070
nab	42,724	10,332,556	3,554,204	42,499	11,629,309	3,559,983	42,779	13,415,024	3,564,339
opc	10,683 [a]	3,514,172	931,935	10,939	4,107,705	1,135,388	11,306 [a]	4,683,302	1,147,191
pch	3,430,927	633,187,916	130,252,348	3,382,783	692,872,811	128,194,954	3,321,787	776,049,247	148,528,993
rca	210,637 [b]	53,999,791 [b]	14,210,966 [b]	211,778 [b]	60,138,720 [b]	15,494,816 [b]	210,700 [b]	62,997,526 [b]	16,750,408 [b]
sda	522,317	98,468,365	216,202,975	535,705	104,044,989	226,692,736	553,089	118,711,906	255,936,372
sbc	13,078,239	1,506,877,921	289,179,711	13,191,394	1,668,120,760	316,462,385	13,372,757	1,864,213,869	355,885,769
ucc	1,785,652	219,878,772	35,522,221	1,769,104	232,593,033	37,789,958	1,745,533	249,443,032	41,100,583
wel	301,944	44,492,259	11,639,834	303,944	50,255,539	12,960,885	306,264	54,983,467	14,230,208
Total	28,713,781	4,026,403,255	1,022,156,020	28,531,973	4,415,123,919	1,092,967,628	28,723,970	4,887,889,743	1,213,633,756

[a] Data obtained from denominational source.

[b] empty tomb review of RCA directory data.

127

Appendix B-1: Church Member Giving 1968-2001 (continued)

	Data Year 1980			Data Year 1981			Data Year 1982		
	Full/Confirmed Members	Congregational Finances	Benevolences	Full/Confirmed Members	Congregational Finances	Benevolences	Full/Confirmed Members	Congregational Finances	Benevolences
abc	1,008,700 a	213,560,656	37,133,159	989,322 a	227,931,461	40,046,261	983,580 a	242,750,027	41,457,745
alc	1,763,067	312,592,610	65,235,739	1,758,452	330,155,588	96,102,638	1,758,239	359,848,865	77,010,444
arp	28,166 a	6,868,650 a	1,054,229 a	28,334 a	7,863,221 a	1,497,838 a	29,087 a	8,580,311 a	1,807,572 a
bcc	13,578 a	6,011,465 a	1,490,334 a	13,993	6,781,857	1,740,711	14,413 a	7,228,612 a	1,594,797 a
ccd	788,394	189,176,399	30,991,519	772,466	211,828,751	31,067,142	770,227	227,178,861	34,307,638
cga	176,429	67,367,485	13,414,112	178,581	78,322,907	14,907,277	184,685	84,896,806	17,171,600
cgg	NA	NA	NA	5,981	1,788,298	403,000	5,781 a	1,864,735 a	418,000 a
chb	170,839	29,813,265	11,663,976	170,267	31,641,019	12,929,076	168,844	35,064,568	12,844,415
chn	483,101	191,536,556	45,786,446 a	490,852	203,145,992	50,084,163 a	497,261	221,947,940	53,232,461 a
ccc	24,410 a	6,017,539 a	2,169,298 a	25,044 a	8,465,804	2,415,233	26,008	9,230,111	2,574,569
cpc	86,941 a	15,973,738 a	2,444,677 a	87,493 a	16,876,846 a	2,531,539 a	88,121 a	17,967,709 a	2,706,361 a
ecc	27,567 a	8,037,564 a	1,630,993 a	27,287 a	8,573,057 a	1,758,025 a	27,203 a	9,119,278 a	1,891,936 a
ecv	77,737	41,888,556 a	10,031,072	79,523	45,206,565 a	8,689,918	81,324	50,209,520 a	8,830,793
elc	ALC & LCA	ALC & LCA	ALC & LCA	ALC & LCA	ALC & LCA	ALC & LCA	ALC & LCA	ALC & LCA	ALC & LCA
els	14,968	3,154,804	876,929 a	14,904	3,461,387	716,624	15,165	3,767,977	804,822
emc	3,782	1,527,945	1,041,447	3,753	1,515,975	908,342	3,832	1,985,890	731,510
feb	4,329	1,250,466	627,536	NA	NA	NA	2,047	696,660	1,020,972
fmc	54,145 a	30,525,352 a	6,648,248 a	54,764 a	32,853,491 a	7,555,713 a	54,198	35,056,434	8,051,593
fum	51,691	9,437,724	2,328,137	51,248	9,551,765	2,449,731	50,601	10,334,180	2,597,215
ggb	74,159	14,967,312	1,547,038	75,028	15,816,060	1,473,070	NA	NA	NA
lca	2,176,991	371,981,816	87,439,137	2,173,558	404,300,509	82,862,299	2,176,265	435,564,519	83,217,264
lms	1,973,958	390,756,268	66,626,364	1,983,198	429,910,406	86,341,102	1,961,260	468,468,156	75,457,846
mch	99,511	28,846,931	16,437,738	99,651	31,304,278	17,448,024	101,501	33,583,338	17,981,274
mgc	36,644 a	6,796,330 a	5,976,652 a	36,609 a	7,857,792 a	7,203,240 a	37,007 a	8,438,680 a	7,705,419 a
mus	MCH & MGC	MCH & MGC	MCH & MGC	MCH & MGC	MCH & MGC	MCH & MGC	MCH & MGC	MCH & MGC	MCH & MGC
mca	24,863	5,178,444	860,399	24,500	5,675,495	831,177	24,669	6,049,857	812,015
nab	43,041	12,453,858	3,972,485	43,146	15,513,286	4,420,403	42,735	17,302,952	4,597,515
opc	11,553 a	5,235,294	1,235,849	11,884 a	5,939,983	1,382,451	11,956 a	6,512,125 a	1,430,061 a
pch	3,262,086	820,218,732	176,172,729	3,202,392	896,641,430	188,576,382	3,157,372	970,223,947	199,331,832
rca	210,762	70,733,297	17,313,239 b	210,312	77,044,709	18,193,793 b	211,168	82,656,050	19,418,165 b
sda	571,141	121,484,768	275,783,385	588,536	133,088,131	297,838,046	606,310	136,877,455	299,437,917
sbc	13,600,126	2,080,375,258	400,976,072	13,782,644	2,336,062,506	443,931,179	13,991,709	2,628,272,553	486,402,607
ucc	1,736,244	278,546,571	44,042,186	1,726,535	300,730,591	48,329,399	1,708,847	323,725,191	52,738,069
wel	308,620	60,624,862	16,037,844	311,351	68,056,396	18,261,099	312,195	71,891,457 a	18,677,343
Total	28,907,543	5,402,940,515	1,348,988,968	29,021,608	5,953,905,556	1,492,894,895	29,103,610	6,517,294,764	1,536,261,770

a Data obtained from denominational source.

b empty tomb review of RCA directory data.

Appendix B-1: Church Member Giving 1968-2001 (continued)

	Data Year 1983			Data Year 1984			Data Year 1985		
	Full/Confirmed Members	Congregational Finances	Benevolences	Full/Confirmed Members	Congregational Finances	Benevolences	Full/Confirmed Members	Congregational Finances	Benevolences
abc	965,117 a	254,716,036	43,683,021	953,945 a	267,556,088	46,232,040	894,732 a	267,694,684	47,201,119
alc	1,756,420	375,500,188	84,633,617	1,756,558	413,876,101	86,601,067	1,751,649	428,861,660	87,152,699
arp	31,738	10,640,050 a	2,180,230 a	31,355	11,221,526 a	3,019,456 a	32,051	12,092,868 a	3,106,994 a
bcc	14,782	7,638,413	1,858,632	15,128	8,160,359	2,586,843	15,535 a	8,504,354 a	2,979,046 a
ccd	761,629	241,934,972	35,809,331	755,233	263,694,210	38,402,791	743,486	274,072,301	40,992,053
cga	182,190	81,309,323	13,896,753	185,404	86,611,269	14,347,570	185,593	91,078,512	15,308,954
cgg	5,759	1,981,300	412,000	4,711	2,211,800	504,200	4,575	2,428,730	582,411
chb	164,680	39,726,743	14,488,192	161,824	37,743,527	15,136,600	159,184	40,658,904	16,509,718
chn	506,439	237,220,642	57,267,073 a	514,937	253,566,280	60,909,810 a	520,741	267,134,078	65,627,515 a
ccc	26,691 a	9,189,221 a	2,980,636	28,383	10,018,982	3,051,425	28,624	11,729,365	3,350,021
cpc	87,186 a	19,252,942 a	3,028,953 a	86,995 a	20,998,768 a	3,331,065 a	85,346 a	22,361,332 a	3,227,932 a
ecc	26,769 a	9,505,479 a	2,019,373 a	26,375 a	10,302,554 a	2,220,852 a	26,016	8,134,641	1,777,172
ecv	82,943	53,279,350 a	10,615,909	84,185	60,295,634 a	11,243,908	85,150	63,590,735 a	13,828,030
elc	ALC & LCA	ALC & LCA	ALC & LCA	ALC & LCA	ALC & LCA	ALC & LCA	ALC & LCA	ALC & LCA	ALC & LCA
els	15,576	3,842,625	838,788	15,396	4,647,714	931,677 a	15,012	4,725,783	791,586
emc	3,857	1,930,689	738,194	3,908	2,017,565	862,350	3,813	2,128,019	1,058,040
feb	2,094	622,467	1,466,399	NA	NA	NA	2,107 a	1,069,851 a	402,611 a
fmc	56,442 a	36,402,355 a	8,334,248 a	56,667 a	39,766,087 a	8,788,189 a	56,242	42,046,626 a	9,461,369 a
fum	49,441	11,723,240	2,886,931	48,713	11,549,163	2,875,370	48,812	12,601,820	3,012,658
ggb	75,133	17,283,259	1,733,755	75,028	17,599,169	1,729,228	73,040	18,516,252	1,683,130
lca	2,176,772	457,239,780	88,909,363	2,168,594	496,228,216	99,833,067	2,161,216	539,142,069	103,534,375
lms	1,984,199	499,220,552	76,991,991 a	1,986,392	539,346,935	81,742,006 a	1,982,753	566,507,516	83,117,011 a
mch	103,350 a	34,153,628	17,581,878	90,347	37,333,306	16,944,094	91,167	34,015,200	25,593,500
mgc	36,318 a	8,702,849 a	7,661,415 a	35,951 a	9,197,458 a	7,795,680 a	35,356 a	9,217,964 a	7,070,700 a
mus	MCH & MGC	MCH & MGC	MCH & MGC	MCH & MGC	MCH & MGC	MCH & MGC	MCH & MGC	MCH & MGC	MCH & MGC
mca	24,913	6,618,339	911,787	24,269	7,723,611	1,183,741	24,396	8,698,949	1,170,349
nab	43,286	18,010,853	5,132,672	43,215	19,322,720	5,724,552	42,863	20,246,236	5,766,686
opc	12,045	6,874,722	1,755,169	12,278 a	7,555,006	2,079,924	12,593 a	8,291,483	2,204,998
pch	3,122,213	1,047,756,995	197,981,080	3,092,151	1,132,098,779	218,412,639	3,057,226 a	1,252,885,684 a	232,487,569 a
rca	211,660	92,071,986	20,632,574	209,968 b	100,378,778	21,794,880	209,395	103,428,950	22,233,299
sda	623,563	143,636,140	323,461,439	638,929	155,257,063	319,664,449	651,594	155,077,180	346,251,406
sbc	14,178,051	2,838,573,815	528,781,000	14,341,822	3,094,913,877	567,467,188	14,477,364	3,272,276,486	609,868,694
ucc	1,701,513	332,613,396	55,716,557	1,696,107	385,786,198	58,679,094	1,683,777	409,543,989	62,169,679 a
wel	313,883	76,133,614 a	24,169,441	315,466	82,884,471 a	22,951,699	316,297 a	87,194,889 a	22,376,423 a
Total	29,346,652	6,975,305,963	1,638,558,401	29,460,234	7,589,863,214	1,727,047,454	29,477,705	8,045,957,110	1,841,897,747

a Data obtained from denominational source.
b empty tomb review of RCA directory data.

129

Appendix B-1: Church Member Giving 1968-2001 (continued)

	Data Year 1986			Data Year 1987			Data Year 1988		
	Full/Confirmed Members	Congregational Finances	Benevolences	Full/Confirmed Members	Congregational Finances	Benevolences	Full/Confirmed Members	Congregational Finances	Benevolences
abc	862,582 a	287,020,378 a	49,070,083 a	868,189 a	291,606,418 a	55,613,855	825,102 a	296,569,316 a	55,876,771
alc	1,740,439	434,641,736	96,147,129	See ELCA	See ELCA	See ELCA	See ELCA	See ELCA	See ELCA
arp	32,438 a	12,336,321 a	3,434,408 a	32,289	13,553,176 a	3,927,030 a	31,922	13,657,776 a	5,063,036 a
bcc	15,911	10,533,883	2,463,558	16,136	11,203,321	3,139,949	16,578 a	13,522,101 a	4,346,690 a
ccd	732,466	288,277,386	42,027,504	718,522	287,464,332	42,728,826	707,985	297,187,996	42,226,128
cga	188,662	91,768,855	16,136,647	198,552	124,376,413	20,261,687	198,842	132,384,232	19,781,941
cgg	NA	NA	NA	4,348	2,437,778	738,818	4,394 a	2,420,600 a	644,000 a
chb	155,967	43,531,293	17,859,101	154,067	45,201,732	19,342,402	151,169	48,008,657	19,701,942 a
chn	529,192	283,189,977	68,438,998 a	541,878	294,160,356	73,033,568 a	550,700	309,478,442	74,737,057 a
ccc	28,948	15,559,846 a	3,961,037	29,429	15,409,349 a	3,740,688	29,015	13,853,547	4,120,974
cpc	84,579 a	22,338,090 a	3,646,356 a	85,781	22,857,711	3,727,681	85,304	23,366,911 e	3,722,607
ecc	25,625	10,977,813 a	2,422,879 a	25,300	14,281,140 a	2,575,415 a	24,980	12,115,762	2,856,766 a
ecv	86,079	67,889,353 a	14,374,707	86,741	73,498,123 a	14,636,000	87,750	77,504,445 a	14,471,178
elc	ALC & LCA	ALC & LCA	ALC & LCA	3,952,663	1,083,293,684	169,685,942	3,931,878	1,150,483,034	169,580,472
els	15,083 a	4,996,111 a	1,050,715 a	15,892	5,298,882	1,082,198	15,518 a	5,713,773 a	1,043,612 a
emc	NA	NA	NA	3,841	2,332,216	1,326,711	3,879	2,522,533	1,438,459
feb	NA	NA	NA	NA	NA	NA	NA	NA	NA
fmc	56,243	46,150,881	9,446,120	57,262	47,743,298	9,938,096	57,432	48,788,041	9,952,103
fum	48,143	12,790,909	2,916,870	47,173	13,768,272	3,631,353	48,325	14,127,491	3,719,125
ggb	72,263	19,743,265	1,883,826	73,515	20,850,827	1,789,578	74,086	21,218,051	1,731,299
lca	2,157,701	569,250,519	111,871,174	See ELCA	See ELCA	See ELCA	See ELCA	See ELCA	See ELCA
lms	1,974,798	605,768,688	87,803,646 a	1,973,347	620,271,274	86,938,723 a	1,962,674	659,288,332	88,587,175 a
mch	91,467 a	40,097,500 a	24,404,200 a	92,673 a	43,295,100	25,033,600	92,682	47,771,200	27,043,900
mgc	35,170	10,101,306 a	7,717,998 a	34,889	11,560,998	8,478,414	34,693	11,399,995	9,638,417
mus	MCH & MGC	MCH & MGC	MCH & MGC	MCH & MGC	MCH & MGC	MCH & MGC	MCH & MGC	MCH & MGC	MCH & MGC
mca	24,260	8,133,127	1,155,350	24,440	9,590,658	1,174,593	23,526	9,221,646	1,210,476
nab	42,084	20,961,799	5,982,391	42,150 a	23,773,844 a	7,873,096 a	42,629	24,597,288	6,611,840
opc	12,919 a	9,333,328 a	2,347,928 a	13,013 a	9,884,288	2,425,480	13,108 a	10,797,786 a	2,648,375 a
pch	3,007,322	1,318,440,264	249,033,881	2,967,781	1,395,501,073	247,234,439	2,929,608	1,439,655,217	284,989,138
rca	207,993	114,231,429	22,954,596	203,581	114,652,192 b	24,043,270	200,631	127,409,263	25,496,802 b
sda	666,199	166,692,974	361,316,753	675,702	166,939,355	374,830,065	687,200	178,768,967	395,849,223
sbc	14,613,638	3,481,124,471	635,196,984	14,722,617	3,629,842,643	662,455,177	14,812,844	3,706,652,161	689,366,904
ucc	1,676,105	429,340,239	63,808,091	1,662,568	451,700,210	66,870,922	1,644,787	470,747,740	65,734,348
wel	316,416	92,662,969 a	22,448,920	317,294	97,567,101 a	22,207,123	316,987	101,975,092 a	22,406,238
Total	29,500,692	8,517,884,710	1,931,321,850	29,641,633	8,943,915,764	1,960,484,699	28,781,126	9,271,207,395	2,054,596,996

a Data obtained from denominational source.

b empty tomb review of RCA directory data.

e A *YACC* prepublication data table listed 23,366,911 for Congregational Finances which, added to Benevolences, equals the published Total of 27,089,518.

Appendix B-1: Church Member Giving 1968-2001 (continued)

	Data Year 1989			Data Year 1990			Data Year 1991		
	Full/Confirmed Members	Congregational Finances	Benevolences	Full/Confirmed Members	Congregational Finances	Benevolences	Full/Confirmed Members	Congregational Finances	Benevolences
abc	789,730 a	305,212,094 a	55,951,539	764,890 a	315,777,005 a	54,740,278	773,838 a	318,150,548 a	52,330,924
alc	See ELCA	See ELCA	See ELCA	See ELCA	See ELCA	See ELCA	See ELCA	See ELCA	See ELCA
arp	32,600	16,053,762 a	4,367,314 a	32,817 a	17,313,355 a	5,031,504 a	33,494 a	17,585,273 a	5,254,738 a
bcc	16,842	12,840,038	3,370,306	17,277	13,327,414	3,336,580	17,456 a	14,491,918 a	3,294,169 a
ccd	690,115	310,043,826	42,015,246	678,750	321,569,909	42,607,007	663,336	331,629,009	43,339,307
cga	199,786	134,918,052	20,215,075	205,884	141,375,027	21,087,504	214,743 a	146,249,447 a	21,801,570 a
cgg	4,415	3,367,000	686,000	4,399	3,106,729	690,000	4,375	2,756,651	662,500
chb	149,681	51,921,820	19,737,714 a	148,253	54,832,226	18,384,483 a	147,954 a	55,035,355 a	19,694,919 a
chn	558,664	322,924,598	76,625,913 a	563,756 a	333,397,255 a	77,991,665 a	572,153	352,654,251	82,276,097 a
ccc	28,413	18,199,823	4,064,111	28,355	16,964,128	4,174,133	28,035	17,760,290	4,304,052
cpc	84,994 a	25,867,112 a	4,086,994 a	85,025 a	27,027,650 a	4,139,967 a	84,706 a	28,069,681 a	5,740,846 a
ecc	24,606	13,274,756 a	2,703,095 a	24,437	12,947,150 a	2,858,077 a	24,124 a	13,100,036 a	3,074,660 a
ecv	89,014	80,621,293 a	15,206,265	89,735	84,263,236 a	15,601,475	89,648	87,321,563 a	16,598,656
elc	3,909,302	1,239,433,257	182,386,940	3,898,478	1,318,884,279	184,174,554	3,890,947	1,375,439,787	186,016,168
els	15,740	6,186,648	1,342,321	16,181	6,527,076	1,193,789	16,004	6,657,338	1,030,445
emc	3,888	2,712,843	1,567,728	4,026	2,991,485	1,800,593	3,958	3,394,563	1,790,115
feb	NA	NA	NA	NA	NA	NA	2,008 a	1,398,968 a	500,092 a
fmc	59,418 a	50,114,090 a	10,311,535 a	58,084	55,229,181	10,118,505	57,794	57,880,464	9,876,739
fum	47,228	16,288,644	4,055,624	45,691	10,036,083	2,511,063	50,803 f	NA	NA
ggb	73,738	23,127,835	1,768,804	74,156	23,127,835	1,737,011	71,119 a	22,362,874 a	1,408,262 a
lca	See ELCA	See ELCA	See ELCA	See ELCA	See ELCA	See ELCA	See ELCA	See ELCA	See ELCA
lms	1,961,114	701,701,168 a	90,974,340 a	1,954,350	712,235,204	96,308,765 a	1,952,845	741,823,412	94,094,637 a
mch	92,517	55,353,313	27,873,241	92,448 a	65,709,827	28,397,083	93,114 a	68,926,324	28,464,199
mgc	33,982	12,096,435	9,054,682	33,535	13,669,288	8,449,395	33,937	13,556,484 a	8,645,993 a
mus	MCH & MGC	MCH & MGC	MCH & MGC	MCH & MGC	MCH & MGC	MCH & MGC	MCH & MGC	MCH & MGC	MCH & MGC
mca	23,802	10,415,640	1,284,233	23,526	10,105,037	1,337,616	22,887	10,095,337	1,205,335
nab	42,629	28,076,077	3,890,017	44,493	31,103,672	7,700,119	43,187 a	27,335,239 a	7,792,876 a
opc	12,573 a	11,062,590 a	2,789,427 a	12,177 a	10,631,166 a	2,738,295 a	12,265	11,700,000	2,700,000
pch	2,886,482	1,528,450,805	295,365,032	2,847,437	1,530,341,707	294,990,441	2,805,548	1,636,407,042	311,905,934 a
rca	198,832	136,796,188 b	29,456,132 b	197,154	144,357,953 b	27,705,029 b	193,531 b	147,532,382 b	26,821,721 b
sda	701,781	196,204,538	415,752,350	717,446	195,054,218	433,035,080	733,026	201,411,183	456,242,995
sbc	14,907,826	3,873,300,782	712,738,838	15,038,409	4,146,285,561	718,174,874	15,232,347	4,283,283,059	731,812,766
ucc	1,625,969	496,825,160	72,300,698	1,599,212	527,378,397	71,984,897	1,583,830	543,803,752	73,149,887
wel	317,117	110,575,539 a	22,811,571	316,813	116,272,092 a	24,088,568	316,929 a	121,835,547 a	24,276,370 a
Total	29,582,798	9,793,965,726	2,134,753,085	29,617,194	10,261,841,145	2,167,088,350	29,719,138	10,659,647,777	2,226,106,972

a Data obtained from denominational source.

b empty tomb review of RCA directory data.

f Inclusive membership, obtained from the denomination and used only in Chapter 5 analysis.

Appendix B-1: Church Member Giving 1968-2000 (continued)

	Data Year 1992			Data Year 1993			Data Year 1994		
	Full/Confirmed Members	Congregational Finances	Benevolences	Full/Confirmed Members	Congregational Finances	Benevolences	Full/Confirmed Members	Congregational Finances	Benevolences
abc	730,009 a	310,307,040 a	52,764,005	764,657 a	346,658,047 a	53,562,811	697,379 a	337,185,885 a	51,553,256 a
alc	See ELCA	See ELCA	See ELCA	See ELCA	See ELCA	See ELCA	See ELCA	See ELCA	See ELCA
arp	33,550	18,175,957 a	5,684,008 a	33,662 a	20,212,390 a	5,822,845 a	33,636	22,618,802 a	6,727,857
bcc	17,646 a	15,981,118 a	3,159,717 a	17,986	13,786,394	4,515,730 a	18,152	14,844,672	5,622,005
ccd	655,652	333,629,412	46,440,333	619,028	328,219,027	44,790,415	605,996	342,352,080	43,165,285
cga	214,743	150,115,497	23,500,213	216,117	158,454,703	23,620,177	221,346 a	160,694,760 a	26,262,049 a
cgg	4,085	2,648,085	509,398	4,239	2,793,000	587,705	3,996	2,934,843	475,799
chb	147,912	57,954,895	21,748,320	146,713	56,818,998	23,278,848	144,282	57,210,682	24,155,595
chn	582,804 a	361,555,793 a	84,118,580 a	589,398	369,896,767	87,416,378 a	595,303	387,385,034	89,721,860
ccc	30,387	22,979,946	4,311,234	36,864	24,997,736 a	5,272,184	37,996 a	23,758,101 a	5,240,805 a
cpc	85,080 a	27,813,626 a	4,339,933 a	84,336 a	27,462,623 a	4,574,550 a	83,733 a	29,212,802 a	4,547,149 a
ecc	24,150	13,451,827 a	3,120,351 a	23,889	13,546,159 a	3,258,595 a	23,504	13,931,409	3,269,986
ecv	90,985 a	93,071,869 a	16,732,701 a	89,511	93,765,006 a	16,482,315	90,919 a	101,746,341 a	17,874,955 a
elc	3,878,055	1,399,419,800	189,605,837	3,861,418	1,452,000,815	188,393,158	3,849,692	1,502,746,601	187,145,886
els	15,929 a	6,944,522 a	1,271,058 a	15,780	6,759,222 a	1,100,660	15,960	7,288,521	1,195,698
emc	4,059	3,839,838 a	1,403,001 a	4,130 a	4,260,307 a	1,406,682 a	4,225 a	4,597,730 a	1,533,157 a
feb	1,872 a	1,343,225 a	397,553 a	1,866 a	1,294,646 a	429,023 a	1,898 a	1,537,041 a	395,719 a
fmc	58,220	60,584,079	10,591,064	59,156	62,478,294	10,513,187	59,354 a	65,359,325 a	10,708,854 a
fum	50,005 f	NA	NA	45,542 f	NA	NA	44,711 f	NA	NA
ggb	72,388 a	21,561,432 a	1,402,330 a	73,129 a	22,376,970 a	1,440,342 a	71,140 a	19,651,624 a	2,052,409 a
lca	See ELCA	See ELCA	See ELCA	See ELCA	See ELCA	See ELCA	See ELCA	See ELCA	See ELCA
lms	1,953,248	777,467,488	97,275,934 a	1,945,077	789,821,559	96,355,945 a	1,944,905	817,412,113	96,048,560 a
mch	94,222 a	68,118,222	28,835,719	95,634	71,385,271	27,973,380	87,911 a	64,651,639	24,830,192
mgc	34,040	14,721,813 a	8,265,700	33,629	14,412,556	7,951,676	32,782	16,093,551	8,557,126 a
mus	MCH & MGC	MCH & MGC	MCH & MGC	MCH & MGC	MCH & MGC	MCH & MGC	MCH & MGC	MCH & MGC	MCH & MGC
mca	22,533	10,150,953	1,208,372	22,223	9,675,502	1,191,131	21,448	9,753,010	1,182,778
nab	43,446	28,375,947	7,327,594	43,045	30,676,902	7,454,087	43,236	32,800,560	7,515,707
opc	12,580 a	12,466,266 a	3,025,824 a	12,924 a	13,158,089 a	3,039,676 a	13,970	14,393,880	3,120,454
pch	2,780,406	1,696,092,968	309,069,530	2,742,192	1,700,918,712	310,375,024	2,698,262	1,800,008,292	307,158,749
rca	190,322 b	147,181,320 b	28,457,900 b	188,551 b	159,715,941 b	26,009,853 b	185,242	153,107,408	27,906,830
sda	748,687	191,362,737	476,902,779	761,703	209,524,570	473,769,831	775,349	229,596,444	503,347,816
sbc	15,358,866	4,462,915,112	751,366,698	15,398,642	4,621,157,751	761,298,249	15,614,060	5,263,421,764	815,360,696
ucc	1,555,382	521,190,413	73,906,372	1,530,178	550,847,702	71,046,517	1,501,310	556,540,722	67,269,762
wel	316,183 a	127,858,970 a	26,426,128 a	315,871	137,187,582	24,587,988	315,302	142,851,919	23,998,935
Total	29,757,441	10,959,280,170	2,283,168,186	29,731,548	11,314,263,241	2,287,518,962	29,792,288	12,195,687,555	2,367,945,929

a Data obtained from denominational source.

b empty tomb review of RCA directory data.

f Inclusive membership, obtained from the denomination and used only in Chapter 5 analysis.

132

Appendix B-1: Church Member Giving 1968-2000 (continued)

	Data Year 1995			Data Year 1996			Data Year 1997		
	Full/Confirmed Members	Congregational Finances	Benevolences	Full/Confirmed Members	Congregational Finances	Benevolences	Full/Confirmed Members	Congregational Finances	Benevolences
abc	726,452 a	365,873,197 a	57,052,333 a	670,363 a	351,362,401 a	55,982,392 a	658,731 a	312,860,507 a	54,236,977 a
alc	See ELCA	See ELCA	See ELCA	See ELCA	See ELCA	See ELCA	See ELCA	See ELCA	See ELCA
arp	33,513	23,399,372 a	5,711,882 a	34,117	23,419,989 a	5,571,337 a	34,344	25,241,384	6,606,829
bcc	18,529	16,032,149	5,480,828	18,424	16,892,154	4,748,871	19,016 a	17,456,379 a	5,934,414 a
ccd	601,237	357,895,652	42,887,958	586,131	370,210,746	42,877,144	568,921	381,463,761	43,009,412
cga	224,061	160,897,147	26,192,559	229,240	180,581,111	26,983,385	229,302	194,438,623	29,054,047
cgg	3,877	2,722,766	486,661	3,920	2,926,516	491,348	3,877	2,987,337	515,247
chb	143,121	60,242,418	22,599,214	141,811	60,524,557 a	19,683,035 a	141,400	60,923,817 a	19,611,047 a
chn	598,946	396,698,137	93,440,095	608,008	419,450,850	95,358,352	615,632	433,821,462	99,075,440
ccc	38,853 a	24,250,819 a	5,483,659 a	38,469 a	25,834,363 a	4,989,062 a	38,956	28,204,355	5,167,644
cpc	81,094 a	31,072,697 a	4,711,934 a	80,122 a	31,875,061 a	5,035,451 a	79,576 a	32,152,971 a	5,152,129 a
ecc	23,422	14,830,454	3,301,060	23,091	14,692,608	3,273,685	22,957	15,658,454	3,460,999
ecv	91,458	109,776,363 a	17,565,085 a	91,823 a	115,693,329 a	18,726,756 a	93,414	127,642,950	20,462,435
elc	3,845,063	1,551,842,465	188,107,066	3,838,750	1,629,909,672	191,476,141	3,844,169	1,731,806,133	201,115,441
els	16,543	7,712,358 a	1,084,136	16,511	8,136,195	1,104,996	16,444	8,937,103	1,150,419
emc	4,284 a	5,321,079 a	1,603,548 a	4,201	5,361,912 a	1,793,267 a	4,348 a	7,017,588 a	2,039,740 a
feb	1,856 a	1,412,281 a	447,544 a	1,751 a	1,198,120 a	507,656 a	1,763 a	1,120,222 a	518,777 a
fmc	59,060	67,687,955	11,114,804	59,343 a	70,262,626	11,651,462	62,191	78,687,325	12,261,465
fum	43,440 f	NA	NA	42,918 f	NA	NA	41,040 f	NA	NA
ggb	70,886 a	24,385,956 a	1,722,662 a	70,562 a	27,763,966 a	1,832,909 a	72,326	28,093,944	1,780,851
lca	See ELCA	See ELCA	See ELCA	See ELCA	See ELCA	See ELCA	See ELCA	See ELCA	See ELCA
lms	1,943,281	832,701,255	98,139,835 a	1,951,730	855,461,015	104,076,876 a	1,951,391	887,928,255	110,520,917
mch	90,139 a	71,641,773	26,832,240	90,959	76,669,365	27,812,549	92,161	76,087,609 a	25,637,872 a
mgc	35,852	15,774,961 a	7,587,049 a	35,333	18,282,833	7,969,999	34,731	14,690,904	6,514,761
mus	MCH & MGC	MCH & MGC	MCH & MGC	MCH & MGC	MCH & MGC	MCH & MGC	MCH & MGC	MCH & MGC	MCH & MGC
mca	21,409	10,996,031	1,167,513	21,140	11,798,536	1,237,349	21,108	12,555,760	1,148,478
nab	43,928	37,078,473	7,480,331	43,744 a	37,172,560 a	7,957,860 a	43,850	37,401,175	7,986,099
opc	14,355	16,017,003	3,376,691	15,072 a	17,883,915 a	3,467,207 a	15,072	20,090,259	3,967,490
pch	2,665,276	1,855,684,719	309,978,224	2,631,466	1,930,179,808	332,336,258	2,609,191	2,064,789,378	344,757,186
rca	183,255	240,250,624	29,995,068	182,342	183,975,696 a	31,271,007	180,980 a	181,977,101 a	32,130,943 a
sda	790,731	240,565,576	503,334,129	809,159	242,316,834	524,977,061	825,654	249,591,109	552,633,569
sbc	15,663,296	5,209,748,503	858,635,435	15,691,249 a	5,987,033,115	891,149,403 a	15,891,514	6,098,933,137	930,176,909
ucc	1,472,213	578,042,965	67,806,448	1,452,565	615,727,028	69,013,791	1,438,181	651,176,773	70,180,193
wel	314,188 a	150,853,785 a	33,193,286 a	314,379 a	156,966,741 a	47,436,904	315,355	164,256,655	52,322,175
Total	29,820,178	12,405,408,933	2,436,519,277	29,755,775	13,489,563,622	2,530,793,513	29,926,555	13,947,992,430	2,649,129,905

a Data obtained from denominational source.

f Inclusive membership, obtained from the denomination and used only in Chapter 5 analysis.

Appendix B-1: Church Member Giving 1968-2001 (continued)

	Data Year 1998			Data Year 1999			Data Year 2000		
	Full/Confirmed Members	Congregational Finances	Benevolences	Full/Confirmed Members	Congregational Finances	Benevolences	Full/Confirmed Members	Congregational Finances	Benevolences
abc	621,232 a	326,046,153 a	53,866,448 a	603,014 a	331,513,521 a	58,675,160	593,113	359,484,902	63,042,002
alc	See ELCA	See ELCA	See ELCA	See ELCA	See ELCA	See ELCA	See ELCA	See ELCA	See ELCA
arp	34,642 a	28,831,982 a	7,378,121 a	35,643 a	33,862,219 a	7,973,285 a	35,022 a	33,004,995 a	25,148,637 a
bcc	19,577	24,116,889	5,274,612	20,010	22,654,566	5,913,551	20,587	25,148,637	5,703,506
ccd	547,875 a	395,699,954 a	45,576,436 a	535,893	410,583,119	47,795,574	527,363	433,965,354	48,726,390
cga	234,311 f	NA	NA	235,849 f	NA	NA	238,891 f	NA	NA
cgg	3,824	3,087,000	689,756	4,083	3,357,300	503,365	4,037	3,232,160	610,113
chb	140,011 a	57,605,960 a	22,283,498 a	138,304 a	63,774,756 a	21,852,687 a	135,978	67,285,361	25,251,272 a
chn	623,028	460,776,715	104,925,922	626,033 a	487,437,668 a	110,818,743 a	633,264	516,708,125	122,284,083
ccc	38,996	28,976,122	5,194,733	40,414	31,165,218	5,931,456	40,974 a	33,537,589 a	6,360,912 a
cpc	80,829 a	33,623,232 a	5,412,917 a	79,452 a	36,303,752 a	5,879,014 a	86,519	39,533,829	6,591,617
ecc	22,868	15,956,209	3,599,440	22,349	16,574,783	3,587,877	21,939	17,656,789	1,982,328
ecv	96,552	140,823,872	20,134,436	98,526 a	161,361,490 a	23,237,513 a	101,317	181,127,526 a	25,983,315 a
elc	3,840,136	1,822,915,831	208,853,359	3,825,228	1,972,950,623	220,647,251	3,810,785	2,067,208,285	231,219,316
els	16,897	9,363,126	1,120,386	16,734	10,062,900	1,129,969	16,569	10,910,109	949,421
emc	4,646 a	6,472,868 a	1,854,222 a	4,511 a	7,528,256 a	1,982,985 a	4,929	8,289,743 a	2,085,475 a
feb	1,828 a	1,433,305 a	502,839 a	1,936 a	1,496,949 a	534,203 a	1,764 a	1,360,133 a	373,057 a
fmc	62,176	82,254,922	12,850,607	62,368 a	86,906,899	12,646,064	62,453	98,853,770	13,430,274
fum	33,908 f	NA	NA	34,863 f	NA	NA	41,297 f	NA	NA
ggb	67,314 a	28,533,439 a	2,594,098 a	55,549 a	22,857,097 a	2,331,087 a	66,296 a	30,470,298 a	2,950,915 a
lca	See ELCA	See ELCA	See ELCA	See ELCA	See ELCA	See ELCA	See ELCA	See ELCA	See ELCA
lms	1,952,020	975,113,229	121,536,226	1,945,846	986,295,136	123,632,549	1,934,057	1,101,690,594	127,554,235
mch	92,002 a	75,796,469 a	26,452,444 a	See MUS	See MUS	See MUS	See MUS	See MUS	See MUS
mgc	36,600	14,786,936 a	5,853,292 a	See MUS	See MUS	See MUS	See MUS	See MUS	See MUS
mus	MCH & MGC	MCH & MGC	MCH & MGC	123,404 a	95,843,112 a	34,821,702 a	120,381 a	NA	NA
mca	20,764	13,082,671	1,131,742	20,400	11,527,684	849,837	20,281	13,391,991	945,165
nab	43,844 a	41,939,978 a	7,731,550 a	45,738	47,207,867	9,055,128	47,097	54,866,431	9,845,352
opc	15,936	22,362,292	4,438,333	17,279 a	24,878,935	4,920,310	17,914	28,120,325	5,978,474
pch	2,587,674	2,173,483,227	355,628,625	2,560,201	2,326,583,688	384,445,608	2,525,330	2,517,278,130	398,602,204
rca	179,085	189,390,759	33,890,048	178,260 a	216,305,458 a	36,158,625 a	177,281	226,555,821	37,221,041
sda	839,915	269,679,595	588,227,010	861,860	301,221,572	629,944,965	880,921	316,562,375	675,000,508
sbc	15,729,356	6,498,607,390	953,491,003	14,001,690 g	6,001,443,051 g	795,207,316 g	15,221,959 g	7,037,516,273 g	936,520,388 g
ucc	1,421,088	678,251,694	74,861,463	1,401,682	700,645,114	76,550,398	1,377,320	744,991,925	78,525,195
wel	315,581 a	178,509,021 a	44,674,782 a	315,637	182,185,390	49,215,524 a	316,386	194,799,255 a	52,998,892 a
Total	29,456,296	14,597,520,840	2,720,028,348	27,639,021	14,594,528,123	2,676,241,746	28,681,455	16,163,550,725	2,888,784,036

a Data obtained from denominational source.

f Inclusive membership, obtained from the denomination and used only in Chapter 5 analysis.

g The 1999 and 2000 data for the Southern Baptist Convention used in the 1968-2000 analysis includes data only for those State Conventions that provided a breakdown of Total Contributions between Congregational Finances and Benevolences for that year. For the Eleven Denominations 1921-2000 analysis, 1999 and 2000 Southern Baptist Convention Total Contributions are $7,772,452,961 and $8,437,177,940, respectively. For the Eleven Denominations 1921-2000 analysis, and the Membership Trends analysis, 1999 and 2000 Southern Baptist Convention Membership is 15,581,756 and 15,960,308, respectively.

Appendix B-1: Church Member Giving 1968-2001 (continued)

Data Year 2001

	Full/Confirmed Members	Congregational Finances	Benevolences
abc	631,771 a	381,080,930 a	74,228,212 a
alc	See ELCA	See ELCA	See ELCA
arp	35,181	36,976,653	7,707,456
bcc	20,739	29,566,287	6,864,936
ccd	518,434	437,447,942	48,609,107
cga	237,222 a	NA	NA
cgg	4,155	3,436,200	477,457
chb	134,828	68,790,933	22,869,690
chn	639,296 a	557,589,101 a	121,203,179 a
ccc	40,857	34,483,917	6,754,192
cpc	85,427	41,216,632	6,744,757
ecc	21,463	17,932,202	2,011,619
ecv	103,549 a	198,202,551 a	25,137,813 a
elc	3,794,969	2,165,092,290	239,910,305
els	16,815	11,361,255	1,246,189
emc	5,278 a	10,563,872 a	2,335,880 a
feb	1,271 a	1,086,582 a	246,296 a
fmc	61,202	111,415,741	14,595,290
fum	40,197 f	NA	NA
ggb	66,636 a	30,152,750 a	3,091,252 a
lca	See ELCA	See ELCA	See ELCA
lms	1,920,949	1,092,453,907	124,703,387
mch	See MUS	See MUS	See MUS
mgc	See MUS	See MUS	See MUS
mus	113,972 a	NA	NA
mca	20,207 a	NA	NA
nab	49,017	50,871,441	9,742,646
opc	18,414	30,012,219	6,077,752
pch	2,493,781	2,526,681,144	409,319,291
rca	173,463	228,677,098	39,313,564
sda	900,985	329,285,946	707,593,100
sbc	15,315,526	7,477,479,269	980,224,243
ucc	1,359,105	772,191,485	80,464,673
wel	315,847 a	204,242,914 a	53,582,183 a
Total	28,728,958	16,848,291,261	2,995,054,469

a Data obtained from denominational source.

f Inclusive membership, obtained from the denomination and used only in Chapter 5 analysis.

g The 2001 data for the Southern Baptist Convention used in the 1968-2001 analysis includes data only for those State Conventions that provided a breakdown of Total Contributions between Congregational Finances and Benevolences for that year. For the Eleven Denominations 1921-2001 analysis, 2001 Southern Baptist Convention Total Contributions is $8,935,013,659. For the Eleven Denominations 1921-2001 analysis, and the Membership Trends analysis, 2001 Southern Baptist Convention Membership is 16,052,920.

Appendix B-2: Church Member Giving for 41 Denominations, 2000-2001

	Data Year 2000			Data Year 2001		
	Full/Confirmed Members	Congregational Finances	Benevolences	Full/Confirmed Members	Congregational Finances	Benevolences
Allegany Wesleyan Methodist Connection (Original Allegheny Conference)	1,734	4,178,221	1,097,005	1,697	3,840,136	1,077,266
Apostolic Faith Mission Church of God	8,291	390,000	579,000	8,301 [a]	420,000 [a]	574,000 [a]
Bible Fellowship Church	7,258	10,342,940	2,620,065	7,197	10,291,710	2,886,202
Christian and Missionary Alliance	185,133	283,603,697	39,671,584	191,318	283,050,637	41,775,305
Church of Christ (Holiness) U.S.A.	10,475	9,106,063	443,937	10,321 [a]	8,584,857 [a]	606,576 [a]
Church of Lutheran Brethren of America	8,207 [a]	11,159,060 [a]	2,064,723 [a]	8,194	11,905,251	2,198,658
Church of the Lutheran Confession	6,527	4,625,633	768,464	6,544	4,777,504	767,004
Churches of God General Conference	32,380	21,078,740	4,495,037	32,429	21,638,897	4,951,042
The Episcopal Church	1,877,271 [a]	1,887,045,141 [a]	256,193,656 [a]	1,897,004 [a]	1,787,480,509 [a]	283,013,410 [a]
Missionary Church	29,948	55,460,687	5,342,763	33,249	61,133,961 [a]	10,604,000 [a]
Presbyterian Church in America	247,010	384,909,043	98,600,797	250,638	405,359,071	93,618,231
Primitive Methodist Church in the U.S.A.	4,499 [a]	4,172,334 [a]	640,538 [a]	4,397	3,971,692 [a]	637,339 [a]
The Romano Byzantine Synod of the Orthodox Catholic Church	25,000	61,000	30,000	30,000	65,000	39,700
The United Methodist Church	8,341,375 [a]	3,854,328,165	906,820,115	8,298,460 [a]	4,067,476,116 [a]	976,217,722 [a]
The Wesleyan Church	114,084	204,711,754	28,136,843	114,211	221,890,922	31,786,700

[a] Data obtained from denominational source.

Appendix B-3.1: Church Member Giving for Eleven Denominations, 1921-1952, in Current Dollars

Year	Total Contributions	Members	Per Capita Giving
1921	$281,173,263	17,459,611	$16.10
1922	345,995,802	18,257,426	18.95
1923	415,556,876	18,866,775	22.03
1924	443,187,826	19,245,220	23.03
1925	412,658,363	19,474,863	21.19
1926	368,529,223	17,054,404	21.61
1927	459,527,624	20,266,709	22.67
1928	429,947,883	20,910,584	20.56
1929	445,327,233	20,612,910	21.60
1930	419,697,819	20,796,745	20.18
1931	367,158,877	21,508,745	17.07
1932	309,409,873	21,757,411	14.22
1933	260,366,681	21,792,663	11.95
1934	260,681,472	22,105,624	11.79
1935	267,596,925	22,204,355	12.05
1936	279,835,526	21,746,023	12.87
1937	297,134,313	21,906,456	13.56
1938	307,217,666	22,330,090	13.76
1939	302,300,476	23,084,048	13.10
1940	311,362,429	23,671,660	13.15
1941	336,732,622	23,120,929	14.56
1942	358,419,893	23,556,204	15.22
1943	400,742,492	24,679,784	16.24
1944	461,500,396	25,217,319	18.30
1945	551,404,448	25,898,642	21.29
1946	608,165,179	26,158,559	23.25
1947	684,393,895	27,082,905	25.27
1948	775,360,993	27,036,992	28.68
1949	875,069,944	27,611,824	31.69
1950	934,723,015	28,176,095	33.17
1951	1,033,391,527	28,974,314	35.67
1952	1,121,802,639	29,304,909	38.28

Appendix B-3.2: Church Member Giving for Eleven Denominations, 1953-1967

	Data Year 1953		Data Year 1954		Data Year 1955	
	Total Contributions	Per Capita Total Contributions	Total Contributions	Per Capita Total Contributions	Total Contributions	Per Capita Total Contributions
American Baptist (Northern)	$66,557,447 a	$44.50 b	$65,354,184	$43.17	$67,538,753 d	$44.19 d
Christian Church (Disciples of Christ)	60,065,545 c	32.50 b	65,925,164	34.77	68,611,162 d	35.96 d
Church of the Brethren	7,458,584	43.78	7,812,806	45.88	9,130,616	53.00
The Episcopal Church	84,209,027	49.02	92,079,668	51.84	97,541,567 d	50.94 b
Evangelical Lutheran Church in America						
The American Lutheran Church						
American Lutheran Church	30,881,256	55.24	34,202,987	58.83	40,411,856	67.03
The Evangelical Lutheran Church	30,313,907	48.70	33,312,926	51.64	37,070,341	55.29
United Evangelical Lutheran Ch.	1,953,163	55.85	2,268,200	50.25	2,635,469	69.84
Lutheran Free Church	Not Reported: YACC 1955, p. 264		2,101,026	44.51	2,708,747	55.76
Evan. Lutheran Churches, Assn. of	Not Reported: YACC 1955, p. 264		Not Reported: YACC 1956, p. 276		Not Reported: YACC 1957, p. 284	
Lutheran Church in America						
United Lutheran Church	67,721,548	45.68	76,304,344	50.25	83,170,787	53.46
General Council Evang. Luth. Ch.						
General Synod of Evan. Luth. Ch.						
United Syn. Evang. Luth. South						
American Evangelical Luth. Ch.	Not Reported: YACC 1955, p. 264		Not Reported: YACC 1956, p. 276		Not Reported: YACC 1957, p. 284	
Augustana Lutheran Church	18,733,019	53.98	22,203,098	62.14	22,090,350	60.12
Finnish Lutheran Ch. (Suomi Synod)	744,971	32.12	674,554	29.47	1,059,682	43.75
Moravian Church in Am. No. Prov.	1,235,534	53.26	1,461,658	59.51	1,241,008	49.15
Presbyterian Church (U.S.A.)						
United Presbyterian Ch. in U.S.A.						
Presbyterian Church in the U.S.A.	141,057,179	56.49	158,110,613	61.47	180,472,698	68.09
United Presbyterian Ch. in N.A.	13,204,897	57.73	14,797,353	62.37	16,019,616	65.39
Presbyterian Church in the U.S.	56,001,996	73.99	59,222,983	75.54	66,033,260	81.43
Reformed Church in America	13,671,897	68.57	14,740,275	71.87	17,459,572	84.05
Southern Baptist Convention	278,851,129	39.84	305,573,654	42.17	334,836,283	44.54
United Church of Christ						
Congregational Christian	64,061,866	49.91	71,786,834	54.76	80,519,810	60.00
Congregational						
Evangelical and Reformed	31,025,133	41.24	36,261,267	46.83	41,363,406	52.74
Evangelical Synod of N.A./German						
Reformed Church in the U.S.						
The United Methodist Church						
The Evangelical United Brethren	36,331,994	50.21	36,609,598	50.43	41,199,631	56.01
The Methodist Church	314,521,214	34.37	345,416,448	37.53	389,490,613	41.82
Methodist Episcopal Church						
Methodist Episcopal Church South						
Methodist Protestant Church						
Total	$1,318,601,306		$1,446,219,640		$1,600,655,226	

a In data year 1953, $805,135 has been subtracted from the 1955 *Yearbook of American Churches* (Edition for 1956) entry. See 1956 *Yearbook of American Churches* (Edition for 1957), p. 276, n.1.

b This Per Capita Total Contributions figure was calculated by dividing (1) revised Total Contributions as listed in this Appendix, by (2) Membership that, for purposes of this report, had been calculated by dividing the unrevised Total Contributions by the Per Capita Total Contributions figures that were published in the *YACC* series.

c In data year 1953, $5,508,883 has been added to the 1955 *Yearbook of American Churches* (Edition for 1956) entry. See 1956 *Yearbook of American Churches* (Edition for 1957), p. 276, n. 4.

d Total Contributions and Per Capita Total Contributions, respectively, prorated based on available data as follows: American Baptist Churches, 1954 and 1957 data; Christian Church (Disciples of Christ), 1954 and 1956 data; and The Episcopal Church, 1954 and 1956 data.

Appendix B-3.2: Church Member Giving for Eleven Denominations, 1953-1967 (continued)

	Data Year 1956		Data Year 1957		Data Year 1958	
	Total Contributions	Per Capita Total Contributions	Total Contributions	Per Capita Total Contributions	Total Contributions	Per Capita Total Contributions
American Baptist (Northern)	$69,723,321 e	$45.21 e	$71,907,890	$46.23	$70,405,404	$45.03
Christian Church (Disciples of Christ)	71,397,159	37.14	73,737,955	37.94	79,127,458	41.17
Church of the Brethren	10,936,285	63.15	11,293,388	64.43	12,288,049	70.03
The Episcopal Church	103,003,465	52.79	111,660,728	53.48	120,687,177	58.33
Evangelical Lutheran Church in America						
The American Lutheran Church						
American Lutheran Church	45,316,809	72.35	44,518,194	68.80	47,216,896	70.89
The Evangelical Lutheran Church	39,096,038	56.47	44,212,046	61.95	45,366,512	61.74
United Evangelical Lutheran Ch.	2,843,527	73.57	2,641,201	65.46	3,256,050	77.38
Lutheran Free Church	2,652,307	53.14	3,379,882	64.70	3,519,017	66.31
Evan. Lutheran Churches, Assn. of	Not Reported: YACC 1958, p. 292		Not Reported: YACC 1959, p. 277		Not Reported: YACC 1960, p. 276	
Lutheran Church in America						
United Lutheran Church	93,321,223	58.46	100,943,860	61.89	110,179,054	66.45
General Council Evang. Luth. Ch.						
General Synod of Evan. Luth. Ch.						
United Syn. Evang. Luth. South						
American Evangelical Luth. Ch.	Not Comparable YACC 1958, p. 292		935,319	59.45	1,167,503	72.98
Augustana Lutheran Church	24,893,792	66.15	28,180,152	72.09	29,163,771	73.17
Finnish Lutheran Ch. (Suomi Synod)	1,308,026	51.56	1,524,299	58.11	1,533,058	61.94
Moravian Church in Am. No. Prov.	1,740,961	67.53	1,776,703	67.77	1,816,281	68.14
Presbyterian Church (U.S.A.)						
United Presbyterian Ch. in U.S.A.					243,000,572	78.29
Presbyterian Church in the U.S.A.	204,208,085	75.02	214,253,598	77.06		
United Presbyterian Ch. in N.A.	18,424,936	73.30	19,117,837	74.24		
Presbyterian Church in the U.S.	73,477,555	88.56	78,426,424	92.03	82,760,291	95.18
Reformed Church in America	18,718,008	88.56	19,658,604	91.10	21,550,017	98.24
Southern Baptist Convention	372,136,675	48.17	397,540,347	49.99	419,619,438	51.04
United Church of Christ						
Congregational Christian	89,914,505	65.18	90,333,453	64.87	97,480,446	69.55
Congregational						
Evangelical and Reformed	51,519,531	64.88	55,718,141	69.56	63,419,468	78.56
Evangelical Synod of N.A./German						
Reformed Church in the U.S.						
The United Methodist Church						
The Evangelical United Brethren	44,727,060	60.57	45,738,332 e	61.75 e	46,749,605 e	62.93 e
The Methodist Church	413,893,955	43.82	462,826,269 e	48.31 e	511,758,582	52.80
Methodist Episcopal Church						
Methodist Episcopal Church South						
Methodist Protestant Church						
Total	$1,753,253,223		$1,880,324,622		$2,012,064,649	

e Total Contributions and Per Capita Total Contributions, respectively, prorated based on available data as follows: American Baptist Churches, 1954 and 1957 data; The Evangelical United Brethren, 1956 and 1960 data; and The Methodist Church, 1956 and 1958 data.

Appendix B-3.2: Church Member Giving for Eleven Denominations, 1953-1967 (continued)

	Data Year 1959		Data Year 1960		Data Year 1961	
	Total Contributions	Per Capita Total Contributions	Total Contributions	Per Capita Total Contributions	Total Contributions	Per Capita Total Contributions
American Baptist (Northern)	$74,877,669	$48.52	$73,106,232	$48.06	$104,887,025	$68.96
Christian Church (Disciples of Christ)	84,375,152 f	51.22	86,834,944	63.26	89,730,589	65.31
Church of the Brethren	12,143,983	65.27	12,644,194	68.33	13,653,155	73.33
The Episcopal Church	130,279,752	61.36	140,625,284	64.51	154,458,809	68.30
Evangelical Lutheran Church in America						
The American Lutheran Church					113,645,260	73.28
American Lutheran Church	50,163,078	73.52	51,898,875	74.49		
The Evangelical Lutheran Church	49,488,063	65.56	51,297,348	66.85		
United Evangelical Lutheran Ch.	Not Reported: YACC 1961, p. 273		Not Reported: YACC 1963, p. 273			
Lutheran Free Church	3,354,270	61.20	3,618,418	63.98	4,316,925	73.46
Evan. Lutheran Churches, Assn. of	Not Reported: YACC 1961, p. 273		Not Reported: YACC 1963, p. 273			
Lutheran Church in America						
United Lutheran Church	114,458,260	68.29	119,447,895	70.86	128,850,845	76.18
General Council Evang. Luth. Ch.						
General Synod of Evan. Luth. Ch.						
United Syn. Evang. Luth. South						
American Evangelical Luth. Ch.	1,033,907	63.83	1,371,600	83.63	1,209,752	74.89
Augustana Lutheran Church	31,279,335	76.97	33,478,865	80.88	37,863,105	89.37
Finnish Lutheran Ch. (Suomi Synod)	1,685,342	68.61	1,860,481	76.32	1,744,550	70.60
Moravian Church in Am. No. Prov.	2,398,565	89.28	2,252,536	82.95	2,489,930	90.84
Presbyterian Church (U.S.A.)						
United Presbyterian Ch. in U.S.A.	259,679,057	82.30	270,233,943	84.31	285,380,476	87.90
Presbyterian Church in the U.S.A.						
United Presbyterian Ch. in N.A.						
Presbyterian Church in the U.S.	88,404,631	99.42	91,582,428	101.44	96,637,354	105.33
Reformed Church in America	22,970,935	103.23	23,615,749	104.53	25,045,773	108.80
Southern Baptist Convention	453,338,720	53.88	480,608,972	55.68	501,301,714	50.24
United Church of Christ						
Congregational Christian	100,938,267	71.12	104,862,037	73.20	105,871,158	73.72
Congregational						
Evangelical and Reformed	65,541,874	80.92	62,346,084	76.58	65,704,662	80.33
Evangelical Synod of N.A./German						
Reformed Church in the U.S.						
The United Methodist Church						
The Evangelical United Brethren	47,760,877 g	64.10 g	48,772,149	65.28	50,818,912	68.12
The Methodist Church	532,854,842 g	53.97 g	553,951,102	55.14	581,504,618	57.27
Methodist Episcopal Church						
Methodist Episcopal Church South						
Methodist Protestant Church						
Total	$2,127,026,579		$2,214,409,136		$2,365,114,612	

f The 1961 *YACC*, p. 273 indicates that data for this year is not comparable with data for the previous year.
g Total Contributions and Per Capita Total Contributions, respectively, prorated based on available data as follows: The Evangelical United Brethren, 1956 and 1960 data; and The Methodist Church, 1958 and 1960 data.

Appendix B-3.2: Church Member Giving for Eleven Denominations, 1953-1967 (continued)

	Data Year 1962		Data Year 1963		Data Year 1964	
	Total Contributions	Per Capita Total Contributions	Total Contributions	Per Capita Total Contributions	Total Contributions	Per Capita Total Contributions
American Baptist (Northern)	$105,667,332	$68.42	$99,001,651	$68.34	$104,699,557	$69.99
Christian Church (Disciples of Christ)	91,889,457	67.20	96,607,038	75.81	102,102,840	86.44
Church of the Brethren	14,594,572	77.88	14,574,688	72.06	15,221,162	76.08
The Episcopal Church	155,971,264	69.80	171,125,464	76.20	175,374,777	76.66
Evangelical Lutheran Church in America						
The American Lutheran Church	114,912,112	72.47	136,202,292	81.11	143,687,165	83.83
American Lutheran Church						
The Evangelical Lutheran Church						
United Evangelical Lutheran Ch.						
Lutheran Free Church	4,765,138	78.68				
Evan. Lutheran Churches, Assn. of						
Lutheran Church in America	185,166,857	84.98	157,423,391	71.45	170,012,096	76.35
United Lutheran Church						
General Council Evang. Luth. Ch.						
General Synod of Evan. Luth. Ch.						
United Syn. Evang. Luth. South						
American Evangelical Luth. Ch.						
Augustana Lutheran Church						
Finnish Lutheran Ch. (Suomi Synod)						
Moravian Church in Am. No. Prov.	2,512,133	91.92	2,472,273	89.29	2,868,694	103.54
Presbyterian Church (U.S.A.)						
United Presbyterian Ch. in U.S.A.	288,496,652	88.08	297,582,313	90.46	304,833,435	92.29
Presbyterian Church in the U.S.A.						
United Presbyterian Ch. in N.A.						
Presbyterian Church in the U.S.	99,262,431	106.96	102,625,764	109.46	108,269,579	114.61
Reformed Church in America	25,579,443	110.16	26,918,484	117.58	29,174,103	126.44
Southern Baptist Convention	540,811,457	53.06	556,042,694	53.49	591,587,981	55.80
United Church of Christ	164,858,968	72.83	162,379,019	73.12	169,208,042	75.94
Congregational Christian						
Congregational						
Evangelical and Reformed						
Evangelical Synod of N.A./German						
Reformed Church in the U.S.						
The United Methodist Church						
The Evangelical United Brethren	54,567,962	72.91	49,921,568	67.37	56,552,783	76.34
The Methodist Church	599,081,561	58.53	613,547,721	59.60	608,841,881	59.09
Methodist Episcopal Church						
Methodist Episcopal Church South						
Methodist Protestant Church						
Total	$2,448,137,339		$2,486,424,360		$2,582,434,095	

Note: Data for the years 1965 through 1967 was not available in a form that could be readily analyzed for the present purposes, and therefore data for 1965-1967 was estimated as described in the introductory comments to Appendix B. See Appendix B-1 for 1968-1991 data except for The Episcopal Church and The United Methodist Church, available data for which is presented in the continuation of Appendix B-3 in the table immediately following.

141

Appendix B-3.3: Church Member Giving for Eleven Denominations,

The Episcopal Church and The United Methodist Church, 1968-2001

The Episcopal Church			The United Methodist Church		
Data Year	Total Contributions	Full/Confirmed Membership	Data Year	Total Contributions	Full/Confirmed Membership
1968	$202,658,092 [c]	2,322,911 [c]	1968	$763,000,434 [a]	10,849,375 [b]
1969	209,989,189 [c]	2,238,538	1969	800,425,000	10,671,774
1970	248,702,969	2,208,773	1970	819,945,000	10,509,198
1971	257,523,469	2,143,557	1971	843,103,000	10,334,521
1972	270,245,645	2,099,896	1972	885,708,000	10,192,265
1973	296,735,919 [c]	2,079,873 [c]	1973	935,723,000	10,063,046
1974	305,628,925	2,069,793	1974	1,009,760,804	9,957,710
1975	352,243,222	2,051,914 [c]	1975	1,081,080,372	9,861,028
1976	375,942,065	2,021,057	1976	1,162,828,991	9,785,534
1977	401,814,395	2,114,638	1977	1,264,191,548	9,731,779
1978	430,116,564	1,975,234	1978	1,364,460,266	9,653,711
1979	484,211,412	1,962,062	1979	1,483,481,986	9,584,771
1980	507,315,457	1,933,080 [c]	1980	1,632,204,336	9,519,407
1981	697,816,298	1,930,690	1981	1,794,706,741	9,457,012
1982	778,184,068	1,922,923 [c]	1982	1,931,796,533	9,405,164
1983	876,844,252	1,906,618	1983	2,049,437,917	9,291,936
1984	939,796,743	1,896,056	1984	2,211,306,198	9,266,853
1985	1,043,117,983	1,881,250	1985	2,333,928,274	9,192,172
1986	1,134,455,479	1,772,271 [c]	1986	2,460,079,431	9,124,575
1987	1,181,378,441	1,741,036	1987	2,573,748,234	9,055,145
1988	1,209,378,098	1,725,581	1988	2,697,918,285	8,979,139
1989	1,309,243,747	1,714,122	1989	2,845,998,177	8,904,824
1990	1,377,794,610	1,698,240	1990	2,967,535,538	8,853,455
1991	1,541,141,356 [c]	1,613,825 [c]	1991	3,099,522,282	8,789,101
1992	1,582,055,527 [c]	1,615,930 [c]	1992	3,202,700,721 [c]	8,726,951 [c]
1993	1,617,623,255 [c]	1,580,339 [c]	1993	3,303,255,279	8,646,595
1994	1,679,250,095 [c]	1,578,282 [c]	1994	3,430,351,778	8,584,125
1995	1,840,431,636 [c]	1,584,225 [c]	1995	3,568,359,334 [c]	8,538,808 [c]
1996	1,731,727,725 [c]	*1,637,584* [c]	1996	3,744,692,223	8,496,047 [c]
1997	1,832,000,448 [c]	*1,757,972* [c]	1997	3,990,329,491 [c]	8,452,042 [c]
1998	1,977,012,320 [c]	*1,807,651* [c]	1998	4,219,596,499 [c]	8,411,503 [c]
1999	2,146,835,718 [c]	*1,843,108* [c]	1999	4,523,284,851	8,377,662
2000	2,143,238,797 [c]	*1,877,271* [c]	2000	4,761,148,280	*8,341,375* [c]
2001	2,070,493,919 [c]	1,897,004 [c]	2001	5,043,693,838 [c]	8,298,460 [c]

[a] The Evangelical United Brethren Data Not Reported: YACC 1970, p. 198-200. This figure is the sum of The Methodist Church in 1968, and the Evangelical United Brethren data for 1967.

[b] This membership figure is an average of the sum of 1967 membership for The Methodist Church and the Evangelical United Brethren and 1969 data for The United Methodist Church.

[c] Data obtained directly from denominational source.

Appendix B-4: Trends in Giving and Membership

Appendix B-4.1: Membership for Seven Denominations, 1968-2001

Year	American Baptist Churches (Total Mem.)	Assemblies of God	Baptist General Conference	Christian and Missionary Alliance	Church of God (Cleveland, TN)	Roman Catholic Church	Salvation Army
1968	1,583,560	610,946	100,000	71,656	243,532	47,468,333	329,515
1969	1,528,019	626,660	101,226	70,573	257,995	47,872,089	331,711
1970	1,472,478	625,027	103,955	71,708	272,276	48,214,729	326,934
1971	1,562,636	645,891	108,474	73,547	287,099	48,390,990	335,684
1972	1,484,393	679,813	111,364	77,991	297,103	48,460,427	358,626
1973	1,502,759	700,071	109,033	77,606	313,332	48,465,438	361,571
1974	1,579,029	751,818	111,093	80,412	328,892	48,701,835	366,471
1975	1,603,033	785,348	115,340	83,628	343,249	48,881,872	384,817
1976	1,593,574	898,711	117,973	83,978	365,124	49,325,752	380,618
1977	1,584,517	939,312	120,222	88,763	377,765	49,836,176	396,238
1978	1,589,610	932,365	131,000	88,903	392,551	49,602,035	414,035
1979	1,600,521	958,418	126,800	96,324	441,385	49,812,178	414,659
1980	1,607,541	1,064,490	133,385	106,050	435,012	50,449,842	417,359
1981	1,621,795	1,103,134	127,662	109,558	456,797	51,207,579	414,999
1982	1,637,099	1,119,686	129,928	112,745	463,992	52,088,774 [a]	419,475
1983	1,620,153	1,153,935	131,594 [a]	117,501	493,904	52,392,934	428,046
1984	1,559,683	1,189,143	131,162 [a]	120,250	505,775	52,286,043	420,971
1985	1,576,483	1,235,403	130,193 [a]	123,602	521,061 [b]	52,654,908	427,825
1986	1,568,778 [a]	1,258,724	132,546 [a]	130,116	536,346 [b]	52,893,217	432,893
1987	1,561,656 [a]	1,275,146	136,688 [a]	131,354	551,632 [b]	53,496,862	434,002
1988	1,548,573 [a]	1,275,148	134,396 [a]	133,575	556,917 [b]	54,918,949 [a]	433,448
1989	1,535,971 [a]	1,266,982	135,125 [a]	134,336	582,203	57,019,948	445,566
1990	1,527,840 [a]	1,298,121	133,742 [a]	138,071	620,393	58,568,015	445,991
1991	1,534,078 [a]	1,324,800	134,717 [a]	141,077	646,201 [b]	58,267,424	446,403
1992	1,538,710 [a]	1,337,321	134,658 [a]	142,346	672,008	59,220,723	450,028 [a]
1993	1,516,505	1,340,400	134,814 [a]	147,367	700,517	59,858,042	450,312 [a]
1994	1,507,934 [a]	1,354,337	135,128	147,560 [a]	722,541	60,190,605	443,246
1995	1,517,400	1,377,320	135,008	147,955	753,230	60,280,454	453,150
1996	1,503,267 [a]	1,407,941	136,120	143,157	773,483 [a]	61,207,914	462,744 [a]
1997	1,478,534 [a]	1,419,717	134,795	146,153	815,042 [a]	61,563,769 [a]	468,262 [a]
1998	1,507,824 [a]	1,453,907	141,445	163,994	839,857 [a]	62,018,436	471,416
1999	1,454,388	1,492,196	142,871 [a]	164,196	870,039	62,391,484	472,871
2000	1,436,909	1,506,834	141,781 [a]	185,133	895,536	63,683,030 [a]	476,887 [a]
2001	1,442,824	1,532,876	144,365 [a]	191,318	920,664 [a]	65,270,444	454,982

a Data obtained from a denominational source.
b Extrapolated fron YACC series.
Note regarding American Baptist Churches in the U.S.A. Total Membership data: Total Membership is used for the American Baptist Churches in the U.S.A. for anlyses that consider membership as a percentage of U.S. population. The ABC denominational office is the source for this data in the years 1968 and 1970. The year 1978 Total Membership data figure is an adjustment of YACC data based on 1981 YACC information.

APPENDIX C: *Income, Deflators, and U.S. Population*

Sources

Income, 1929-2001

Per Capita Disposable Personal Income in Current Dollars: U.S. Department of Commerce, Bureau of Economic Analysis; "Table 8.7. Selected Per Capita Product and Income Series in Current and Chained Dollars;" Line 4: "Disposable personal income;" National Income and Product Accounts Tables; <http://www.bea.doc.gov/bea/dn/nipaweb/ TableViewFixed.asp#Mid> via <http://www.bea.doc.gov/bea/dn/nipaweb/SelectTable.asp>: Selections: First Year = 1929-A, Last Year = 2002-A & Q, Annual; Last Revised on July 31, 2003; (Generated by empty tomb, inc.: August 15, 2003).

Deflator, 1996 Dollars, 1929-2001

Gross National Product: Implicit Price Deflators for Gross National Product [1996=100]: U.S. Bureau of Economic Analysis; "Table 7.3. Quantity and Price Indexes for Gross National Product and Command-Basis Gross National Product;" Line 4: "Implicit price deflator;" National Income and Product Accounts Tables; <http://www.bea.doc.gov/bea/dn/ nipaweb/TableViewFixed.asp#Mid> via <http://www.bea.doc.gov/bea/dn/nipaweb/ SelectTable.asp>: Selections: First Year = 1929-A, Last Year = 2002-A & Q, Annual; Last Revised on July 31, 2003; (Generated by empty tomb, inc.: August 15, 2003).

Population, 1929-2001

U.S Bureau of Economic Analysis; "Table 8.7. Selected Per Capita Product and Income Series in Current and Chained Dollars;" Line 16: "Population (mid-period, thousands)"; National Income and Product Accounts Tables; <http://www.bea.doc.gov/bea/dn/nipaweb/ TableViewFixed.asp#Mid> via <http://www.bea.doc.gov/bea/dn/nipaweb/SelectTable.asp>: Selections: First Year = 1929-A, Last Year = 2002-A & Q, Annual; Last Revised on July 31, 2003; (Generated by empty tomb, inc.: August 15, 2003).

Appendix C.1: Per Capita Disposable Personal Income and Deflators, 1921-2001

Year	Current $s Per Capita Disposable Personal Income	Implicit Price Deflator GNP [1958=100]	Implicit Price Deflator GNP [1996=100]	Year	Current $s Per Capita Disposable Personal Income	Implicit Price Deflator GNP [1996=100]
1921	$555	54.5		1962	2,174	22.74
1922	$548	50.1		1963	2,249	22.99
1923	$623	51.3		1964	2,412	23.34
1924	$626	51.2		1965	2,567	23.77
1925	$630	51.9		1966	2,742	24.45
1926	$659	51.1		1967	2,899	25.21
1927	$650	50.0		1968	3,119	26.29
1928	$643	50.8		1969	3,329	27.59
1929	$683		12.60	1970	3,591	29.05
1930	$605		12.14	1971	3,860	30.52
1931	$517		10.87	1972	4,138	31.82
1932	$393		9.60	1973	4,619	33.60
1933	$365		9.35	1974	5,013	36.62
1934	$417		9.87	1975	5,470	40.03
1935	$465		10.06	1976	5,960	42.31
1936	$525		10.18	1977	6,519	45.03
1937	$560		10.61	1978	7,253	48.24
1938	$512		10.29	1979	8,033	52.26
1939	$545		10.18	1980	8,869	57.05
1940	$581		10.33	1981	9,773	62.38
1941	$703		11.02	1982	10,364	66.26
1942	$880		11.89	1983	11,036	68.89
1943	$990		12.52	1984	12,215	71.45
1944	$1,072		12.81	1985	12,941	73.70
1945	$1,087		13.16	1986	13,555	75.32
1946	$1,145		14.76	1987	14,246	77.58
1947	$1,194		16.34	1988	15,312	80.22
1948	$1,307		17.28	1989	16,235	83.28
1949	$1,281		17.25	1990	17,176	86.53
1950	$1,388		17.45	1991	17,669	89.67
1951	$1,499		18.70	1992	18,527	91.84
1952	$1,552		18.99	1993	18,981	94.06
1953	$1,622		19.24	1994	19,626	96.02
1954	$1,629		19.43	1995	20,361	98.11
1955	$1,715		19.77	1996	21,072	100.00
1956	$1,800		20.45	1997	21,887	101.93
1957	$1,867		21.12	1998	23,037	103.17
1958	$1,899		21.63	1999	23,749	104.65
1959	$1,983		21.88	2000	25,237	106.86
1960	$2,026		22.18	2001	25,957	109.38
1961	$2,081		22.43			

The State of Church Giving through 2001

Appendix C.2: U.S. Population, 1921-2001

Year	U.S. Population	Year	U.S. Population
1921	108,538,000	1962	186,590,000
1922	110,049,000	1963	189,300,000
1923	111,947,000	1964	191,927,000
1924	114,109,000	1965	194,347,000
1925	115,829,000	1966	196,599,000
1926	117,397,000	1967	198,752,000
1927	119,035,000	1968	200,745,000
1928	120,509,000	1969	202,736,000
1929	121,878,000	1970	205,089,000
1930	123,188,000	1971	207,692,000
1931	124,149,000	1972	209,924,000
1932	124,949,000	1973	211,939,000
1933	125,690,000	1974	213,898,000
1934	126,485,000	1975	215,981,000
1935	127,362,000	1976	218,086,000
1936	128,181,000	1977	220,289,000
1937	128,961,000	1978	222,629,000
1938	129,969,000	1979	225,106,000
1939	131,028,000	1980	227,726,000
1940	132,122,000	1981	230,008,000
1941	133,402,000	1982	232,218,000
1942	134,860,000	1983	234,332,000
1943	136,739,000	1984	236,394,000
1944	138,397,000	1985	238,506,000
1945	139,928,000	1986	240,682,000
1946	141,389,000	1987	242,842,000
1947	144,126,000	1988	245,061,000
1948	146,631,000	1989	247,387,000
1949	149,188,000	1990	249,983,000
1950	151,684,000	1991	253,253,000
1951	154,287,000	1992	256,634,000
1952	156,954,000	1993	260,011,000
1953	159,565,000	1994	263,194,000
1954	162,391,000	1995	266,327,000
1955	165,275,000	1996	269,448,000
1956	168,221,000	1997	272,687,000
1957	171,274,000	1998	275,891,000
1958	174,141,000	1999	279,062,000
1959	177,073,000	2000	282,128,000
1960	180,760,000	2001	284,822,000
1961	183,742,000		